# 帆船竞赛规则
## 2017—2020

世界帆船运动联合会　编著
中国帆船帆板运动协会　审定
总编译：曲春
翻译：辛婧　姜作儒　孟淑霞　康鹏

人民体育出版社

# RACE SIGNALS

The meanings of visual and sound signals are stated below. An arrow pointing up or down ( ↑ ↓ ) means that a visual signal is displayed or removed. A dot ( • ) means a sound; five short dashes (– – – – –) mean repetitive sounds; a long dash (—) means a long sound. When a visual signal is displayed over a class flag, the signal applies only to that class.

### Postponement Signals

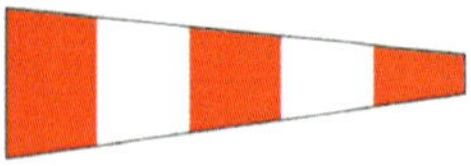

↑•• ↓•

**AP** Races not started are *postponed*. The warning signal will be made 1 minute after removal unless at that time the race is *postponed* again or *abandoned*.

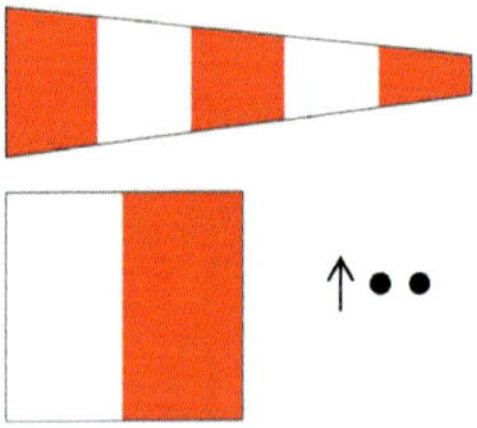

↑••

**AP over H** Races not started are *postponed*. Further signals ashore.

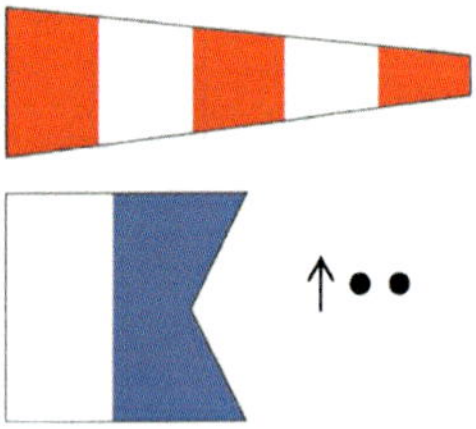

↑••

**AP over A** Races not started are *postponed*. No more racing today.

**AP over a numeral pennant 1–9**

*Postponement* of 1-9 hours from the scheduled starting time.

**Pennant 1** ↑•• ↓•

**Pennant 2** ↑•• ↓•

**Pennant 3** ↑•• ↓•

**Pennant 4** ↑•• ↓•

**Pennant 5** ↑•• ↓•

**Pennant 6** ↑•• ↓•

**Pennant 7** ↑•• ↓•

**Pennant 8** ↑•• ↓•

**Pennant 9** ↑•• ↓•

### Abandonment Signals

↑••• ↓•

**N** All races that have started are *abandoned*. Return to the starting area. The warning signal will be made 1 minute after removal unless at that time the race is *abandoned* again or *postponed*.

**N over H** All races are *abandoned*. Further signals ashore.

**N over A** All races are *abandoned*. No more racing today.

## 竞赛信号

下面是对视觉和音响信号含义的说明。一个向上或向下指的箭头（↑↓）意为一个视觉信号的展示或移除。一个点（•）意为一声音响信号；5个半字线（-----）意为重复的音响信号；一个一字线（—）意为一声长音响信号。当一个视觉信号在一个级别旗之上展示，该信号只适用那个级别。

### 推迟信号

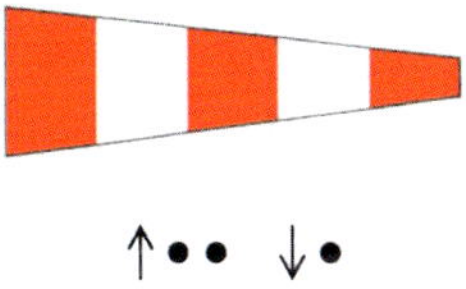


AP旗：*推迟*未起航的竞赛。移除后1分钟发出预告信号，除非那时竞赛再次被*推迟*或*放弃*。

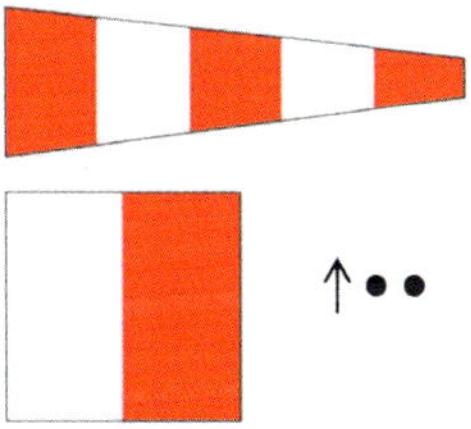


AP 旗在 H 旗之上：*推迟*未起航的竞赛。岸上等信号。

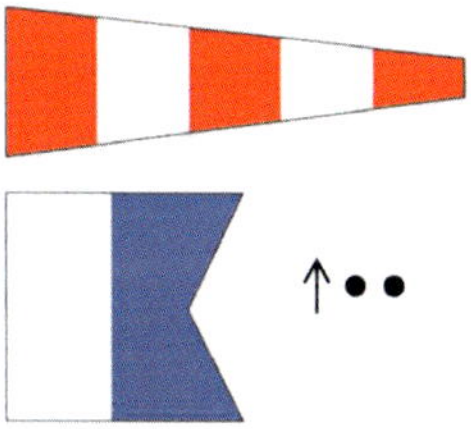


AP旗在A 旗之上：*推迟*未起航的竞赛。今天没有比赛了。

AP旗在1~9中一个数字的三角旗之上：

比预定的起航时间*推迟*1~9小时。

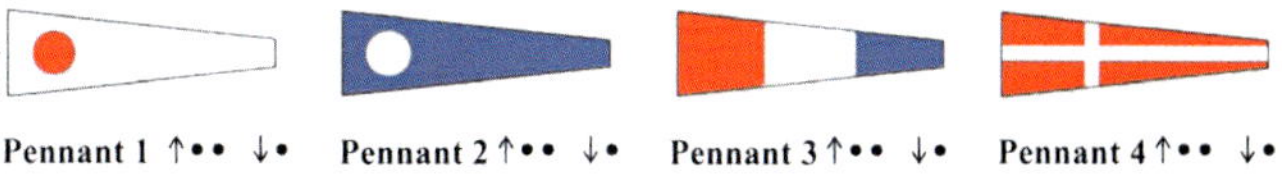


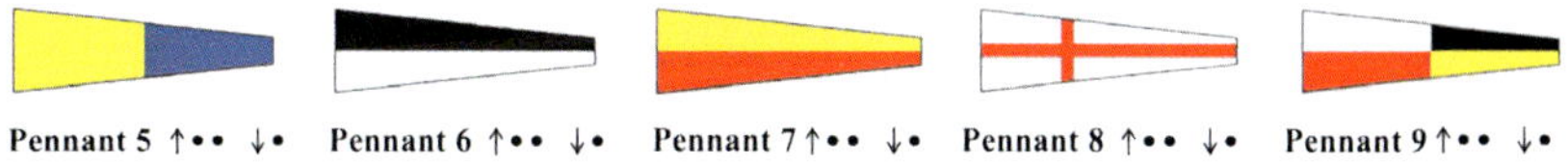


### 放弃信号

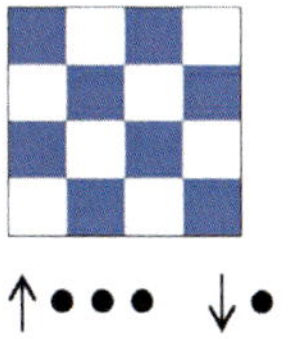


N旗：*放弃*所有已起航的竞赛，回到起航区。移除后1分钟发出预告信号，除非那时竞赛再次被*放弃*或*推迟*。

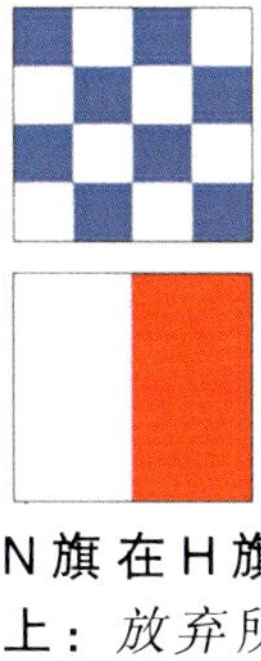

N 旗在 H 旗之上：*放弃*所有的竞赛，岸上等信号。

N 旗在 A 旗之上：*放弃*所有竞赛，今天没有比赛了。

## Preparatory Signals

↑• ↓—

**P** Preparatory signal.

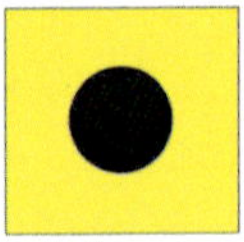

↑• ↓—

**I** Rule 30.1 is in effect.

↑• ↓—

**Z** Rule 30.2 is in effect.

↑• ↓—

**U** Rule 30.3 is in effect.

↑• ↓—

**Black** flag. Rule 30.4 is in effect.

---

## Recall Signals

↑•

**X** Individual recall.

↑•• ↓•

**First Substitute** General recall. The warning signal will be made 1 minute after removal.

## Shortened Course

↑••

**S** The course has been shortened. Rule 32.2 is in effect.

---

## Changing the Next Leg

– – – – –

**C** The position of the next *mark* has been changed:

to starboard;

to port;

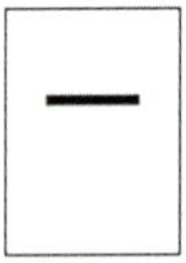

to decrease the length of the leg;

to increase the length of the leg.

---

## Other Signals

↑•

**L** Ashore: A notice to competitors has been posted.
Afloat: Come within hail or follow this vessel.

– – – – –

**M** The object displaying this signal replaces a missing *mark*.

↑•

**Y** Wear a personal flotation device (see rule 40).

(no sound)

**Blue** flag or shape. This race committee vessel is in position at the finishing line.

## 准备信号

↑• ↓—

**P旗：**准备信号。

↑• ↓—

**I旗：**规则30.1生效。

↑• ↓—

**Z旗：**规则30.2生效。

↑• ↓—

**U旗：**规则30.3 生效。

↑• ↓—

**黑旗：**规则30.4 生效。

---

## 召回信号

↑•

**X 旗：**个别召回。

↑•• ↓•

**代一旗：**全部召回。移除后1 分钟发出准备信号。

## 缩短航线

↑••

**S旗：**缩短航线。规则 32.2 生效。

---

## 改变下一个航段

— — — — — —

**C旗：**下一个标志的位置改变了。

向右边改变。

向左边改变。

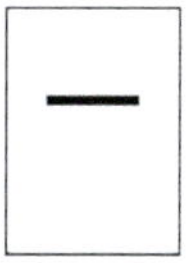

减少航段的长度。

增加航段的长度。

---

## 其他信号

↑•

**L旗在岸上：**贴出了一个选手通知。

**L 旗在水上：**靠近或跟随这条船。

— — — — — —

**M旗：**展示此信号的物体代替了一个丢失的标志。

↑•

**Y旗：**穿戴个人漂浮装备（参见规则40）。

（无音响）**蓝旗或蓝色物体：**该竞赛委员会的船在终点线就位。

作为帆船运动的领导机构，世界帆联在全球所有帆船竞赛和相关活动中推行并支持环境保护。

世界帆联执委办公室联络信息：
Ariadne House
Town Quay
Southampton
Hampshire SO14 2AQ
UK

Tel +44 (0) 2380 635111
Fax +44 (0) 2380 635789
Email office@sailing.org
网站：sailing.org

World Sailing (UK) Limited, Southampton, UK出版

2016年7月

# CONTENTS

# 目　录

# ONLINE RULES DOCUMENTS

*World Sailing has established a single internet address at which readers will find links to all the documents available on the World Sailing website that are mentioned in this book. Those documents are listed below. Links to other rules documents will also be provided at that address.*

*The address is:* ***sailing.org/racingrules/documents.***

# 在线规则文件

*世界帆联已经发布了独立的网络地址，读者可以在世界帆联的网站查找到这本书所有相关的文件。这些文件如下所列。其他规则的链接也将在此网络地址提供。*

*网址是：sailing.org/racingrules/documents.*

# INTRODUCTION

*The Racing Rules of Sailing* includes two main sections. The first, Parts 1–7, contains rules that affect all competitors. The second, the appendices, provides details of rules, rules that apply to particular kinds of racing, and rules that affect only a small number of competitors or officials.

**Terminology**

A term used in the sense stated in the Definitions is printed in italics or, in preambles, in bold italics (for example, *racing* and ***racing***).

Each of the terms in the table below is used in *The Racing Rules of Sailing* with the meaning given.

| *Term* | *Meaning* |
|---|---|
| Boat | A sailboat and the crew on board. |
| Competitor | A person who races or intends to race in the event. |
| National authority | A World Sailing member national authority. |
| Race committee | The race committee appointed under rule 89.2(c) and any other person or committee performing a race committee function. |
| Racing rule | A rule in *The Racing Rules of Sailing.* |
| Technical committee | The technical committee appointed under rule 89.2(c) and any other person or committee performing a technical committee function. |
| Vessel | Any boat or ship. |

Other words and terms are used in the sense ordinarily understood in nautical or general use.

**Notation** The notation '[DP]' in a *rule* means that the penalty for a breach of the *rule* may, at the discretion of the protest committee, be less than disqualification. Guidelines for discretionary penalties are available on the World Sailing website.

# 导言

*《帆船竞赛规则》*包括两个主要部分。第一部分为1—7章，包含了与所有选手有关的规则。第二部分为附录部分，包含规则的细节、适用于特定比赛形式的规则，以及只涉及少数选手或官员的规则。

**术语：**与定义中所述意义相同的术语用斜体印刷，在各章前言中用***粗斜体***印刷（例如：*竞赛*与***竞赛***）。
下表中的每一个术语都以其对应的含义在*《帆船竞赛规则》*中出现。

| *术语* | *含义* |
|---|---|
| 船 | 帆船及船上的人员 |
| 选手 | 参加或者计划参加比赛的人 |
| 国家管理机构 | 世界帆联会员国国家管理机构 |
| 竞赛委员会 | 根据规则89.2(c)任命的竞赛委员会以及其他任何履行竞赛委员会职能的个人或组织 |
| 竞赛规则 | *《帆船竞赛规则》*中的规则 |
| 技术委员会 | 根据规则89.2(c)任命的技术委员会以及其他任何履行技术委员会职能的个人或组织 |
| 船舶 | 任意小船或者轮船 |

其他的词语和术语按照其在航海和日常使用情况下的意义使用。

**注释：***规则*中的注释标记“［DP］”表示抗议委员会对所违反*规则*做出的自由裁量的惩罚，可能会轻于取消资格。关于自由裁量的判罚指南可以在世界帆联网站查询。

**Revision** The racing rules are revised and published every four years by World Sailing, the international authority for the sport. This edition becomes effective on 1 January 2017 except that for an event beginning in 2016 the date may be postponed by the notice of race and sailing instructions. Marginal markings indicate important changes to Parts 1–7 and the Definitions in the 2013–2016 edition. No changes are contemplated before 2021, but any changes determined to be urgent before then will be announced through national authorities and posted on the World Sailing website.

**Appendices** When the rules of an appendix apply, they take precedence over any conflicting rules in Parts 1–7 and the Definitions. Each appendix is identified by a letter. A reference to a rule in an appendix will contain the letter and the rule number (for example, 'rule A1'). The letters I, O and Q are not used to designate appendices in this book.

**World Sailing Codes** The World Sailing Codes are listed in the table below. The codes are published in the World Sailing Regulations.

| *Title* | *Racing Rule* | *Regulation* |
|---|---|---|
| Advertising Code | 80 | 20 |
| Anti-Doping Code | 5 | 21 |
| Betting and Anti-Corruption Code | 6 | 37 |
| Disciplinary Code | 7 | 35 |
| Eligibility Code | 75.2 | 19 |
| Sailor Classification Code | 79 | 22 |

These Codes are referred to in the definition *Rule* but are not included in this book because they can be changed at any time. The most recent versions of the codes are published on the World Sailing website; new versions will be announced through national authorities.

**修订：**本竞赛规则由帆船运动的国际管理机构——世界帆联负责每四年一次的修订和出版。除了2016年开始的被竞赛通知和航行细则推迟的赛事外，本版规则于 2017 年 1 月 1 日生效。页边标记表明该处是对 2013—2016 年版规则中1—7章和定义的重要修改。2021 年前无意对本规则进行修改，但在此之前被认定需紧急修改的地方将通过国家管理机构公布，并在世界帆联网站发布。

**附录：**附录中的规则适用时，优先于1—7章和定义中任何与之冲突的规则。每个附录以一个字母为代码来识别。涉及到某附录中某一条规则时要包含附录字母和规则号码（如："规则A1"）。字母 I、O 和 Q 在本书中不作为指定附录的字母。

**世界帆联守则：**世界帆联守则如下表所列。这些守则公布在世界帆联规章中。

| *标题* | *竞赛规则* | *规章* |
| --- | --- | --- |
| 广告守则 | 80 | 20 |
| 反兴奋剂守则 | 5 | 21 |
| 博彩和反腐败守则 | 6 | 37 |
| 纪律守则 | 7 | 35 |
| 资格法规 | 75.2 | 19 |
| 选手分级法规 | 79 | 22 |

这些守则是*规则*定义中提到的，但本书未包括其内容，因为此类守则可随时进行修改。最新版本的守则会在世界帆联网站上发布，新版本将通过国家管理机构公布。

**Cases and Calls** World Sailing publishes interpretations of the racing rules in *The Case Book for 2017–2020* and recognizes them as authoritative interpretations and explanations of the rules. It also publishes *The Call Book for Match Racing for 2017–2020* and *The Call Book for Team Racing for 2017–2020*, and it recognizes them as authoritative only for umpired match or team racing. These publications are available on the World Sailing website.

**案例和判例**：世界帆联出版的*《2017—2020年规则案例书》*对竞赛规则进行了解释，该解释被认为是对规则的权威解释。世界帆联还出版了*《2017—2020年对抗赛判例》*和*《2017—2020年队赛判例》*，被认为是仅针对水上现场裁决的对抗赛或队赛的权威文本。这些出版物发布在世界帆联的网站上。

规则新增与更改部分在段落旁用竖线指示。

# DEFINITIONS

*A term used as stated below is shown in italic type or, in preambles, in bold italic type. The meaning of several other terms is given in Terminology in the Introduction.*

***Abandon*** A race that a race committee or protest committee *abandons* is void but may be resailed.

***Clear Astern* and *Clear Ahead*; *Overlap*** One boat is *clear astern* of another when her hull and equipment in normal position are behind a line abeam from the aftermost point of the other boat's hull and equipment in normal position. The other boat is *clear ahead.* They *overlap* when neither is *clear astern.* However, they also *overlap* when a boat between them *overlaps* both. These terms always apply to boats on the same *tack.* They apply to boats on opposite *tacks* only when rule 18 applies between them or when both boats are sailing more than ninety degrees from the true wind.

***Conflict of Interest*** A person has a *conflict of interest* if he

(a) may gain or lose as a result of a decision to which he contributes,

(b) may reasonably appear to have a personal or financial interest which could affect his ability to be impartial, or

(c) has a close personal interest in a decision.

***Fetching*** A boat is *fetching* a *mark* when she is in a position to pass to windward of it and leave it on the required side without changing *tack.*

***Finish*** A boat *finishes* when any part of her hull, or crew or equipment in normal position, crosses the finishing line from the course side. However, she has not *finished* if after crossing the finishing line she

# 定义

*下列术语以斜体字出现或在各章前言中以粗斜体出现。其他一些术语的释义已经在导言中列举。*

***放弃*** 竞赛委员会或抗议委员会*放弃*的一轮竞赛是无效的，但是可以重赛。

***明显在后与明显在前；相联*** 当一条船的船体和其处于正常位置的装备位于另一条船船体和其处于正常位置的装备的最后一点的正横线之后，该船为*明显在后*。另一条船为*明显在前*。当没有任何一条船为*明显在后*时，她们为*相联*。但是，当她们中间有一条船跟她俩均*相联*时，这两条船也*相联*。这些术语总是适用于相同*舷风*的船。除非规则18适用或两船均同真风风向的角度大于90度，否则这些术语不适用于处于相对*舷风*的船。

***利益冲突*** 一个人如果有以下情况，就有*利益冲突*：

（a）所做的决定可能会导致其获利或损失，

（b）可能会影响到其公正性的个人利益或经济利益，或者

（c）在一个裁决中有密切的个人利益。

***飞驰*** 船处于从一个*标志*上风通过并从规定的一侧离开该*标志*时无需换*舷*的位置时，该船为正在*飞驰*该*标志*。

***到达终点*** 当一条船处于正常位置时的船体、船员或装备的任何部分从航线一侧越过终点线即为*到达终点*。但是，如果在越过终点线

(a) takes a penalty under rule 44.2,

(b) corrects an error under rule 28.2 made at the line, or

(c) continues to sail the course.

***Keep Clear*** A boat *keeps clear* of a right-of-way boat

(a) if the right-of-way boat can sail her course with no need to take avoiding action and,

(b) when the boats are *overlapped*, if the right-of-way boat can also change course in both directions without immediately making contact.

***Leeward* and *Windward*** A boat's *leeward* side is the side that is or, when she is head to wind, was away from the wind. However, when sailing by the lee or directly downwind, her *leeward* side is the side on which her mainsail lies. The other side is her *windward* side. When two boats on the same *tack overlap*, the one on the *leeward* side of the other is the *leeward* boat. The other is the *windward* boat.

***Mark*** An object the sailing instructions require a boat to leave on a specified side, and a race committee vessel surrounded by navigable water from which the starting or finishing line extends. An anchor line or an object attached accidentally to a *mark* is not part of it.

***Mark-Room*** *Room* for a boat to leave a *mark* on the required side. Also,

(a) *room* to sail to the *mark* when her *proper course* is to sail close to it, and

(b) *room* to round the *mark* as necessary to sail the course.

However, *mark-room* for a boat does not include *room* to tack unless she is *overlapped* inside and to *windward* of the boat required to give *mark-room* and she would be *fetching* the *mark* after her tack.

后她有如下情况，则为没有*到达终点*：

（a）根据规则 44.2 做解脱，

（b）根据规则28.2 改正在终点线上犯的错误，或者

（c）继续行驶航线。

***避让*** 如果符合以下条件，一条船就*避让*了另一条有航行权的船：

（a）有航行权的船不需要做出避让动作就可以航行在其航线上，并且

（b）当两条船*相联*时，有航行权的船在两个方向上都能改变航线而不会立刻造成接触。

***下风和上风*** 船的*下风*边就是离开风的那一边，或当她行驶正顶风时刚刚离开风的那一边。但当背风航行或正顺风航行时，她的*下风*边就是其主帆所在的一边。另外一边为其*上风*边。当两条船同*舷风相联*时，处在一条船的*下风*边的船是*下风*船，这条船是*上风*船。

***标志/标*** 航行细则规定船从特定一侧驶离的物体和由可航行水域包围的、由此延伸出起航线或终点线的竞赛委员会船舶。锚绳或偶然附着在*标志*上的物体不是它的一部分。

***绕标空间*** 船在其所要求一侧驶离*标志*时所需的*空间*。也包括：

（a）当她的*正当航线*是需要驶近*标志*时行驶到*标志*的*空间*，以及

（b）行驶航线所需要的绕行或通过*标志*的*空间*。

但是，对于一条船来说*绕标空间*不包括迎风换舷的*空间*，除非该船建立*上风相联*并且处于需要给予她*绕标空间*的船的内侧，而且在迎风换舷后该船可以*飞驰*该*标志*。

***Obstruction*** An object that a boat could not pass without changing course substantially, if she were sailing directly towards it and one of her hull lengths from it. An object that can be safely passed on only one side and an area so designated by the sailing instructions are also *obstructions*. However, a boat *racing* is not an *obstruction* to other boats unless they are required to *keep clear* of her or, if rule 23 applies, avoid her. A vessel under way, including a boat *racing*, is never a continuing *obstruction*.

***Overlap*** See ***Clear Astern*** **and** ***Clear Ahead; Overlap***.

***Party*** A *party* to a hearing is

(a) for a protest hearing: a protestor, a protestee;

(b) for a request for redress: a boat requesting redress or for which redress is requested, a race committee acting under rule 60.2(b), a technical committee acting under rule 60.4(b);

(c) for a request for redress under rule 62.1(a): the body alleged to have made an improper action or omission;

(d) a person against whom an allegation of a breach of rule 69 is made; a person presenting an allegation under rule 69;

(e) a *support person* subject to a hearing under rule 60.3(d) or 69; any boat that person supports; a person appointed to present an allegation under rule 60.3(d).

However, the protest committee is never a *party*.

***Postpone*** A *postponed* race is delayed before its scheduled start but may be started or *abandoned* later.

***Proper Course*** A course a boat would sail to *finish* as soon as possible in the absence of the other boats referred to in the rule using the term. A boat has no *proper course* before her starting signal.

***Protest*** An allegation made under rule 61.2 by a boat, a race committee, a technical committee or a protest committee that a boat has broken a *rule*.

***障碍物*** 船正直接驶向一个物体并且距其有1倍船长时，若她不明显改变航线就不能通过的物体。只能从一侧安全通过的物体和航行细则中特指的区域也可作为*障碍物*。但是，正在*竞赛*的船对其他船不构成*障碍物*，除非这些船应该*避让*她，或若规则23适用，躲避她。正在行驶的各种船舶，包括正在*竞赛*的船，永远不是连续*障碍物*。

***相联*** 参见***明显在后***和***明显在前；相联*** 。

***一方*** 审理一方是指：

（a）对于抗议审理：抗议者，被抗议者；

（b）对于要求补偿：提出补偿要求或被要求补偿的船，按规则60.2(b)行动的竞赛委员会，按规则60.4(b)行动的技术委员会；

（c）对于依规则62.1(a)提出的要求补偿：被指责为有不当行为或疏漏的个人或机构；

（d）被指控违反规则 69.1(a)的；根据规则 69.2(e)(1)提出指控的人；

（e）根据规则60.3(d)或69接受某一审理的*后援人员*；受该后援人员支持的船；根据规则60.3(d)被指定去指控违规过程的人。

但抗议委员会从来都不能作为一方。

***推迟*** *推迟*竞赛是在计划起航前延迟，但随后可以起航或*放弃*。

***正当航线*** 在规则中该术语提到的在无其他船只影响下尽快*到达终点*的那条航线。在起航信号前船没有*正当航线*。

***抗议*** 由船、竞赛委员会、技术委员会或抗议委员会根据规则61.2所提出的关于某条船违反*规则*的指控。

***Racing*** A boat is *racing* from her preparatory signal until she *finishes* and clears the finishing line and *marks* or retires, or until the race committee signals a general recall, *postponement* or *abandonment*.

***Room*** The space a boat needs in the existing conditions, including space to comply with her obligations under the rules of Part 2 and rule 31, while manoeuvring promptly in a seamanlike way.

***Rule***

(a) The rules in this book, including the Definitions, Race Signals, Introduction, preambles and the rules of relevant appendices, but not titles;

(b) World Sailing Advertising Code, Anti-Doping Code, Betting and Anti-Corruption Code, Disciplinary Code, Eligibility Code, Sailor Classification Code, respectively Regulations 20, 21, 37, 35, 19 and 22;

(c) the prescriptions of the national authority, unless they are changed by the notice of race or sailing instructions in compliance with the national authority's prescription, if any, to rule 88.2;

(d) the class rules (for a boat racing under a handicap or rating system, the rules of that system are 'class rules');

(e) the notice of race;

(f) the sailing instructions; and

(g) any other documents that govern the event.

***Start*** A boat *starts* when, having been entirely on the pre-start side of the starting line at or after her starting signal, and having complied with rule 30.1 if it applies, any part of her hull, crew or equipment crosses the starting line in the direction of the first *mark*.

*竞赛*　*竞赛*是指船从其准备信号开始直至她*到达终点*并完全离开终点线和标志或退出，或直至竞赛委员会发出全部召回、*推迟*或*放弃*信号。

*空间*　船在现有条件下以正常的方式快速进行航行操作所需的空间，包括履行规则第二章和规则31规定的义务所需要的空间。

*规则*

（a）本书中的规则，包括定义、竞赛信号、导言、各章前言和有关的附录规则但不包括标题；

（b）世界帆联广告守则、反兴奋剂守则、博彩和反腐败守则、纪律守则、资格法规、选手分级法规，以及相对应的规章20、21、37、35、19和22；

（c）国家管理机构的规定，除非其依据国家管理机构的规定在竞赛通知或航行细则中做出了更改，如果有此更改，按规则88.2执行；

（d）级别规则（对于以让分或分级办法进行比赛的船来说，该办法中的规则就是“级别规则”）；

（e）竞赛通知；

（f）航行细则；以及

（g）所有该赛事执行的其他文件。

*起航*　在起航信号发出时或发出后，船完全位于起航线准备区一侧并且遵守了规则30.1（如果采用该规则），其船体、船员或装备的任何部分向第一个*标志*越过起航线即为*起航*。

***Support Person*** Any person who

(a) provides, or may provide, physical or advisory support to a competitor, including any coach, trainer, manager, team staff, medic, paramedic or any other person working with, treating or assisting a competitor in or preparing for the competition, or

(b) is the parent or guardian of a competitor.

***Tack, Starboard* or *Port*** A boat is on the *tack*, *starboard* or *port*, corresponding to her *windward* side.

***Windward*** See ***Leeward* and *Windward***.

***Zone*** The area around a *mark* within a distance of three hull lengths of the boat nearer to it. A boat is in the *zone* when any part of her hull is in the *zone*.

***后援人员*** 满足以下条件的任何人：

（a）提供，或可以为选手提供有形或咨询支持，包括教练、陪练、管理人员、后勤人员、医务人员、护理人员，或者其他与选手一起工作、治疗或协助选手做比赛准备工作的人员，或者

（b）是选手的父母或者监护人。

***舷风、右舷或左舷*** 船的*舷风*边、*右舷*或*左舷*是与其*上风*边一致的。

***上风*** 参见***上风***和***下风*** 。

***标区*** 一船距离标志周围3倍船长的区域范围。当船体的任何部分在此*标区*内即为该船在此*标区*内。

# BASIC PRINCIPLES

**SPORTSMANSHIP AND THE RULES**

Competitors in the sport of sailing are governed by a body of *rules* that they are expected to follow and enforce. A fundamental principle of sportsmanship is that when competitors break a *rule* they will promptly take a penalty, which may be to retire.

**ENVIRONMENTAL RESPONSIBILITY**

Participants are encouraged to minimize any adverse environmental impact of the sport of sailing.

# **PART 1** FUNDAMENTAL RULES

**1 SAFETY**

**1.1 Helping Those in Danger**

A boat or competitor shall give all possible help to any person or vessel in danger.

**1.2 Life-Saving Equipment and Personal Flotation Devices**

A boat shall carry adequate life-saving equipment for all persons on board, including one item ready for immediate use, unless her class rules make some other provision. Each competitor is individually responsible for wearing a personal flotation device adequate for the conditions.

**2 FAIR SAILING**

A boat and her owner shall compete in compliance with recognized principles of sportsmanship and fair play. A boat may be penalized under this rule only if it is clearly established that these principles

# 基本原则

**体育道德与规则**

参加帆船项目的选手要遵守执行的全部*规则*。体育道德的基本原则是当选手违反某条*规则*时应尽快接受惩罚，惩罚可能是退出比赛。

**环保责任**

赛事参与者应当尽力将对环境的不利影响最小化。

# 第一章　基本规则

**1 安全**

**1.1 援助处于危险中的船只或人员**

船只或选手应对处于危险中的任何人员或船舶给予一切尽可能的援助。

**1.2 救生装备和个人漂浮装备**

每条船应为船上所有的人员携带足够的救生装备，包括一件应急使用的装备，除非该船级别规则另有其他规定。穿用符合条件的个人漂浮装备是每位选手个人的责任。

**2 公平航行**

船及其船东应按照公认的体育道德和公平竞赛的原则进行比赛。船只有在被清晰地确定违背了这些原则时方可能因本规则

have been violated. The penalty shall be either disqualification or disqualification that is not excludable.

## 3 ACCEPTANCE OF THE RULES

**3.1** (a) By participating or intending to participate in a race conducted under these *rules*, each competitor and boat owner agrees to accept these *rules*.

(b) A *support person* by providing support, or a parent or guardian by permitting their child to enter a race, agrees to accept the *rules*.

**3.2** Each competitor and boat owner agrees, on behalf of their *support persons*, that such *support persons* are bound by the *rules*.

**3.3** Acceptance of the *rules* includes agreement

(a) to be governed by the *rules*;

(b) to accept the penalties imposed and other action taken under the *rules*, subject to the appeal and review procedures provided in them, as the final determination of any matter arising under the *rules*;

(c) with respect to any such determination, not to resort to any court of law or tribunal not provided for in the *rules*; and

(d) by each competitor and boat owner to ensure that their *support persons* are aware of the *rules*.

**3.4** The person in charge of each boat shall ensure that all competitors in the crew and the boat's owner are aware of their responsibilities under this rule.

**3.5** This rule may be changed by a prescription of the national authority of the venue.

## 4 DECISION TO RACE

The responsibility for a boat's decision to participate in a race or to continue *racing* is hers alone.

## 5 ANTI-DOPING

A competitor shall comply with the World Anti-Doping Code, the rules of the World Anti-Doping Agency, and World Sailing Regulation 21, Anti-Doping Code. An alleged or actual breach of this rule shall be dealt with under Regulation 21. It shall not be grounds for a *protest* and rule 63.1 does not apply.

受到惩罚。违反本规则的判罚可以是取消资格（DSQ）或是不能去掉的取消资格（DNE）。

## 3 接受规则

3.1 （a）参加或准备参加执行这些*规则*的比赛，表明每位选手和船东都同意接受这些*规则*。

（b）*后援人员*在提供支持时，或者允许他们的子女参加比赛的父母中的某位或监护人同意接受*规则*。

3.2 代表其*后援人员*的每位选手和船东同意这些*后援人员*同样受*规则*的约束。

3.3 接受*规则*包括同意：

（a）受*规则*的约束；

（b）接受强制的判罚和其他根据*规则*采取的措施，接受*规则*规定的上诉和审查的程序，并根据*规则*将此作为最终决议；

（c）关于任何诸如此类的决议，不诉诸于*规则*中未规定的任何法院或特别法庭；同时

（d）每位选手和船东要确保其*后援人员*都清楚*规则*。

3.4 船只负责人应确保该船的所有选手和船东了解本条规则要他们承担的责任。

3.5 本规则可以根据场馆所在地国家管理机构的规定进行更改。

## 4 参赛的决定

决定是否参加比赛或继续*竞赛*是该船自己的权利。

## 5 反兴奋剂

选手必须遵守世界反兴奋剂守则，世界反兴奋剂协会的规则和世界帆联规章21，即反兴奋剂守则。被指控或实际违反了该规则者将按规章21处理。它不能成为*抗议*的理由，同时规则63.1不适用。

6 **BETTING AND ANTI-CORRUPTION**

Each competitor, boat owner and *support person* shall comply with World Sailing Regulation 37, Betting and Anti-Corruption Code. An alleged or actual breach of this rule shall be dealt with under Regulation 37. It shall not be grounds for a *protest* and rule 63.1 does not apply.

7 **DISCIPLINARY CODE**

Each competitor, boat owner and *support person* shall comply with World Sailing Regulation 35, Disciplinary, Appeals and Review Code (referred to as 'Disciplinary Code' elsewhere). An alleged or actual breach of this rule shall be dealt with under Regulation 35. It shall not be grounds for a *protest* and rule 63.1 does not apply.

## 6 博彩和反腐败

每位选手、船东和*后援人员*必须遵守世界帆联规章37，博彩和反腐败守则。被指控或者实际违反该规则者应按照规章37处理。它不能成为*抗议*的理由，同时规则 63.1不适用。

## 7 纪律守则

每位选手、船东和*后援人员*要接受世界帆联规章35，纪律、上诉和重审守则（简称纪律守则）。被指控或者实际违反该规则者应按照规章35处理。它不能成为*抗议*的理由，同时规则63.1不适用。

# PART 2 WHEN BOATS MEET

*The rules of Part 2 apply between boats that are sailing in or near the racing area and intend to **race**, are **racing**, or have been **racing**. However, a boat not **racing** shall not be penalized for breaking one of these rules, except rule 14 when the incident resulted in injury or serious damage, or rule 24.1.*

*When a boat sailing under these rules meets a vessel that is not, she shall comply with the* International Regulations for Preventing Collisions at Sea (IRPCAS) *or government right-of-way rules. If the sailing instructions so state, the rules of Part 2 are replaced by the right-of-way rules of the* IRPCAS *or by government right-of-way rules.*

## SECTION A RIGHT OF WAY

*A boat has right of way over another boat when the other boat is required to **keep clear** of her. However, some rules in Sections B, C and D limit the actions of a right-of-way boat.*

### 10 ON OPPOSITE TACKS

When boats are on opposite *tacks*, a *port-tack* boat shall *keep clear* of a *starboard-tack* boat.

### 11 ON THE SAME TACK, OVERLAPPED

When boats are on the same *tack* and *overlapped*, a *windward* boat shall *keep clear* of a *leeward* boat.

### 12 ON THE SAME TACK, NOT OVERLAPPED

When boats are on the same *tack* and not *overlapped*, a boat *clear astern* shall *keep clear* of a boat *clear ahead*.

# 第二章　船只相遇时

*第二章的规则适用于在比赛场地区域内或场地区域附近航行及准备**竞赛**、**正在竞赛**或一直在**竞赛**的船之间的船只。但是，不参加**竞赛**的船将不会因触犯这些规则中的某一条而受到处罚，事件造成受伤或者严重损坏时的规则14和规则24.1除外。*
*一条按照这些规则航行的船与一艘未按这些规则航行的船舶相遇时，应遵守《**国际海上避碰规则（IRPCAS）**》或政府有关航行权的规定。如果航行细则中做出了这样的说明，那么，IRPCAS或政府有关航行权的规定将替代第二章的规则。*

## A节　航行权

*当另一条船需要**避让**这一条船时，这条船对另一条船拥有航行权。但是，B节、C节和D节中的部分规则对有航行权的船的行为有所限制。*

### 10　相对舷风

当船相对*舷风*行驶时，*左舷*船应*避让右舷*船。

### 11　同舷风、相联

当船同*舷风相联*行驶时，*上风*船应*避让下风*船。

### 12　同舷风、不相联

当船同*舷风*但未*相联*时，*明显在后*的船应*避让明显在前*的船。

**13 WHILE TACKING**

After a boat passes head to wind, she shall *keep clear* of other boats until she is on a close-hauled course. During that time rules 10, 11 and 12 do not apply. If two boats are subject to this rule at the same time, the one on the other's port side or the one astern shall *keep clear.*

## SECTION B GENERAL LIMITATIONS

**14 AVOIDING CONTACT**

A boat shall avoid contact with another boat if reasonably possible. However, a right-of-way boat or one entitled to *room* or *mark-room*

(a) need not act to avoid contact until it is clear that the other boat is not *keeping clear* or giving *room* or *mark-room*, and

(b) shall be exonerated if she breaks this rule and the contact does not cause damage or injury.

**15 ACQUIRING RIGHT OF WAY**

When a boat acquires right of way, she shall initially give the other boat *room* to *keep clear*, unless she acquires right of way because of the other boat's actions.

**16 CHANGING COURSE**

16.1 When a right-of-way boat changes course, she shall give the other boat *room* to *keep clear.*

16.2 In addition, when after the starting signal a *port-tack* boat is *keeping clear* by sailing to pass astern of a *starboard-tack* boat, the *starboard tack* boat shall not change course if as a result the *port-tack* boat would immediately need to change course to continue *keeping clear.*

**17 ON THE SAME TACK; PROPER COURSE**

If a boat *clear astern* becomes *overlapped* within two of her hull lengths to *leeward* of a boat on the same *tack*, she shall not sail above her *proper course* while they remain on the same *tack* and *overlapped* within that distance, unless in doing so she promptly sails astern of the other boat. This rule does not apply if the *overlap* begins while the *windward* boat is required by rule 13 to *keep clear.*

### 13 迎风换舷时

一条船越过正顶风后，应*避让*其他船直至行驶在近迎风航线上。在这期间规则10、11和12不适用。如果两条船同时受本规则约束，在另一条船的左舷或在后的船应*避让*。

## B节 一般限制

### 14 避免接触

在合理且可能的情况下，一条船应避免与另外一条船接触。但是，有航行权的船、有权拥有*空间*或*绕标空间*的船

（a）在另外一条船很明显*不避让*或不给予*空间*或*绕标空间*前，无需采取避免接触的行为，并且

（b）如果接触没有造成损坏或损伤，违反这条规则者应该免责。

### 15 获取航行权

当一条船获取航行权时，她应于一开始时给另外一条船*避让*的*空间*，除非该船是因另外那条船的行为而获得航行权。

### 16 改变航线

16.1 当有航行权的船改变航线时，她应给予另外一条船*空间*去*避让*。

16.2 另外，起航信号后，一条*左舷*船以从*右舷*船尾通过的方式*避让*时，如果*右舷*船改变航线会造成*左舷*船需要马上改变航线继续*避让*，*右舷*船就不应改变航线。

### 17 同舷风；正当航线

同*舷风*时，如果一条*明显在后*的船在其2倍船长间距内与另一条船建立*下风相联*，当她们在此间距内仍保持同*舷风*和*相联*时，她不应高于其*正当航线*，除非在这样做时她立刻行驶到另一条船的船尾后面。当*上风*船根据规则13被要求*避让*时建立*相联*，此规则不适用。

## SECTION C AT MARKS AND OBSTRUCTIONS

*Section C rules do not apply at a starting **mark** surrounded by navigable water or at its anchor line from the time boats are approaching them to **start** until they have passed them.*

### 18 MARK-ROOM

**18.1 When Rule 18 Applies**

Rule 18 applies between boats when they are required to leave a *mark* on the same side and at least one of them is in the *zone*. However, it does not apply

(a) between boats on opposite *tacks* on a beat to windward,

(b) between boats on opposite *tacks* when the *proper course* at the *mark* for one but not both of them is to tack,

(c) between a boat approaching a *mark* and one leaving it, or

(d) if the *mark* is a continuing *obstruction*, in which case rule 19 applies.

**18.2 Giving Mark-Room**

(a) When boats are *overlapped* the outside boat shall give the inside boat *mark-room*, unless rule 18.2(b) applies.

(b) If boats are *overlapped* when the first of them reaches the *zone*, the outside boat at that moment shall thereafter give the inside boat *mark-room*. If a boat is *clear ahead* when she reaches the *zone*, the boat *clear astern* at that moment shall thereafter give her *mark-room*.

(c) When a boat is required to give *mark-room* by rule 18.2(b),

(1) she shall continue to do so even if later an *overlap* is broken or a new *overlap* begins;

(2) if she becomes *overlapped* inside the boat entitled to *mark-room*, she shall also give that boat *room* to sail her *proper course* while they remain *overlapped*.

## C节 在标志和障碍物旁

*从船接近被航行水域围绕的起航***标志***或其锚绳去***起航***直至船通过它们时，C节的规则不适用。*

### 18 绕标空间

**18.1 规则18适用时**

在被要求同侧离开*标志*且至少其中一条船处于*标区*内的两船之间，规则18适用。然而，其不适用于：

（a）以相对*舷风*迎风行驶的船之间，

（b）两条相对*舷风*的船之间，其中仅有一条船在*标*旁的*正当航线*是做迎风换舷，

（c）在一条正接近*标志*的船和一条正离开*标志*的船之间，或者

（d）如果*标志*是一个连续*障碍物*，规则19适用。

**18.2 给予绕标空间**

（a）当船只*相联*时，外侧船应给予内侧船*绕标空间*，除非18.2(b)适用。

（b）当其中的第一条船到达*标区*时，如果船*相联*，此时的外侧船之后应给予内侧船*绕标空间*。如果到达*标区*时一条船*明显在前*，此时*明显在后*的船之后应给予其*绕标空间*。

（c）当规则18.2(b)要求一条船给予*绕标空间*时，

（1）即使稍后*相联*被打破或者新的*相联*建立，她应当继续这样做；

（2）如果该船已经与有权要求*绕标空间*的船建立了内侧*相联*，只要*相联*没有打破，她仍然应该给予对方行驶*正当航线*的空间。

(d) Rules 18.2(b) and (c) cease to apply when the boat entitled to *mark-room* has been given that *mark-room*, or if she passes head to wind or leaves the *zone*.

(e) If there is reasonable doubt that a boat obtained or broke an *overlap* in time, it shall be presumed that she did not.

(f) If a boat obtained an inside *overlap* from *clear astern* or by tacking to *windward* of the other boat and, from the time the *overlap* began, the outside boat has been unable to give *mark-room*, she is not required to give it.

**18.3 Tacking in the Zone**

If a boat in the *zone* of a *mark* to be left to port passes head to wind from *port* to *starboard tack* and is then *fetching* the *mark*, she shall not cause a boat that has been on *starboard tack* since entering the *zone* to sail above close-hauled to avoid contact and she shall give *mark-room* if that boat becomes *overlapped* inside her. When this rule applies between boats, rule 18.2 does not apply between them.

**18.4 Gybing**

When an inside *overlapped* right-of-way boat must gybe at a *mark* to sail her *proper course*, until she gybes she shall sail no farther from the *mark* than needed to sail that course. Rule 18.4 does not apply at a gate *mark*.

## 19 ROOM TO PASS AN OBSTRUCTION

**19.1 When Rule 19 Applies**

Rule 19 applies between two boats at an *obstruction* except

(a) when the *obstruction* is a *mark* the boats are required to leave on the same side, or

(b) when rule 18 applies between the boats and the *obstruction* is another boat *overlapped* with each of them.

However, at a continuing *obstruction*, rule 19 always applies and rule 18 does not.

**19.2 Giving Room at an Obstruction**

(a) A right-of-way boat may choose to pass an *obstruction* on either side.

（d）当有权利要求*绕标空间*的船被给予*绕标空间*后，或者如果该船越过正顶风或离开*标区*时，规则18.2(b)和(c)终止生效。

（e）如果对船是否及时建立或打破了*相联*有合理的质疑，应假定其没有。

（f）如果一条船从*明显在后*或通过迎风换舷至另一条船*上风*建立内侧*相联*，*相联*开始的时候，外侧船已经不能够给予*绕标空间*，她就不必给予*绕标空间*。

**18.3 在标区迎风换舷**

一条船如果在*标区*内*左舷*一侧离开*标志*，该船从*左舷*越过正顶风至*右舷*航行，处于飞驰该*标志*状态时，她不能造成*右舷*进入*标区*的船高于近迎风行驶来避免接触，而且，如果那条船与该船建立了内侧*相联*，则该船必须给予*绕标空间*。当此规则适用于船之间时，规则18.2在她们之间就不适用。

**18.4 顺风换舷**

当一条内侧*相联*并有航行权的船在*标志*旁必须顺风换舷来行驶她的*正当航线*时，顺风换舷前她离*标志*的距离不得远于行驶那个*正当航线*所需的距离。在门标时规则18.4不适用。

## 19 通过障碍物的空间

**19.1 规则 19 适用时**

规则19适用于在*障碍物*旁的两船之间，以下情况除外：

（a）当*障碍物*是一个*标志*时，两船被要求从同一侧驶离，或

（b）当规则18适用于两船之间时，该*障碍物*是另一条与她俩分别*相联*的船。

然而，在通过连续*障碍物*时，规则19总是适用，而规则18却不适用。

**19.2 在障碍物旁给予空间**

（a）拥有航行权的船可以选择从任意一侧通过*障碍物*。

(b) When boats are *overlapped*, the outside boat shall give the inside boat *room* between her and the *obstruction*, unless she has been unable to do so from the time the *overlap* began.

(c) While boats are passing a continuing *obstruction*, if a boat that was *clear astern* and required to *keep clear* becomes *overlapped* between the other boat and the *obstruction* and, at the moment the *overlap* begins, there is not *room* for her to pass between them, she is not entitled to *room* under rule 19.2(b). While the boats remain *overlapped*, she shall *keep clear* and rules 10 and 11 do not apply.

## 20 ROOM TO TACK AT AN OBSTRUCTION

### 20.1 Hailing

A boat may hail for *room* to tack and avoid a boat on the same *tack*. However, she shall not hail unless

(a) she is approaching an *obstruction* and will soon need to make a substantial course change to avoid it safely, and

(b) she is sailing close-hauled or above.

In addition, she shall not hail if the *obstruction* is a *mark* and a boat that is *fetching* it would be required to change course as a result of the hail.

### 20.2 Responding

(a) After a boat hails, she shall give a hailed boat time to respond.

(b) A hailed boat shall respond even if the hail breaks rule 20.1.

(c) A hailed boat shall respond either by tacking as soon as possible, or by immediately replying 'You tack' and then giving the hailing boat *room* to tack and avoid her.

(d) When a hailed boat responds, the hailing boat shall tack as soon as possible.

(e) From the time a boat hails until she has tacked and avoided a hailed boat, rule 18.2 does not apply between them.

### 20.3 Passing On a Hail to an Additional Boat

When a boat has been hailed for *room* to tack and she intends to respond by tacking, she may hail another boat on the same *tack* for *room* to tack and avoid her. She may hail even if her hail does not meet the conditions of rule 20.1. Rule 20.2 applies between her and a boat she hails.

（b）当船*相联*时，外侧船应给予内侧船在她和*障碍物*之间的*空间*，除非从*相联*开始的时候她已经做不到这一点。

（c）当船正在通过一个连续*障碍物*的时候，如果一条*明显在后*应该进行*避让*的船与另一条船和*障碍物*之间形成*相联*，当*相联*开始的时候，其间她没有可通过的*空间*，根据规则19.2(b)，她无权拥有*空间*，并且当两船保持*相联*时，她应该*避让*，规则 10 和 11不适用。

## 20 障碍物旁迎风换舷的空间

### 20.1 呼喊

船可通过呼喊要求*空间*去迎风换舷并避让另一条同*舷风*的船。但仅可以在发生以下情况时呼喊：

（a）她正在接近一个*障碍物*而且很快需要改变其原有航线来安全地避开它，和

（b）她正在近迎风或者高于近迎风航行。

此外，如果*障碍物*是一个*标志*，而一条飞*驰*她的船会因为该呼喊而被要求改变航线，她就不应该呼喊。

### 20.2 回应

（a）一条船呼喊后，她应给予被呼喊的船时间以回应。

（b）即使呼喊违反了规则20.1，被呼喊的船也应当做出回应。

（c）被呼喊的船应尽快通过迎风换舷，或马上回答“你迎风换舷（You tack）”来回应并且给予呼喊的船迎风换舷和避让的*空间*。

（d）当被呼喊的船做出回应，呼喊的船应立即迎风换舷。

（e）从船呼喊的那一刻起，直到其完成换舷并避让了被呼喊的船为止，规则18.2在这两船之间不适用。

### 20.3 向另一条船传递呼喊

当一条船被呼喊给予迎风换舷的*空间*并且她也计划做迎风换舷来回应呼喊时，她应该呼喊另一条与其同*舷风*的船给予其*空间*来迎风换舷以避让她。即使她的呼喊不符合规则20.1的条件，她

## SECTION D OTHER RULES

*When rule 22 or 23 applies between two boats, Section A rules do not.*

**21 EXONERATION**

When a boat is sailing within the *room* or *mark-room* to which she is entitled, she shall be exonerated if, in an incident with a boat required to give her that *room* or *mark-room*,

(a) she breaks a rule of Section A, rule 15 or rule 16, or

(b) she is compelled to break rule 31.

**22 STARTING ERRORS; TAKING PENALTIES; BACKING A SAIL**

**22.1** A boat sailing towards the pre-start side of the starting line or one of its extensions after her starting signal to *start* or to comply with rule 30.1 shall *keep clear* of a boat not doing so until she is completely on the pre-start side.

**22.2** A boat taking a penalty shall *keep clear* of one that is not.

**22.3** A boat moving astern, or sideways to windward, through the water by backing a sail shall *keep clear* of one that is not.

**23 CAPSIZED, ANCHORED OR AGROUND; RESCUING**

If possible, a boat shall avoid a boat that is capsized or has not regained control after capsizing, is anchored or aground, or is trying to help a person or vessel in danger. A boat is capsized when her masthead is in the water.

**24 INTERFERING WITH ANOTHER BOAT**

**24.1** If reasonably possible, a boat not *racing* shall not interfere with a boat that is *racing*.

**24.2** If reasonably possible, a boat shall not interfere with a boat that is taking a penalty, sailing on another leg or subject to rule 22.1. However, after the starting signal this rule does not apply when the boat is sailing her *proper course*.

依然应当呼喊。规则20.2在她和被她呼喊的那条船之间适用。

## D节　其他规则

*当规则22和23适用于两船之间时，A节规则不适用。*

### 21　免责

当一条船在有权拥有的*空间*或者*绕标空间*内航行时，如果事件中的另一条船需要给她这个*空间*或者*绕标空间*的话，那么该船在下列情况下应该免责：

（a）她违反了规则A节、规则15或规则16，或者

（b）她被迫违反了规则31。

### 22　起航失误；解脱；帆反受风

22.1　起航信号发出后向起航线或者其两端延长线的准备区一侧航行去*起航*的船，或执行规则30.1的船应*避让*没有这样做的船直至自己完全处于起航准备区一侧。

22.2　正在解脱的船应*避让*其他正常航行的船。

22.3　通过让帆反受风使船相对于水体向后移动或向上风横移的船应*避让*没有这样做的船。

### 23　翻船、抛锚或搁浅；救援

一条船如有可能应躲避翻倒的船或翻倒后未能重新获得操纵能力的船，躲避抛锚或搁浅的船，以及正在帮助处在危险中的人或船舶的船。当船桅杆顶部在水中时即为翻船。

### 24　妨碍另外一条船

24.1　如有合理的可能，不参加*竞赛*的船不应妨碍正在*竞赛*的船。

24.2　如有合理的可能，一条船不应妨碍正在做解脱的船，不应妨碍航行在另外一个航段上的船或规则22.1所描述的船。但是，起航信号发出后，该规则不适用于正在行驶*正当航线*的船。

# PART 3 CONDUCT OF A RACE

**25 NOTICE OF RACE, SAILING INSTRUCTIONS AND SIGNALS**

25.1 The notice of race and sailing instructions shall be made available to each boat before a race begins.

25.2 The meanings of the visual and sound signals stated in Race Signals shall not be changed except under rule 86.1(b). The meanings of any other signals that may be used shall be stated in the notice of race or sailing instructions.

25.3 When the race committee is required to display a flag as a visual signal, it may use a flag or other object of a similar appearance.

**26 STARTING RACES**

Races shall be started by using the following signals. Times shall be taken from the visual signals; the absence of a sound signal shall be disregarded.

| *Minutes before starting signal* | *Visual signal* | *Sound signal* | *Means* |
|---|---|---|---|
| 5* | Class flag | One | Warning signal |
| 4 | P, I, Z, Z with I, U, or black flag | One | Preparatory signal |
| 1 | Preparatory flag removed | One long | One minute |
| 0 | Class flag removed | One | Starting signal |

*or as stated in the sailing instructions

The warning signal for each succeeding class shall be made with or after the starting signal of the preceding class.

# 第三章　竞赛的实施

## 25　竞赛通知、航行细则和信号

25.1　竞赛通知和航行细则应在比赛开始前提供给每条参赛船。

25.2　除规则86.1(b)外，竞赛信号中所述的视觉和音响信号的含义不得改变。其他可能使用的信号的含义应在竞赛通知或航行细则中说明。

25.3　当竞赛委员会需要展示一面旗帜作为视觉信号时，可使用一面旗帜或其他近似外观的物体。

## 26　竞赛起航

竞赛起航将使用下列信号。计时以视觉信号为准，音响信号的缺失不必理会。

| *起航信号前时间（分钟）* | *视觉信号* | *音响信号* | *含义* |
|---|---|---|---|
| 05* | 级别旗 | 一声 | 预告信号 |
| 4 | P，I，Z，Z和I，U旗或黑旗 | 一声 | 准备信号 |
| 1 | 移除准备信号 | 一长声 | 1分钟 |
| 0 | 移除级别信号 | 一声 | 起航信号 |

*或按航行细则中的描述

后续每个级别比赛的预告信号将与前一个级别的起航信号同时或在其之后发出。

## 27 OTHER RACE COMMITTEE ACTIONS BEFORE THE STARTING SIGNAL

27.1 No later than the warning signal, the race committee shall signal or otherwise designate the course to be sailed if the sailing instructions have not stated the course, and it may replace one course signal with another and signal that wearing personal flotation devices is required (display flag Y with one sound).

27.2 No later than the preparatory signal, the race committee may move a starting *mark.*

27.3 Before the starting signal, the race committee may for any reason *postpone* (display flag AP, AP over H, or AP over A, with two sounds) or *abandon* the race (display flag N over H, or N over A, with three sounds).

## 28 SAILING THE COURSE

28.1 A boat shall *start*, sail the course described in the sailing instructions and *finish.* While doing so, she may leave on either side a *mark* that does not begin, bound or end the leg she is sailing. After *finishing* she need not cross the finishing line completely.

28.2 A string representing a boat's track from the time she begins to approach the starting line from its pre-start side to *start* until she *finishes* shall, when drawn taut,

(a) pass each *mark* on the required side and in the correct order,

(b) touch each rounding *mark*, and

(c) pass between the *marks* of a gate from the direction of the previous *mark.*

She may correct any errors to comply with this rule, provided she has not *finished.*

## 29 RECALLS

### 29.1 Individual Recall

When at a boat's starting signal any part of her hull, crew or equipment is on the course side of the starting line or she must comply with rule 30.1, the race committee shall promptly display flag X with one sound. The flag shall be displayed until all such boats have sailed completely to the pre-start side of the starting line or one of its extensions and have complied with rule 30.1 if it

## 27　发出起航信号之前竞赛委员会的其他行动

27.1　如果航行细则中未指明行驶的航线，竞赛委员会应不晚于预告信号发出时用信号通知或用其他方法指明要行驶的航线，可以用一个场地信号代替另外一个，并发出需穿着个人救生衣的信号（展示Y旗并伴随一声音响）。

27.2　竞赛委员会可以在不晚于准备信号时移动起航*标志*。

27.3　起航信号之前，竞赛委员会可能以任何理由*推迟*比赛（展示AP旗、AP旗在H旗之上或 AP旗在A旗之上，并伴随两声音响）或*放弃*比赛（展示N旗在H旗之上或N旗在A旗之上，并伴随三声音响）。

## 28　行驶航线

28.1　船应该先*起航*，按照航行细则中所描述的航线航行并*到达终点*。在这个过程中，可以在不具有标示所行驶航段的起点、边界或结束功能的*标志*的任意一侧离开。*到达终点*后她不需要完全通过终点线。

28.2　一条船开始从准备起航一侧靠近起航线*起航*后直到她*到达终点*，代表她的轨迹的一条线被拉紧时，应该

（a）在规定的一侧按照正确的顺序通过每个*标志*，

（b）触及每个所绕的*标志*，并且

（c）以上一个*标志*来的方向，从两个门*标*之间通过。

只要还没有*到达终点*，该船可遵照本规则改正任何错误。

## 29　召回

29.1　**个别召回**

当起航信号发出时，一条船的船体、船员或装备的任何一部分处于起航线的航线一侧或她必须执行规则 30.1 时，竞赛委员会应尽快展示 X 旗并伴随一声音响。该旗要展示至所有这样的船完全处于起航线或其两端延长线的起航准备区一侧，

applies, but no later than four minutes after the starting signal or one minute before any later starting signal, whichever is earlier. If rule 30.3 or 30.4 applies this rule does not.

**29.2 General Recall**

When at the starting signal the race committee is unable to identify boats that are on the course side of the starting line or to which rule 30 applies, or there has been an error in the starting procedure, the race committee may signal a general recall (display the First Substitute with two sounds). The warning signal for a new start for the recalled class shall be made one minute after the First Substitute is removed (one sound), and the starts for any succeeding classes shall follow the new start.

**30 STARTING PENALTIES**

**30.1 I Flag Rule**

If flag I has been displayed, and any part of a boat's hull, crew or equipment is on the course side of the starting line or one of its extensions during the last minute before her starting signal, she shall sail across an extension to the pre-start side before *starting*.

**30.2 Z Flag Rule**

If flag Z has been displayed, no part of a boat's hull, crew or equipment shall be in the triangle formed by the ends of the starting line and the first *mark* during the last minute before her starting signal. If a boat breaks this rule and is identified, she shall receive, without a hearing, a 20% Scoring Penalty calculated as stated in rule 44.3(c). She shall be penalized even if the race is restarted or resailed, but not if it is *postponed* or *abandoned* before the starting signal. If she is similarly identified during a subsequent attempt to start the same race, she shall receive an additional 20% Scoring Penalty.

**30.3 U Flag Rule**

If flag U has been displayed, no part of a boat's hull, crew or equipment shall be in the triangle formed by the ends of the starting

并在规则30.1适用时遵从它的规定，但展示时间不得晚于起航信号发出后 4 分钟或下一起航信号前1分钟，以这两个时刻先到的一个为限。如果规则30.3或 30.4适用，则本规则不适用。

29.2 **全部召回**

当发出起航信号时，竞赛委员会无法识别在起航线的航线一侧的船或规则30适用的那些船，或起航程序有误时，竞赛委员会可发出全部召回信号（展示代一旗并伴随两声音响）。被全部召回的级别新的起航预告信号将在代一旗移除（一声音响）后1分钟发出，后续所有级别的起航应该随这个新起航顺延。

## 30 起航惩罚

30.1 **I 旗规则**

如果I旗已经展示，当一条船在其起航信号发出前的最后1分钟内，船体、船员或装备的任何一部分处于起航线或其两端延长线的航线一侧，她应航行通过任一端延长线返回起航准备区一侧再去*起航*。

30.2 **Z 旗规则**

如果Z旗已经展示，当一条船在其起航信号发出前的最后1分钟内，船体、船员或装备的任何部分不得处于起航线两端与第一个*标志*形成的三角区域内。如某船违反了本规则并被识别，无须审理，她将被处以规则44.3(c)规定的20%的记分惩罚。除非该轮比赛在起航信号发出前被*推迟*或*放弃*，否则即使该轮比赛再次起航或重新比赛，此判罚仍有效。如果在同一轮竞赛的再次起航过程中，她同样被确定有相似行为，她应被加判20%的记分惩罚。

30.3 **U 旗规则**

如果U旗已经展示，一条船在其起航信号发出前的最后1分

line and the first *mark* during the last minute before her starting signal. If a boat breaks this rule and is identified, she shall be disqualified without a hearing, but not if the race is restarted or resailed.

30.4 **Black Flag Rule**

If a black flag has been displayed, no part of a boat's hull, crew or equipment shall be in the triangle formed by the ends of the starting line and the first *mark* during the last minute before her starting signal. If a boat breaks this rule and is identified, she shall be disqualified without a hearing, even if the race is restarted or resailed, but not if it is *postponed* or *abandoned* before the starting signal. If a general recall is signalled or the race is *abandoned* after the starting signal, the race committee shall display her sail number before the next warning signal for that race, and if the race is restarted or resailed she shall not sail in it. If she does so, her disqualification shall not be excluded in calculating her series score.

31 **TOUCHING A MARK**

While *racing*, a boat shall not touch a starting *mark* before *starting*, a *mark* that begins, bounds or ends the leg of the course on which she is sailing, or a finishing *mark* after *finishing*.

32 **SHORTENING OR ABANDONING AFTER THE START**

32.1 After the starting signal, the race committee may shorten the course (display flag S with two sounds) or *abandon* the race (display flag N, N over H, or N over A, with three sounds),

(a) because of foul weather,

(b) because of insufficient wind making it unlikely that any boat will *finish* within the time limit,

(c) because a *mark* is missing or out of position, or

钟内，船体、船员或装备的任何部分不得处于起航线两端和第一个*标志*形成的三角区域内。如某船违反本规则并被识别，无须审理，她将被记为取消资格，但该轮比赛再次起航或重新比赛的情况除外。

30.4 **黑旗规则**

如果黑旗已经展示，一条船在其起航信号发出前的最后1分钟内，船体、船员或装备的任何部分不得处于起航线两端与第一个*标志*形成的三角区域内。如某船违反了本规则并被识别，无须审理，她将被记为取消资格，除非在起航信号发出前该轮比赛被*推迟*或*放弃*，否则即使该轮比赛再次起航或重新比赛，此判罚仍有效。如在起航信号后发出全部召回或*放弃*竞赛的信号，竞赛委员会将在该轮比赛的下一个预告信号前展示该船帆号；如果该轮再次起航或重新比赛，该船不得再参加该轮比赛。如果她再参加该轮比赛，她被取消资格的分数将不能从总分中去掉。

## 31 碰标

*竞赛*时，船在*起航*前不允许触碰起点*标志*以及标示她正在行驶的航段的起始、边界和结束的*标志*，并且*到达终点*后也不许触碰终点*标志*。

## 32 起航后缩短航线或放弃竞赛

32.1 起航信号发出后，竞赛委员会可根据下列情况缩短航线（展示S旗并伴随两声音响）或*放弃*比赛（展示N旗，或N旗在H或A旗之上，并伴随三声音响）：

（a）因恶劣天气，

（b）因风力不足使得这轮竞赛中的任何一条船不可能在限定的时间内*到达终点*，

（c）因*标志*丢失或移位，或者

(d) for any other reason directly affecting the safety or fairness of the competition.

In addition, the race committee may shorten the course so that other scheduled races can be sailed, or *abandon* the race because of an error in the starting procedure. However, after one boat has sailed the course and *finished* within the time limit, if any, the race committee shall not *abandon* the race without considering the consequences for all boats in the race or series.

**32.2** If the race committee signals a shortened course (displays flag S with two sounds), the finishing line shall be,

(a) at a rounding *mark*, between the *mark* and a staff displaying flag S;

(b) a line the course requires boats to cross; or

(c) at a gate, between the gate *marks*.

The shortened course shall be signalled before the first boat crosses the finishing line.

## 33 CHANGING THE NEXT LEG OF THE COURSE

The race committee may change a leg of the course that begins at a rounding *mark* or at a gate by changing the position of the next *mark* (or the finishing line) and signalling all boats before they begin the leg. The next *mark* need not be in position at that time.

(a) If the direction of the leg will be changed, the signal shall be the display of flag C with repetitive sounds and one or both of

(1) the new compass bearing,

(2) a green triangle for a change to starboard or a red rectangle for a change to port.

(b) If the length of the leg will be changed, the signal shall be the display of flag C with repetitive sounds and a '–' if the length will be decreased or a '+' if it will be increased.

(c) Subsequent legs may be changed without further signalling to maintain the course shape.

（d）因直接影响竞赛安全或公平的任何其他理由。

此外，竞赛委员会可以缩短航线以便日程中其他比赛可以正常进行或者由于起航流程中的一个错误而*放弃*本轮比赛。但是，如有任何一条船在时限内行驶了整个航线并且*到达终点*后，竞赛委员会不应该在不考虑所有船在该轮比赛或系列赛中的结果的前提下*放弃*该轮比赛。

32.2 如果竞赛委员会发出了缩短航线的信号（展示S旗并伴随两声音响），终点线：

（a）若在一个绕行的*标志*旁，将在该*标志*与展示S旗的旗杆之间；

（b）将为航线要求船通过的一条线；或者

（c）若在门标处，将在两个门标之间。

缩短航线的信号应该在第一条船通过终点线之前发出。

## 33 改变下一航段

竞赛委员会可以从一个绕行的*标志*或者门标开始改变航线中的一个航段，方法是改变下一个*标志*（或终点线）的位置并在所有船开始这个航段前用信号通知她们。下一*标志*无须在那时到位。

（a）如果将改变航段的方向，信号应是展示C旗并伴随重复音响，并且有下面的一种或两种展示：

（1）新的罗径方位，

（2）一个绿色的三角形以示改变至右舷，或是一个红色的长方形以示改变至左舷。

（b）如果将改变航段的长度，信号应是展示C旗伴随重复音响，并且“–”表示将减少长度或者“+”表示将增加长度。

（c）为保持整个航线的形状可以不再发信号就改变后续航段。

## 34 MARK MISSING

If a *mark* is missing or out of position, the race committee shall, if possible,

(a) replace it in its correct position or substitute a new one of similar appearance, or

(b) substitute an object displaying flag M and make repetitive sound signals.

## 35 TIME LIMIT AND SCORES

If one boat sails the course as required by rule 28 and *finishes* within the time limit, if any, all boats that *finish* shall be scored according to their finishing places unless the race is *abandoned*. If no boat *finishes* within the time limit, the race committee shall *abandon* the race.

## 36 RACES RESTARTED OR RESAILED

If a race is restarted or resailed, a breach of a *rule* in the original race, or in any previous restart or resail of that race, shall not

(a) prohibit a boat from competing unless she has broken rule 30.4; or

(b) cause a boat to be penalized except under rule 2, 30.2, 30.4 or 69 or under rule 14 when she has caused injury or serious damage.

## 34　标志丢失

当一个*标志*丢失或移位，如有可能，竞赛委员会应：

（a）把*标志*重新放在正确的位置，或用新的相似外观的*标志*代替，或

（b）由一个展示M旗的物体代替并伴随重复音响。

## 35　时间限制和记分

如一条船按规则28的要求行驶了整个航线并在时间限制内（如果有的话）*到达终点*，除非比赛被*放弃*，否则所有*到达终点*的船应按终点位置顺序记分。如果没有一条船在时间限制内*到达终点*，竞赛委员会应*放弃*该轮竞赛。

## 36　重新起航或重新竞赛

如果一轮比赛重新起航或重新竞赛，或者该轮竞赛在此之前的任意一次重新起航或重新竞赛的比赛中违反了*规则*，将不能

（a）禁止某条船比赛，除非她违反了规则30.4；或者

（b）导致一条船被判罚，除非她违反了规则2（译者注：经2018世界帆联年会规则委员会决定，将于2020年的规则版本中正式加入规则2，目前在实践中已开始酌情考虑此点）、30.2、30.4或69，或根据规则14当她造成了损伤或严重损坏。

# PART 4 OTHER REQUIREMENTS WHEN RACING

*Part 4 rules apply only to boats **racing** unless the rule states otherwise.*

**40 PERSONAL FLOTATION DEVICES**

When flag Y is displayed with one sound before or with the warning signal, competitors shall wear personal flotation devices, except briefly while changing or adjusting clothing or personal equipment. When flag Y is displayed ashore, this rule applies at all times while afloat. Wet suits and dry suits are not personal flotation devices.

**41 OUTSIDE HELP**

A boat shall not receive help from any outside source, except

(a) help for a crew member who is ill, injured or in danger;

(b) after a collision, help from the crew of the other vessel to get clear;

(c) help in the form of information freely available to all boats;

(d) unsolicited information from a disinterested source, which may be another boat in the same race.

However, a boat that gains a significant advantage in the race from help received under rule 41(a) may be protested and penalized; any penalty may be less than disqualification.

**42 PROPULSION**

**42.1 Basic Rule**

Except when permitted in rule 42.3 or 45, a boat shall compete by using only the wind and water to increase, maintain or decrease her speed. Her crew may adjust the trim of sails and hull, and perform other acts of seamanship, but shall not otherwise move their bodies to propel the boat.

# 第四章　竞赛时的其他规定

*规则第四章只适用于参加**竞赛**的船，除非规则另有说明。*

## 40　个人漂浮装备

当在预告信号发出之前或同时展示Y旗并伴随一声音响时，除了暂时更换、调整衣物或个人装备外，选手应穿戴个人漂浮装备。当在岸上展示Y旗时，在水上时这条规则也一直生效。干式或湿式保暖服不是个人漂浮装备。

## 41　外部援助

一条船不得从任何外部途径接受援助，以下情况例外：

（a）援助生病、受伤或遇险的选手；

（b）在碰撞后可接受另外一条船舶上船员的援助以达到脱离接触的目的；

（c）所有船都可得到的信息形式的援助；

（d）非利益方主动提供的信息，这可能来自于同一轮竞赛中另一条船。

然而，一条船根据规则41(a)在该轮竞赛接受援助后明显获益，她可能被抗议并被判罚；判罚可轻于取消资格。

## 42　推进

### 42.1　基本规则

除规则42.3或规则45允许外，一条船在比赛中仅可以利用风和水来增加、保持或降低船的速度。其船员可以调整帆和船体并采用其他的海上操作动作，而不应靠额外移动身体去推进船只。

**42.2 Prohibited Actions**

Without limiting the application of rule 42.1, these actions are prohibited:

(a) pumping: repeated fanning of any sail either by pulling in and releasing the sail or by vertical or athwartship body movement;

(b) rocking: repeated rolling of the boat, induced by

(1) body movement,

(2) repeated adjustment of the sails or centreboard, or

(3) steering;

(c) ooching: sudden forward body movement, stopped abruptly;

(d) sculling: repeated movement of the helm that is either forceful or that propels the boat forward or prevents her from moving astern;

(e) repeated tacks or gybes unrelated to changes in the wind or to tactical considerations.

**42.3 Exceptions**

(a) A boat may be rolled to facilitate steering.

(b) A boat's crew may move their bodies to exaggerate the rolling that facilitates steering the boat through a tack or a gybe, provided that, just after the tack or gybe is completed, the boat's speed is not greater than it would have been in the absence of the tack or gybe.

(c) Except on a beat to windward, when surfing (rapidly accelerating down the front of a wave) or planing is possible, the boat's crew may pull in any sail in order to initiate surfing or planing, but each sail may be pulled in only once for each wave or gust of wind.

(d) When a boat is above a close-hauled course and either stationary or moving slowly, she may scull to turn to a close-hauled course.

(e) If a batten is inverted, the boat's crew may pump the sail until the batten is no longer inverted. This action is not permitted if it clearly propels the boat.

(f) A boat may reduce speed by repeatedly moving her helm.

### 42.2 禁止动作

在不限制规则42.1适用的情况下，下列属于禁止动作：

（a）摇帆：利用收帆并松帆或上下左右晃动身体来反复扇动某面帆；

（b）滚动：通过下述动作使船反复滚动：

（1）身体的运动，

（2）对帆或稳向板的反复调节，或

（3）转向；

（c）前冲：身体突然前移、突然停止；

（d）摇舵：用力地或者能推进船体向前或防止其向后移动的舵的反复运动；

（e）反复进行与风的变化或战术考虑无关的迎风换舷或顺风换舷。

### 42.3 例外

（a）船可以滚动协助转向。

（b）船上的船员可移动他们的身体加大滚动，以助力完成迎风换舷或顺风换舷，只要在完成迎风换舷或顺风换舷之后，船速不超过原来不做迎风换舷或顺风换舷时的速度。

（c）除在驶向上风的迎风航线上之外，在有可能冲浪（在浪的前方突然加速下滑）或滑行时，船上的船员为了促使冲浪或滑行，可以拉动任意帆，但每一个涌浪或一次阵风只能拉动一次。

（d）当一条船处在高于近迎风航线上不动或前进速度很慢时，她可摇舵转向近迎风航线。

（e）如果帆骨翻转，船上的船员可以摇帆直到帆骨不再翻转。如果该动作明显推动了船只，那么就不被允许。

（f）船可以通过快速移动舵来减速。

(g) Any means of propulsion may be used to help a person or another vessel in danger.

(h) To get clear after grounding or colliding with a vessel or object, a boat may use force applied by her crew or the crew of the other vessel and any equipment other than a propulsion engine. However, the use of an engine may be permitted by rule 42.3(i).

(i) Sailing instructions may, in stated circumstances, permit propulsion using an engine or any other method, provided the boat does not gain a significant advantage in the race.

*Note: Interpretations of rule 42 are available at the World Sailing website or by mail upon request.*

## 43 COMPETITOR CLOTHING AND EQUIPMENT

**43.1** (a) Competitors shall not wear or carry clothing or equipment for the purpose of increasing their weight.

(b) Furthermore, a competitor's clothing and equipment shall not weigh more than 8 kilograms, excluding a hiking or trapeze harness and clothing (including footwear) worn only below the knee. Class rules or sailing instructions may specify a lower weight or a higher weight up to 10 kilograms. Class rules may include footwear and other clothing worn below the knee within that weight. A hiking or trapeze harness shall have positive buoyancy and shall not weigh more than 2 kilograms, except that class rules may specify a higher weight up to 4 kilograms. Weights shall be determined as required by Appendix H.

**43.2** Rule 43.1(b) does not apply to boats required to be equipped with lifelines.

## 44 PENALTIES AT THE TIME OF AN INCIDENT

### 44.1 Taking a Penalty

A boat may take a Two-Turns Penalty when she may have broken one or more rules of Part 2 in an incident while *racing*. She may take a One-Turn Penalty when she may have broken rule 31. Alternatively, sailing instructions may specify the use of the Scoring Penalty or some other penalty, in which case the specified penalty shall replace the One-Turn and the Two-Turns Penalty. However, （g）援助处在危险中的个人或船舶时，任何推进方式均可使用。

（h）船在搁浅后或与另外一条船或物体碰撞后，可借用另外一条船舶上船员的外力或装备使船脱离困境，但不能借助于推进引擎。然而，规则42.3(i)规定的情况可以使用引擎。

（i）在规定的情况下，航行细则可以允许使用引擎或其他方式提供的推进，前提是该船在比赛中没有获得明显优势。

*注：规则42 的解释在世界帆联网站可以查到或要求函寄。*

## 43 选手的服装与装备

43.1 （a）选手不应穿着或携带专为增加他们体重的服装或装备。

（b）此外，选手的服装和装备称重时不得超过8公斤，不包括压舷裤或吊带和只穿在膝盖以下的服装（包括鞋袜）。级别规则或航行细则中可能会规定一个更低的重量或不能超出10 公斤的更高标准。级别规则可在规定的重量中包括鞋袜和其他膝盖以下的服装。压舷裤或吊带应有正浮力，除级别规则中注明可有高达4公斤的更高重量标准外，其重量不得超过2 公斤。重量的决定可按附录 H执行。

43.2 规则43.1(b)不适用于需要装备安全护栏的船。

## 44 事件发生时的惩罚

### 44.1 解脱

在竞赛中当船违反了规则第二章中的一条或多条规则时，她将转两圈解脱。她违反规则31时可转一圈解脱。或者，航行细则可详细说明分数惩罚或其他惩罚的用法，在这种情况下，特别规定的惩罚方法将替换一圈或者两圈解脱。然而，

(a) when a boat may have broken a rule of Part 2 and rule 31 in the same incident she need not take the penalty for breaking rule 31;

(b) if the boat caused injury or serious damage or, despite taking a penalty, gained a significant advantage in the race or series by her breach her penalty shall be to retire.

**44.2 One-Turn and Two-Turns Penalties**

After getting well clear of other boats as soon after the incident as possible, a boat takes a One-Turn or Two-Turns Penalty by promptly making the required number of turns in the same direction, each turn including one tack and one gybe. When a boat takes the penalty at or near the finishing line, she shall sail completely to the course side of the line before *finishing*.

**44.3 Scoring Penalty**

(a) A boat takes a Scoring Penalty by displaying a yellow flag at the first reasonable opportunity after the incident.

(b) When a boat has taken a Scoring Penalty, she shall keep the yellow flag displayed until *finishing* and call the race committee's attention to it at the finishing line. At that time she shall also inform the race committee of the identity of the other boat involved in the incident. If this is impracticable, she shall do so at the first reasonable opportunity and within the protest time limit.

(c) The race score for a boat that takes a Scoring Penalty shall be the score she would have received without that penalty, made worse by the number of places stated in the sailing instructions. When the sailing instructions do not state the number of places, the penalty shall be 20% of the score for Did Not *Finish*, rounded to the nearest whole number (0.5 rounded upward). The scores of other boats shall not be changed; therefore, two boats may receive the same score. However, the penalty shall not cause the boat's score to be worse than the score for Did Not *Finish*.

（a）当一条船在同一事件中违反了规则第二章和规则31时，她不必接受违反规则31的惩罚；

（b）如果船造成了损伤或严重损坏，或尽管做了解脱，但由于犯规她在该轮竞赛或系列赛中获得了明显优势，对她的惩罚应该是退出比赛。

**44.2 一圈和两圈解脱**

船在事件发生后尽快完全避让其他船后做一圈或两圈解脱，她应尽快在同样的方向做被要求次数的转圈，每一圈包括一个迎风换舷和一个顺风换舷。在终点线或终点线附近做解脱的船，应该在*到达终点*前完全回到终点线的航线一侧。

**44.3 分数惩罚**

（a）在事件发生后，一条船应在最先出现的合理时机展示黄旗以表示接受分数惩罚。

（b）当一条船已经接受了分数惩罚，她应展示黄旗直至*到达终点*，并且在到达终点线时提醒竞赛委员会注意黄旗。此时，她也应通知竞赛委员会事件中相关的另一条船的帆号。如不可行，她应在抗议时限内第一合理的时机进行报告。

（c）接受分数惩罚的船的轮次分数应是其在没有受到惩罚前得到的分数加上航行细则中规定的名次数得出的更差分数。当航行细则中没有注明加罚的名次数时，该罚分应为没有*到达终点*对应的分数的20%（四舍五入取整数）。其他船的分数不应被改变；因此，两条船可能有相同的分数。但是，罚分不能导致该船成绩差于**没有***到达终点*对应的分数。

**45 HAULING OUT; MAKING FAST; ANCHORING**

A boat shall be afloat and off moorings at her preparatory signal. Thereafter, she shall not be hauled out or made fast except to bail out, reef sails or make repairs. She may anchor or the crew may stand on the bottom. She shall recover the anchor before continuing in the race unless she is unable to do so.

**46 PERSON IN CHARGE**

A boat shall have on board a person in charge designated by the member or organization that entered the boat. See rule 75.

**47 LIMITATIONS ON EQUIPMENT AND CREW**

**47.1** A boat shall use only the equipment on board at her preparatory signal.

**47.2** No person on board shall intentionally leave, except when ill or injured, or to help a person or vessel in danger, or to swim. A person leaving the boat by accident or to swim shall be back on board before the boat continues in the race.

**48 FOG SIGNALS AND LIGHTS; TRAFFIC SEPARATION SCHEMES**

**48.1** When safety requires, a boat shall sound fog signals and show lights as required by the *International Regulations for Preventing Collisions at Sea (IRPCAS)* or applicable government rules.

**48.2** A boat shall comply with rule 10, Traffic Separation Schemes, of the *IRPCAS.*

**49 CREW POSITION; LIFELINES**

**49.1** Competitors shall use no device designed to position their bodies outboard, other than hiking straps and stiffeners worn under the thighs.

**49.2** When lifelines are required by the class rules or any other *rule*, competitors shall not position any part of their torsos outside them, except briefly to perform a necessary task. On boats equipped with upper and lower lifelines, a competitor sitting on the deck facing outboard with his waist inside the lower lifeline may have the upper part of his body outside the upper lifeline. Unless a class rule or any

## 45　拖船上岸；系留；抛锚

船应在准备信号发出后浮于水上和解开系泊索。之后她不可被拖上岸或系留，除非是在排空舱底水、缩帆或修理船时。她可抛锚或船员可站在水底。在继续竞赛前她应起锚，除非她办不到。

## 46　负责人

船上应有一名由给该船报名的成员或组织指定的负责人。参见规则75。

## 47　装备和船员的限制

47.1　在准备信号发出时，参赛船应该只使用船上的装备。

47.2　除因伤病、救援处在危险中的个人和船舶或游泳外，船上的人员不得故意离开船。因偶然或游泳离开了船的船员应在船继续参加竞赛前返回。

## 48　雾中信号与灯光；分道通航制

48.1　在安全航行需要时，每条船应遵守*《国际海上避碰规则（IRPCAS）》*或适用的政府规定，发出雾中音响信号和灯光信号。

48.2　船必须遵守*IRPCAS*中的第10条，即分道通航制。

## 49　船员位置；安全护栏

49.1　选手不应使用任何使身体置于船舷外的装置，除非使用吊裤和大腿以下穿着的坚硬装备。

49.2　当级别*规则*或其他规则要求有安全护栏时，除非短时执行一项必要的任务，否则选手不得将其身体躯干的任何部分置于安全护栏之外。在装有上下安全护栏的船上，如选手坐在甲板上，面向舷外，腰部在下安全护栏内侧，可以使其身体上

other *rule* specifies a maximum deflection, lifelines shall be taut. If | the class rules do not specify the material or minimum diameter of lifelines, they shall comply with the corresponding specifications in the *World Sailing Offshore Special Regulations*.

*Note: Those regulations are available at the World Sailing website.*

**50 SETTING AND SHEETING SAILS**

**50.1 Changing Sails**

When headsails or spinnakers are being changed, a replacing sail may be fully set and trimmed before the replaced sail is lowered. However, only one mainsail and, except when changing, only one spinnaker shall be carried set at a time.

**50.2 Spinnaker Poles; Whisker Poles**

Only one spinnaker pole or whisker pole shall be used at a time except when gybing. When in use, it shall be attached to the foremost mast.

**50.3 Use of Outriggers**

(a) No sail shall be sheeted over or through an outrigger, except as permitted in rule 50.3(b) or 50.3(c). An outrigger is any fitting or other device so placed that it could exert outward pressure on a sheet or sail at a point from which, with the boat upright, a vertical line would fall outside the hull or deck. For the purpose of this rule, bulwarks, rails and rubbing strakes are not part of the hull or deck and the following are not outriggers: a bowsprit used to secure the tack of a sail, a bumkin used to sheet the boom of a sail, or a boom of a boomed headsail that requires no adjustment when tacking.

(b) Any sail may be sheeted to or led above a boom that is regularly used for a sail and is permanently attached to the mast from which the head of the sail is set.

(c) A headsail may be sheeted or attached at its clew to a spinnaker pole or whisker pole, provided that a spinnaker is not set.

半部分探出到上安全护栏外侧。除非有级别规则或其他*规则*规定了护栏索的最大偏离度，安全护栏应当是拉紧的。如果级别规则没有规定安全护栏的材质和最小直径，应当执行世界帆联《离岸赛特别规则》中相应的规格规定。

*注：以上提到的规则都可以在世界帆联网站查到。*

## 50 升帆与调帆

### 50.1 换帆

在更换前帆或球帆时，替换帆在被替换的帆降下之前可以全部升起并调好，但是，除换帆外，一次只能使用一面主帆和一面球帆。

### 50.2 球帆杆和球帆底边撑杆

除顺风换舷外，一次只限使用一根球帆杆或球帆撑杆（译者注：一端与桅杆连接，另一端与球帆后角连接的杆状物）。使用时，它应被固定在最前面的桅杆上。

### 50.3 舷外撑杆的使用

（a）除规则50.3(b)或50.3(c)允许的外，缭绳不应从舷外撑杆上或通过舷外撑杆来操控。舷外撑杆是这样设置的任何配件或其他装置：它能从某一点对缭绳或帆施加向外的张力，当船处于直立状态时，从该点引出的垂直线将落在船体或甲板的外边。对本条规则来说，舷墙、护舷木和护舷条不是船体或甲板的组成部分。下面部件不属于舷外撑杆：用来固定帆前下角的船首撑杆，用来操控帆杆缭绳的伸到船尾之外的撑杆或迎风换舷时不需要调整的前帆用帆杆。

（b）任何帆都可以被升在或绑在帆杆上方，这个帆杆通常为张帆所用，并永久性地固定在张挂工作帆上角的桅杆上。

（c）只要不升起球帆，前帆后角可以连到球帆杆或球帆撑杆上来操作。

**50.4 Headsails**

For the purposes of rules 50 and 54 and Appendix G, the difference between a headsail and a spinnaker is that the width of a headsail, measured between the midpoints of its luff and leech, is less than 75% of the length of its foot. A sail tacked down behind the foremost mast is not a headsail.

## 51 MOVABLE BALLAST

All movable ballast, including sails that are not set, shall be properly stowed. Water, dead weight or ballast shall not be moved for the purpose of changing trim or stability. Floorboards, bulkheads, doors, stairs and water tanks shall be left in place and all cabin fixtures kept on board. However, bilge water may be bailed out.

## 52 MANUAL POWER

A boat's standing rigging, running rigging, spars and movable hull appendages shall be adjusted and operated only by the power provided by the crew.

## 53 SKIN FRICTION

A boat shall not eject or release a substance, such as a polymer, or have specially textured surfaces that could improve the character of the flow of water inside the boundary layer.

## 54 FORESTAYS AND HEADSAIL TACKS

Forestays and headsail tacks, except those of spinnaker staysails when the boat is not close-hauled, shall be attached approximately on a boat's centreline.

## 55 TRASH DISPOSAL

A competitor shall not intentionally put trash in the water. This rule applies at all times while afloat. The penalty for a breach of this rule may be less than disqualification.

### 50.4 前帆

对于规则50、54和附录G而言，前帆和球帆的不同在于前帆从其前缘和后缘的中间点所量得的宽度小于其底边长度的75%。帆前下角固定在最前面的桅杆后方的帆不是前帆。

## 51 可移动的压舱物

所有可移动的压舱物应合理放置，包括未使用的帆。不能通过移动压舱水、固定配重或压舱物来达到改变船的纵倾度或稳定性的目的。船舱底板、隔舱板、门、梯子和水箱应放置到位，并且所有舱室设施都应保留在船上。但是，可以排出舱底积水。

## 52 人力

船的固定支索、调帆索具、桅帆杆及可移动的船体附属物只能依靠船员的人力来调整和操作。

## 53 船的表面磨擦

船不得排出或释放出某种物质，比如聚合物，也不应有能够提高边界层内水流特性的特殊质地的船体表面。

## 54 前支索和前帆前下角

前支索和前帆前下角应大致被固定在船的中心线上，船不在近迎风航行时所使用的球帆支索除外。

## 55 垃圾处理

选手不得故意往水中丢垃圾。该条规则适用于整个水上时段。对于违反该条规则的判罚可以轻于取消资格。

# **PART 5** PROTESTS, REDRESS, HEARINGS, MISCONDUCT AND APPEALS

## **SECTION A** PROTESTS; REDRESS; RULE 69 ACTION

### 60 RIGHT TO PROTEST; RIGHT TO REQUEST REDRESS OR RULE 69 ACTION

**60.1** A boat may

(a) protest another boat, but not for an alleged breach of a rule of Part 2 or rule 31 unless she was involved in or saw the incident; or

(b) request redress.

**60.2** A race committee may

(a) protest a boat, but not as a result of information arising from a request for redress or an invalid *protest*, or from a report from a person with a *conflict of interest* other than the representative of the boat herself;

(b) request redress for a boat; or

(c) report to the protest committee requesting action under rule 69.2(b).

**60.3** A protest committee may

(a) protest a boat, but not as a result of information arising from a request for redress or an invalid *protest*, or from a report from a person with a *conflict of interest* other than the representative of the boat herself. However, it may protest a boat

(1) if it learns of an incident involving her that may have resulted in injury or serious damage, or

(2) if during the hearing of a valid *protest* it learns that the boat, although not a *party* to the hearing, was involved in the incident and may have broken a *rule*;

(b) call a hearing to consider redress;

# 第五章　抗议、补偿、审理、品行不端和上诉

## A节　抗议；补偿；规则 69 的措施

### 60　抗议的权利；要求补偿的权利或规则 69 的措施

60.1　一条船可以

（a）抗议另外一条船，但对涉嫌违反规则第二章或规则31的抗议只能当其自己是当事船或目睹事件时才能提出；或

（b）要求补偿。

60.2　竞赛委员会可以

（a）抗议一条船，但不能从一份补偿要求、一份无效的*抗议*或有*利益冲突*的人而不是船本身的代表的报告中获取信息后提出抗议。

（b）要求给予某条船补偿；或

（c）向抗议委员会报告要求按规则69.2(b)采取措施。

60.3　抗议委员会可以

（a）抗议一条船，但不能从一份补偿要求、一份无效的*抗议*或有有*利益冲突*的人而不是船本身的代表的报告中获取信息后提出抗议。然而可在下列情况下对一条船提出抗议：

（1）如果了解到涉及她的事件中可能已经导致损伤或严重损坏，或

（2）如果在审理一个有效*抗议*时，了解到该船虽不是审理的一方，但也涉及该事件并有可能违反了*规则*；

（b）召集审理考虑给予补偿；

(c) act under rule 69.2(b); or

(d) call a hearing to consider whether a *support person* has broken a *rule*, based on its own observation or information received from any source, including evidence taken during a hearing.

**60.4** A technical committee may

(a) protest a boat, but not as a result of information arising from a request for redress or an invalid *protest*, or from a report from a person with a *conflict of interest* other than the representative of the boat herself. However, it shall protest a boat if it decides that

(1) a boat has broken a rule of Part 4, but not rules 41, 42, 44 and 46, or

(2) a boat or personal equipment does not comply with the class rules;

(b) request redress for a boat; or

(c) report to the protest committee requesting action under rule 69.2(b).

**60.5** However, neither a boat nor a committee may protest for an alleged breach of rule 5, 6, 7 or 69.

## 61 PROTEST REQUIREMENTS

### 61.1 Informing the Protestee

(a) A boat intending to protest shall inform the other boat at the first reasonable opportunity. When her *protest* will concern an incident in the racing area that she was involved in or saw, she shall hail 'Protest' and conspicuously display a red flag at the first reasonable opportunity for each. She shall display the flag until she is no longer *racing*. However,

(1) if the other boat is beyond hailing distance, the protesting boat need not hail but she shall inform the other boat at the first reasonable opportunity;

(2) if the hull length of the protesting boat is less than 6 metres, she need not display a red flag;

(3) if the incident was an error by the other boat in sailing the course, she need not hail or display a red flag but she

（c）按规则69.2(b)采取措施；或

（d）以其自身的观察或者从任何来源获取到的信息为基础，包括在审理过程中取得的证据召集审理来考虑*后援人员*是否已经违反*规则*。

60.4 技术委员会可以

（a）抗议一条船，但不能从一份补偿要求、一份无效的*抗议*或有*利益冲突*的人而不是船本身的代表的报告中获取信息后提出抗议。然而如果确认了如下情况，其应该抗议：

（1）某船违反规则第四章，但没有违反规则 41、42、44 和 46，或

（2）某船或个人装备不符合级别规则；

（b）为一条船要求补偿；或

（c）向抗议委员会报告要求按规则69.2(b)采取措施。

60.5 然而，任何一条船或委员会都不可以就涉嫌违反规则5、6、7或69的情况提出抗议。

## 61 对抗议的要求

### 61.1 通知被抗议人

（a）一条有意提出抗议的船应在最先出现的合理时机通知另外一条船。当她的*抗议*是在竞赛区域中涉及到她或她所看到的事件，她应呼喊“Protest（抗议）”并在每一次最先出现的合理时机明显地展示一面红旗，她应将这面旗展示到她不再*竞赛*为止。但

（1）如果另外一条船远于可呼喊距离，抗议船无需呼喊，但需在最先出现的合理时机通知那条船；

（2）如果提出抗议的船的船体长度短于6米则无须展示红旗；

（3）如果该事件是另一条船所犯的行驶航线的错误，她不需要呼喊或展示红旗，但是她应当在该船*到*

shall inform the other boat either before or at the first reasonable opportunity after the other boat *finishes*;

(4) if as a result of the incident a member of either crew is in danger, or there is injury or serious damage that is obvious to the boat intending to protest, the requirements of this rule do not apply to her, but she shall attempt to inform the other boat within the time limit of rule 61.3.

(b) If the race committee, technical committee or protest committee intends to protest a boat concerning an incident the committee observed in the racing area, it shall inform her after the race within the time limit of rule 61.3. In other cases the committee shall inform the boat of its intention to protest as soon as reasonably possible.

(c) If the protest committee decides to protest a boat under rule 60.3(a)(2), it shall inform her as soon as reasonably possible, close the current hearing, proceed as required by rules 61.2 and 63, and hear the original and the new *protests* together.

**61.2 Protest Contents**

A *protest* shall be in writing and identify

(a) the protestor and protestee;

(b) the incident;

(c) where and when the incident occurred;

(d) any *rule* the protestor believes was broken; and

(e) the name of the protestor's representative.

However, if requirement (b) is met, requirement (a) may be met at any time before the hearing, and requirements (d) and (e) may be met before or during the hearing. Requirement (c) may also be met before or during the hearing, provided the protestee is allowed reasonable time to prepare for the hearing.

**61.3 Protest Time Limit**

A *protest* by a boat, or by the race committee, technical committee or protest committee about an incident the committee observed in the racing area, shall be delivered to the race office within the protest time limit stated in the sailing instructions. If none is stated, the time limit is two hours after the last boat in the race *finishes*. Other race committee, technical committee or protest committee *protests* shall

*达终点*前或在其*到达终点*后的最先出现的合理时机告知该船；

（4）如果事件结果造成任何一方的船员处于危险中，或打算提出抗议的船有明显的损伤或严重损坏，那么此条规则的要求对她不适用，但是她应尽力在规则61.3规定的时限内通知另外那条船。

（b）如果竞赛委员会、技术委员会或抗议委员会有意抗议一条与该委员会在竞赛水域观察到的事件有关的船时，应在该轮赛后，在规则61.3所规定的抗议时限内通知该船。在其他情况下，该委员会应当尽可能早地告知该船其将被抗议。

（c）如果抗议委员会决定根据规则60.3(a)(2)向一条船提出抗议，应在最先出现的合理时间内通知该船，结束当前的审理，按照规则61.2和63的要求进行审理，将原*抗议*和新*抗议*一同审理。

**61.2 抗议内容**

应以书面形式提出*抗议*并明确：

（a）抗议者和被抗议者；

（b）事件；

（c）事件发生的时间和地点；

（d）抗议者所确信违反的*规则*；和

（e）抗议者代表的姓名。

但是，如已满足(b)项要求，可在审理前任何时间满足(a)项要求，在审理前或审理中满足(d)项和(e)项要求。也可以在审理前或者审理中满足(c)项要求，前提是允许被抗议者有合理的时间来做好审理准备。

**61.3 抗议时限**

一个由船或竞赛委员会、技术委员会或抗议委员会提出的关于该委员会在竞赛水域观察到的事件的*抗议*，应在航行细则

be delivered to the race office no later than two hours after the committee receives the relevant information. The protest committee shall extend the time if there is good reason to do so.

**62 REDRESS**

**62.1** A request for redress or a protest committee's decision to consider redress shall be based on a claim or possibility that a boat's score or place in a race or series has been or may be, through no fault of her own, made significantly worse by

(a) an improper action or omission of the race committee, protest committee, organizing authority or technical committee for the event, but not by a protest committee decision when the boat was a *party* to the hearing;

(b) injury or physical damage because of the action of a boat that was breaking a rule of Part 2 or of a vessel not *racing* that was required to keep clear;

(c) giving help (except to herself or her crew) in compliance with rule 1.1; or

(d) an action of a boat, or a member of her crew, that resulted in a penalty under rule 2 or a penalty or warning under rule 69.2(h).

**62.2** A request shall be in writing and identify the reason for making it. If the request is based on an incident in the racing area, it shall be delivered to the race office within the protest time limit or two hours after the incident, whichever is later. Other requests shall be delivered as soon as reasonably possible after learning of the reasons for making the request. The protest committee shall extend the time if there is good reason to do so. No red flag is required.

规定的抗议时限内递交到竞赛办公室。如未注明时限，该时限为该轮比赛最后一条船*到达终点*后两个小时。竞赛委员会、技术委员会或抗议委员会提出的其他*抗议*应在该委员会收到相关信息后两小时内递交至竞赛办公室。若理由充足，抗议委员会可延长递交抗议的时间。

## 62 补偿

62.1 补偿的要求或抗议委员会考虑给予补偿的决定应建立在如下要求和可能的基础上，即一船因非自身失误，在一轮比赛或系列赛中的得分或名次已经或有可能由于以下原因明显变差：

（a）由于赛事的竞赛委员会、抗议委员会、组织机构或技术委员会的不当行为或疏忽，但不是由于当船作为审理一方时由抗议委员会做出的裁决；

（b）由于另外一条船违反规则第二章或一条应避让的不参加竞赛的船舶的行为而造成的损伤或有形损坏；

（c）根据规则1.1向别人（对自己或对自己的船员除外）提供帮助；或

（d）一条船或其船员的行为导致根据规则2被判罚或根据69.2(b)被判罚或警告。

62.2 补偿要求应以书面形式提出并写明要求补偿的原因。如果要求是基于在竞赛水域发生的事件，补偿要求应在不晚于抗议时限或在事件发生后的两小时内提交到竞赛办公室，以后到的时间为准。其他的补偿要求应在得知要求补偿的原因后尽快提交。如果有充分的理由，抗议委员会可延长该时间。不要求展示红旗。

## SECTION B HEARINGS AND DECISIONS

### 63 HEARINGS

#### 63.1 Requirement for a Hearing

A boat or competitor shall not be penalized without a protest hearing, except as provided in rules 30.2, 30.3, 30.4, 64.3(d), 64.4(b), 69, 78.2, A5 and P2. A decision on redress shall not be made without a hearing. The protest committee shall hear all *protests* and requests for redress that have been delivered to the race office unless it allows a *protest* or request to be withdrawn.

#### 63.2 Time and Place of the Hearing; Time for Parties to Prepare

All *parties* to the hearing shall be notified of the time and place of the hearing, the *protest* or redress information shall be made available to them, and they shall be allowed reasonable time to prepare for the hearing.

#### 63.3 Right to Be Present

(a) A representative of each *party* to the hearing has the right to be present throughout the hearing of all the evidence. When a *protest* claims a breach of a rule of Part 2, 3 or 4, the representatives of boats shall have been on board at the time of the incident, unless there is good reason for the protest committee to rule otherwise. Any witness, other than a member of the protest committee, shall be excluded except when giving evidence.

(b) If a *party* to the hearing of a *protest* or request for redress does not come to the hearing, the protest committee may nevertheless decide the *protest* or request. If the *party* was unavoidably absent, the committee may reopen the hearing.

#### 63.4 Conflict of Interest

(a) A protest committee member shall declare any possible *conflict of interest* as soon as he is aware of it. A *party* to the hearing

## B节 审理和裁决

### 63 审理

#### 63.1 审理的要求

船或选手不应在没有审理的情况下被判罚，规则30.2、30.3、30.4、64.3(d)、64.4(b)［译者注：经2018世界帆联年会规则委员会决定，将在2020年的规则版本中正式加入规则64.4(b)，目前的实践中已开始酌情考虑此点］、69、78.2、A5 和 P2 规定的情况例外。在没有审理的情况下不得对补偿做出裁决。抗议委员会应审理所有递交到竞赛办公室的*抗议*和补偿的要求，除非其允许撤销一个*抗议*或要求。

#### 63.2 审理的时间和地点；抗议各方准备的时间

审理的时间和地点应通知到参加审理的每一方，并且他们可以拿到*抗议*或补偿信息，还应给予他们合理的时间为审理做好准备。

#### 63.3 出席的权利

（a）每一方的代表都有权出席对所有证据的审理过程。当抗议中指出违反了第二、第三或第四章中某条规则时，事件发生时船的代表应在船上，除非抗议委员会有适当的理由另行决定。除抗议委员会的成员外，所有证人只有提供证据时在场，此外不得出席审理。

（b）如果*抗议*或要求补偿审理的一方未参加审理，抗议委员会仍然可裁决*抗议*或要求。如果有一方不可避免地缺席审理，委员会可重新进行审理。

#### 63.4 利益冲突

（a）抗议委员会的成员一旦意识到有可能存在*利益冲突*，需要尽快声明。审理的一方如果认定一名抗议委员会成员存在*利益冲突*，应当尽快提出反对意见。抗议委

who believes a member of the protest committee has a *conflict of interest* shall object as soon as possible. A *conflict of interest* declared by a protest committee member shall be included in the written information provided under rule 65.2.

*(b)* A member of a protest committee with a *conflict of interest* shall not be a member of the committee for the hearing, unless

(1) all *parties* consent, or

*(2)* the protest committee decides that the *conflict of interest* is not significant.

(c) When deciding whether a *conflict of interest* is significant, the protest committee shall consider the views of the *parties*, the level of the conflict, the level of the event, the importance to each *party*, and the overall perception of fairness.

(d) However, for World Sailing major events, or for other events as prescribed by the national authority of the venue, rule 63.4(b) does not apply and a person who has a *conflict of interest* shall not be a member of the protest committee.

**63.5 Validity of the Protest or Request for Redress**

At the beginning of the hearing the protest committee shall take any evidence it considers necessary to decide whether all requirements for the *protest* or request for redress have been met. If they have been met, the *protest* or request is valid and the hearing shall be continued. If not, the committee shall declare the *protest* or request invalid and close the hearing. If the *protest* has been made under rule 60.3(a)(1), the committee shall also determine whether or not injury or serious damage resulted from the incident in question. If not, the hearing shall be closed.

**63.6 Taking Evidence and Finding Facts**

The protest committee shall take the evidence of the *parties* present at the hearing and of their witnesses and other evidence it considers necessary. A member of the protest committee who saw the incident shall, while the *parties* are present, state that fact and may give evidence. A *party* present at the hearing may question any person who gives evidence. The committee shall then find the facts and base its decision on them.

**63.7 Conflict Between Rules**

If there is a conflict between two or more *rules* that must be resolved before the protest committee makes a decision, the committee shall apply the *rule* that it believes will provide the fairest result for all

员会的成员所做的*利益冲突*声明应包含在规则65.2规定的书面信息中。

(b) 有*利益冲突*的一个抗议委员会成员不能作为该审理的抗议委员会的一员，除非

(1) 每一方都同意，或

(2) 抗议委员会认定这个*利益冲突*并不突出。

(c) 在判断*利益冲突*是否突出时，抗议委员会应该考虑每一方的意见、冲突的程度、赛事的等级、对每一方的重要性以及整体公平性。

(d) 但是，对于世界帆联的主要赛事，或者赛事举办地国家管理机构规定的其他赛事，规则63.4(b)不适用。同时，有*利益冲突*的人不应作为抗议委员会的成员。

**63.5 抗议或补偿要求的有效性**

审理开始时，抗议委员会应该核实其认为必要的一切证据来决定*抗议*或者补偿的要求是否有效。如果符合所有的要求，且*抗议*或补偿要求有效，将继续审理。如果不符合要求，抗议委员会将宣布*抗议*或补偿要求无效并结束审理。如果*抗议*是根据规则60.3(a)(1)提出的，抗议委员会也应决定事件是否造成了损伤或严重损坏。如果没有，应结束审理。

**63.6 取证和认定事实**

抗议委员会应在审理中从参加审理的每一方及其证人处获取证据，以及获取其认为必要的证据。目睹了事件的抗议委员会成员也应在每一方在场时说明事实并提供证据。出席审理的一方可向任何提供证据的人提问。抗议委员会此时可认定事实并以此做出裁决。

**63.7 规则间的冲突**

如果两条或多条规则之间发生冲突，该问题必须在抗议委员会做出裁决之前解决，委员会应按照确定的给所有受影响的船提供公平结果的*规则*执行。只有冲突发生在竞赛通知、航

boats affected. Rule 63.7 applies only if the conflict is between rules in the notice of race, the sailing instructions, or any of the other documents that govern the event under item (g) of the definition *Rule*.

**63.8 Protests Between Boats in Different Races**

A *protest* between boats sailing in different races conducted by different organizing authorities shall be heard by a protest committee acceptable to those authorities.

**63.9 Hearings under Rule 60.3(d) – Support Persons**

If the protest committee decides to call a hearing under rule 60.3(d), it shall promptly follow the procedures in rules 63.2, 63.3, 63.4 and 63.6, except that the information given to the *parties* shall be details of the alleged breach and a person may be appointed by the protest committee to present the allegation.

**64 DECISIONS**

**64.1 Penalties and Exoneration**

When the protest committee decides that a boat that is a *party* to a protest hearing has broken a *rule* and is not exonerated, it shall disqualify her unless some other penalty applies. A penalty shall be imposed whether or not the applicable *rule* was mentioned in the *protest*. If a boat has broken a *rule* when not *racing*, her penalty shall apply to the race sailed nearest in time to that of the incident. However,

(a) when as a consequence of breaking a *rule* a boat has compelled another boat to break a *rule*, the other boat shall be exonerated.

(b) if a boat has taken an applicable penalty, she shall not be further penalized under this rule unless the penalty for a *rule* she broke is a disqualification that is not excludable from her series score.

(c) if the race is restarted or resailed, rule 36 applies.

**64.2 Decisions on Redress**

When the protest committee decides that a boat is entitled to redress under rule 62, it shall make as fair an arrangement as possible for all boats affected, whether or not they asked for redress. This may be to adjust the scoring (see rule A10 for some examples) or finishing

行细则中的规则或*规则*定义中(g)所说的约束赛事的其他文件中的规则时，规则63.7适用。

63.8 **不同竞赛中的船之间的抗议**

不同组织机构组织的不同竞赛中的船之间发生*抗议*时，应由这些组织机构接受的抗议委员会进行审理。

63.9 **根据规则60.3(d)审理——后援人员**

如果抗议委员会决定根据规则60.3(d)召集审理，它应该立即根据规则63.2、63.3、63.4和63.6的程序进行，但向*各方*提供的信息应该包括涉嫌违规的细节，抗议委员会可能会指定一人出面说明违规经过。

## 64 裁决

64.1 **惩罚和免责**

当抗议委员会裁定*抗议*审理中一*方*违反了*规则*并不被免责时，她应被取消资格，除非有其他适用的惩罚。不管抗议中是否提及所适用的*规则*，惩罚都应当被执行。如果一条船不是在*竞赛*时违反了*规则*，对其的惩罚应当在距离违反*规则*的事件发生时间最近的已航行轮次执行。但是，

（a）当一条船违反*规则*的结果造成了另一条船被迫违反*规则*的话，另外一条船应被免责。

（b）如果一条船已经接受了适用的惩罚，根据规则不能对其做出进一步惩罚，除非其违反*规则*的取消资格的惩罚是不能从系列赛积分中去掉的。

（c）如果该轮竞赛再次起航或者重赛，规则36适用。

64.2 **补偿的决定**

当抗议委员会决定根据规则62给予某条船补偿时，不管其是否提出补偿要求，应尽可能对所有受影响的船做出合理公平的安排。可通过调整得分（见规则A10的例子）或船到达终点的时间、*放弃*比赛、使成绩有效或做出其他安排。当对事

times of boats, to *abandon* the race, to let the results stand or to make some other arrangement. When in doubt about the facts or probable results of any arrangement for the race or series, especially before *abandoning* the race, the protest committee shall take evidence from appropriate sources.

**64.3 Decisions on Protests Concerning Class Rules**

(a) When the protest committee finds that deviations in excess of tolerances specified in the class rules were caused by damage or normal wear and do not improve the performance of the boat, it shall not penalize her. However, the boat shall not *race* again until the deviations have been corrected, except when the protest committee decides there is or has been no reasonable opportunity to do so.

(b) When the protest committee is in doubt about the meaning of a class rule, it shall refer its questions, together with the relevant facts, to an authority responsible for interpreting the rule. In making its decision, the committee shall be bound by the reply of the authority.

(c) When a boat is penalized under a class rule and the protest committee decides that the boat also broke the same rule in earlier races in the same event, the penalty may be imposed for all such races. No further *protest* is necessary.

(d) When a boat penalized under a class rule states in writing that she intends to appeal, she may compete in subsequent races without changes to the boat. However, if she fails to appeal or the appeal is decided against her, she shall be disqualified without a further hearing from all subsequent races in which she competed.

(e) Measurement costs arising from a *protest* involving a class rule shall be paid by the unsuccessful *party* unless the protest committee decides otherwise.

**64.4 Decisions Concerning Support Persons**

(a) When the protest committee decides that a *support person* who is a *party* to a hearing under rule 60.3(d) or 69 has broken a *rule*, it may

(1) issue a warning,

(2) exclude the person from the event or venue or remove any privileges or benefits, or

(3) take other action within its jurisdiction as provided by the *rules*.

实、比赛或系列赛成绩任何结果的安排有疑问时，特别是在*放弃*比赛前，抗议委员会应从适当的来源中找出证据。

64.3 **涉及级别规则抗议的裁决**

（a）当抗议委员会发现由于受损或正常磨损而使船的误差超过了级别规则的规定，但并不会提高该船的性能时，不应对其做出惩罚。但是，该船在修正误差之前将不允许再参加竞赛，除非抗议委员会认为该船没有合理的机会进行修正。

（b）当抗议委员会对某一级别规则的含义有疑问时，它应将问题连同有关事实一起提交给负责解释规则的一个管理机构。抗议委员会应依据管理机构的回复进行裁决。

（c）当一条船由于违反级别规则被判罚，抗议委员会判定该船在该赛事其他已经完成的轮次中也违反了同样的规则时，该判罚可以适用于所有这样的轮次。无须进一步*抗议*。

（d）当根据级别规则被判罚的船以书面形式声明她准备提出上诉时，她可在不改变船的情况下继续参加后面的比赛。但是，如果她没有上诉或在上诉中败诉，那么她将被取消后面所有已经参加过的轮次的资格，无须进一步审理。

（e）涉及级别规则的*抗议*所产生的丈量费用应由败诉一方支付，除非抗议委员会做出了其他的裁决。

64.4 **涉及后援人员的裁决**

（a）当抗议委员会认定依规则60.3(d)或69而作为审理一方的*后援人员*违反了*规则*，它可以

（1）给予一个警告，

（2）将其逐出赛事或场地，或者剥夺其享有的权利或受益，或

（3）在*规则*提供的权限内采取其他措施。

(b) The protest committee may also penalize a boat that is a *party* to a hearing under rule 60.3(d) or 69 for the breach of a *rule* by a *support person* by changing the boat's score in a single race, up to and including DSQ, when the protest committee decides that

(1) the boat may have gained a competitive advantage as the result of the breach by the *support person*, or

(2) the *support person* committed a further breach after the protest committee warned the boat in writing, following a previous hearing, that a penalty may be imposed.

## 65 INFORMING THE PARTIES AND OTHERS

**65.1** After making its decision, the protest committee shall promptly inform the *parties* to the hearing of the facts found, the applicable *rules*, the decision, the reasons for it, and any penalties imposed or redress given.

**65.2** A *party* to the hearing is entitled to receive the above information in writing, provided she asks for it in writing from the protest committee no later than seven days after being informed of the decision. The committee shall then promptly provide the information, including, when relevant, a diagram of the incident prepared or endorsed by the committee.

**65.3** When the protest committee penalizes a boat under a class rule, it shall send the above information to the relevant class rule authorities.

## 66 REOPENING A HEARING

The protest committee may reopen a hearing when it decides that it may have made a significant error, or when significant new evidence becomes available within a reasonable time. It shall reopen a hearing when required by the national authority under rule 71.2 or R5. A *party* to the hearing may ask for a reopening no later than 24 hours after being informed of the decision. On the last scheduled day of racing the request shall be delivered

(a) within the protest time limit if the requesting *party* was informed of the decision on the previous day;

(b) no later than 30 minutes after the *party* was informed of the decision on that day.

（b）抗议委员会也可以由于*后援人员*违反*规则*对依规则60.3(d)或69而作为审理一方的船做出惩罚，改变该船单轮得分，判罚最高可至DSQ且包括DSQ，条件是当抗议委员会裁定

（1）该船可能通过*后援人员*违反*规则*的结果获得竞赛优势，或

（2）在抗议委员会上一次审理后书面警告某船可能对她进行判罚后，其*后援人员*继续违反*规则*。

## 65 通知每一方和其他人

65.1 做出裁决后，抗议委员会应尽快通知参加审理的每一*方*审理所认定的事实、适用的*规则*、裁决及其理由和所给予的惩罚或补偿。

65.2 参加审理的一方只要在被通知裁决后不晚于7天内以书面形式要求抗议委员会提供有关上述裁决的书面材料，她就有资格获取该材料。抗议委员会应尽快提供其所要求的信息，包括委员会准备或认可的相关的事件图示。

65.3 当抗议委员会依据级别规则对某船进行惩罚时，她应将上述材料递交给相关级别规则管理机构。

## 66 重新审理

当抗议委员会认为自己可能有明显的错误或在合理的时间内又获得实质性的新证据时，可重新召集审理。当国家管理机构依据规则71.2和R5要求重审时，抗议委员会应重新审理。在被通知裁决后的24小时之内，参加审理的一方可要求重新审理。在竞赛时间表的最后一天应按如下要求送达请求：

（a）如果提出请求的一方是在前一天被告知裁决的，在抗议时限内；

（b）如果一方在当天被告知裁决的，在被告知时间后30分钟内。

When a hearing is reopened, a majority of the members of the protest committee shall, if possible, be members of the original protest committee.

## 67 DAMAGES

The question of damages arising from a breach of any *rule* shall be governed by the prescriptions, if any, of the national authority.

*Note: There is no rule 68.*

# SECTION C MISCONDUCT

## 69 MISCONDUCT

### 69.1 Obligation not to Commit Misconduct; Resolution

(a) A competitor, boat owner or *support person* shall not commit an act of misconduct.

(b) Misconduct is:

(1) conduct that is a breach of good manners, a breach of good sportsmanship, or unethical behaviour; or

(2) conduct that may bring the sport into disrepute.

(c) An allegation of a breach of rule 69.1(a) shall be resolved in accordance with the provisions of rule 69. It shall not be grounds for a *protest* and rule 63.1 does not apply.

### 69.2 Action by a Protest Committee

(a) A protest committee acting under this rule shall have at least three members.

(b) When a protest committee, from its own observation or from information received from any source, including evidence taken during a hearing, believes a person may have broken rule 69.1(a), it shall decide whether or not to call a hearing.

(c) When the protest committee needs more information to make the decision to call a hearing, it shall consider appointing a person or persons to conduct an investigation. These investigators shall not be members of the protest committee that will decide the matter.

当重新审理时，如果可能的话，该抗议委员会大多数成员应是原抗议委员会的成员。

### 67　损坏

由于违反任一*规则*而引起的损失问题，如果该国家管理机构有此方面的规定，可参照进行处理。

*注：此处没有规则68。*

## C节　品行不端

### 69　品行不端

69.1 不做品行不端的错事的义务；决议

（a）选手、船东或*后援人员*不应做出品行不端的错误行为。

（b）品行不端指的是

（1）不文明礼貌、破坏体育精神的举止或不道德的行为；或

（2）给体育运动抹黑的行为。

（c）关于违反规则69.1(a)的指控应当依据规则69的条款进行裁决。但它不应该作为*抗议*的依据，规则63.1不适用。

**69.2 抗议委员会的措施**

（a）根据此规则行事的抗议委员会至少需要3名成员。

（b）当抗议委员会根据自己的观察或从任何其他渠道得来的信息，包括审理中得到的证据，认为某人违反了规则69.1(a)，委员会应该决定是否要召集审理。

（c）当抗议委员会需要更多的信息来决定召集审理时，其应考虑任命一名或多名人员来进行调查。这些调查人员不应该是抗议委员会中对此事有决定作用的人员。

(d) When an investigator is appointed, all relevant information he gathers, favourable or unfavourable, shall be disclosed to the protest committee, and if the protest committee decides to call a hearing, to the *parties*.

(e) If the protest committee decides to call a hearing, it shall promptly inform the person in writing of the alleged breach and of the time and place of the hearing and follow the procedures in rules 63.2, 63.3(a), 63.4 and 63.6 except that:

(1) unless a person has been appointed by World Sailing, a person may be appointed by the protest committee to present the allegation.

(2) a person against whom an allegation has been made under this rule shall be entitled to have an advisor and a representative with him who may act on his behalf.

(f) If the person is unable to attend the hearing and

(1) provides good reason, the protest committee shall reschedule it; or

(2) does not provide good reason and does not come to it, the protest committee may conduct it without the person present.

(g) The standard of proof to be applied is the test of the comfortable satisfaction of the protest committee, bearing in mind the seriousness of the alleged misconduct. However, if the standard of proof in this rule conflicts with the laws of a country, the national authority may, with the approval of World Sailing, change it with a prescription to this rule.

(h) When the protest committee decides that a competitor or boat owner has broken rule 69.1(a), it may take one or more of the following actions

(1) issue a warning;

(2) change their boat's score in one or more races, including disqualification(s) that may or may not be excluded from her series score;

(3) exclude the person from the event or venue or remove any privileges or benefits; and

（d）调查人员被任命之后，他所搜集的所有相关信息，不管是有利的还是不利的，都应对抗议委员会公开，如果抗议委员会决定召集审理，这些信息对每一方都应该公开。

（e）如果抗议委员会决定召集审理，委员会应立刻以书面形式通知此人其被控违反规则，以及审理的时间和地点，应该遵守规则63.2、63.3(a)、63.4 和 63.6 中的相关程序，除了：

（1）除非此人是世界帆联任命的，否则应由抗议委员会指定人员提出控诉。

（2）在此规则下，控诉针对的那个人有权拥有一名顾问及一名能代表其言行的代表。

（f）如果此人不能参加审理，并

（1）提供了充足的理由，抗议委员会应重新安排审理；或

（2）不能提供充足的理由也无法到场时，抗议委员会可以进行缺席审理。

（g）所运用的证据标准是测试抗议委员会是否完全满意，同时记住被控的品行不端的严重性。然而，如果此规则中的证据标准与某个国家的法律相冲突，那么国家管理机构在征得世界帆联同意的前提下，可以参考本规则对其进行更改。

（h）当抗议委员会认定选手或船东违反了规则69.1(a)，可以采取以下一个或多个措施：

（1）发布警告；

（2）更改他们的船在一轮或多轮比赛中的得分，包括可以和不可以从系列赛得分中去掉的取消资格；

（3）将其逐出赛事或场馆，或者剥夺其享有的权利或受益，以及

(4) take any other action within its jurisdiction as provided by the *rules*.

(i) When the protest committee decides that a *support person* has broken rule 69.1(a), rule 64.4 applies.

(j) If the protest committee

(1) imposes a penalty greater than one DNE;

(2) excludes the person from the event or venue; or

(3) in any other case if it considers it appropriate,

it shall report its findings, including the facts found, its conclusions and decision to the national authority of the person or, for specific international events listed in the World Sailing Regulations, to World Sailing. If the protest committee has acted under rule 69.2(f)(2), the report shall also include that fact and the reasons for it.

(k) If the protest committee decides not to conduct the hearing without the person present, or if the protest committee has left the event and a report alleging a breach of rule 69.1(a) is received, the race committee or organizing authority may appoint the same or a new protest committee to proceed under this rule. If it is impractical for the protest committee to conduct a hearing, it shall collect all available information and, if the allegation seems justified, make a report to the national authority of the person or, for specific international events listed in the World Sailing Regulations, to World Sailing.

**69.3 Action by a National Authority and World Sailing**

The disciplinary powers, procedures and responsibilities of national authorities and World Sailing that apply are specified in World Sailing Regulation 35, Disciplinary Code. National authorities and World Sailing may impose further penalties, including suspension of eligibility, under that regulation.

（4）在*规则*提供的权限内采取其他措施。

（i）当抗议委员会认定*后援人员*违反了规则 69.1(a)，规则 64.4适用。

（j）如果抗议委员会

（1）采取给予一个比 DNE 更严重的判罚；

（2）将此人从赛事或者场馆中驱逐出去；或

（3）若考虑到其合理性的其他情况。

委员会应该就发现的内容，包括找到的事实、其结论及裁决向此人所在的国家管理机构汇报，或对于世界帆联规章中列举出来的一些特定的国际赛事，向世界帆联汇报这些内容。如果抗议委员会依据规则69.2(f)(2)采取措施，该报告也同样要包括事实及其原因。

（k）如果抗议委员会决定在当事人不在现场的情况下不能召集审理，或者如果抗议委员会在离开了赛事的情况下收到了违反规则69.1(a)的指控，竞赛委员会或组织机构可以任命相同或新的抗议委员会依据此规则处理。如果抗议委员会无法组织审理，则应该收集所有可用的信息，如果指控是合理的，向当事人所在的国家管理机构汇报，对于世界帆联规章中列举的一些特定的国际赛事，应该向世界帆联汇报。

**69.3 国家管理机构与世界帆联的措施**

国家管理机构和世界帆联适用的纪律处分权力、程序及责任在世界帆联规章35，即纪律守则一章中有详细的说明。国家管理机构和世界帆联有可能会追加处罚，包括依据规章延缓参赛资格。

## SECTION D APPEALS

### 70 APPEALS AND REQUESTS TO A NATIONAL AUTHORITY

**70.1** (a) Provided that the right of appeal has not been denied under rule 70.5, a *party* to a hearing may appeal a protest committee's decision or its procedures, but not the facts found.

(b) A boat may appeal when she is denied a hearing required by rule 63.1.

**70.2** A protest committee may request confirmation or correction of its decision.

**70.3** An appeal under rule 70.1 or a request by a protest committee under rule 70.2 shall be sent to the national authority with which the organizing authority is associated under rule 89.1. However, if boats will pass through the waters of more than one national authority while *racing*, the sailing instructions shall identify the national authority to which appeals or requests are required to be sent.

**70.4** A club or other organization affiliated to a national authority may request an interpretation of the *rules*, provided that no *protest* or request for redress that may be appealed is involved. The interpretation shall not be used for changing a previous protest committee decision.

**70.5** There shall be no appeal from the decisions of an international jury constituted in compliance with Appendix N. Furthermore, if the notice of race and the sailing instructions so state, the right of appeal may be denied provided that

(a) it is essential to determine promptly the result of a race that will qualify a boat to compete in a later stage of an event or a subsequent event (a national authority may prescribe that its approval is required for such a procedure);

(b) a national authority so approves for a particular event open only to entrants under its own jurisdiction; or

(c) a national authority after consultation with World Sailing so approves for a particular event, provided the protest committee is constituted as required by Appendix N, except that only two members of the protest committee need be International Judges.

## D节　上诉

### 70　上诉及寻求国家管理机构的确认

70.1　（a）只要没有依据规则70.5被驳回上诉权，审理的一方可对抗议委员会的裁决或程序提出上诉。但不能对认定的事实提出上诉。

（b）当一条船根据规则63.1 要求的审理被拒绝时，可以要求上诉。

70.2　抗议委员会可要求对其裁决进行确认和修正。

70.3　根据规则70.1提出的上诉或者根据规则70.2由抗议委员会提出的要求应被送交根据规则89.1与组织机构相关的国家管理机构。然而，当船在*竞赛*中会通过不止一个国家管理机构的水域时，航行细则应该确定上诉或要求需要提交至哪个国家管理机构。

70.4　只要不涉及有可能上诉的*抗议*或补偿要求，隶属某一个国家管理机构的俱乐部或其他组织可要求对*规则*进行解释。解释不得被用来改变抗议委员会之前做出的裁决。

70.5　对于按附录N要求组成的国际仲裁委员会做出的裁决不可提出上诉。而且，如竞赛通知和航行细则中有如此规定，上诉权就可被驳回，前提是

（a）必须尽快确定竞赛的结果，以使船有资格参加该赛事后阶段的比赛或后续的赛事（国家管理机构可以规定这样的程序需得到其批准）；

（b）在只向其管辖范围内的报名者公开的特定赛事上，国家管理机构批准这样做时；或

（c）抗议委员会是按附录N的要求组成，但经国家管理机构与世界帆联协商后同意的某一特定赛事中，该抗议委

**70.6** Appeals and requests shall conform to Appendix R.

## 71 NATIONAL AUTHORITY DECISIONS

**71.1** A person who has a *conflict of interest* or was a member of the protest committee shall not take any part in the discussion or decision on an appeal or a request for confirmation or correction.

**71.2** The national authority may uphold, change or reverse a protest committee's decision including a decision on validity or a decision under rule 69. Alternatively, the national authority may order that a hearing be reopened, or that a new hearing be held by the same or a different protest committee. When the national authority decides that there shall be a new hearing, it may appoint the protest committee.

**71.3** When from the facts found by the protest committee the national authority decides that a boat that was a *party* to a protest hearing broke a *rule* and is not exonerated, it shall penalize her, whether or not that boat or that *rule* was mentioned in the protest committee's decision.

**71.4** The decision of the national authority shall be final. The national authority shall send its decision in writing to all *parties* to the hearing and the protest committee, who shall be bound by the decision.

员会可以只需要2名国际仲裁。

70.6 上诉和要求必须符合附录R的规定。

## 71 国家管理机构的裁决

71.1 有*利益冲突*的人或曾是抗议委员会的成员，不得参加对上诉及确认或修正要求的讨论或裁决。

71.2 国家管理机构可维持、更改或推翻抗议委员会做出的裁决，包括有效性的裁决或者根据规则69做出的裁决。或者，国家管理机构可以要求重新审理，或者由一个相同或不同的抗议委员会进行新的审理。当国家管理机构决定应该重新审理时，它可以任命抗议委员会。

71.3 当从抗议委员会发现的事实中，国家管理机构认定参加抗议审理一方的某条船违反了*规则*且没有被免责，国家管理机构应对其进行惩罚，不管抗议委员会的裁决中是否提到该船或某条*规则*。

71.4 国家管理机构的裁决是最终的裁决。国家管理机构应将其裁决以书面形式发至出席审理的每一方及抗议委员会，他们应遵守该裁决。

# PART 6 ENTRY AND QUALIFICATION

## 75 ENTERING A RACE

75.1 To enter a race, a boat shall comply with the requirements of the organizing authority of the race. She shall be entered by

(a) a member of a club or other organization affiliated to a World Sailing member national authority,

(b) such a club or organization, or

(c) a member of a World Sailing member national authority.

75.2 Competitors shall comply with World Sailing Regulation 19, Eligibility Code.

## 76 EXCLUSION OF BOATS OR COMPETITORS

76.1 The organizing authority or the race committee may reject or cancel the entry of a boat or exclude a competitor, subject to rule 76.3, provided it does so before the start of the first race and states the reason for doing so. On request the boat shall promptly be given the reason in writing. The boat may request redress if she considers that the rejection or exclusion is improper.

76.2 The organizing authority or the race committee shall not reject or cancel the entry of a boat or exclude a competitor because of advertising, provided the boat or competitor complies with World Sailing Regulation 20, Advertising Code.

76.3 At world and continental championships no entry within stated quotas shall be rejected or cancelled without first obtaining the approval of the relevant World Sailing Class Association (or the Offshore Racing Council) or World Sailing.

## 77 IDENTIFICATION ON SAILS

A boat shall comply with the requirements of Appendix G governing class insignia, national letters and numbers on sails.

# 第六章　报名与资格

## 75　比赛报名

75.1　船在报名参加一个比赛时，应符合赛事组织机构的要求，并应以下列名义报名：

（a）隶属世界帆联会员国管理机构的俱乐部或其他组织的会员，

（b）这样的俱乐部或组织，或

（c）世界帆联会员国家管理机构的会员。

75.2　选手应符合世界帆联规章19，即资格法规的有关规定。

## 76　船或选手的禁赛

76.1　按规则76.3，组织机构或竞赛委员会可以拒绝或取消接纳某条船或选手报名，但要在第一轮比赛开始之前并声明此做法的理由。如有疑问，应当立刻将该理由以书面形式告知该船。如果该船认为拒绝或取消其报名资格是不合适的，她可以要求补偿。

76.2　组织机构或者竞赛委员会不应因广告拒绝或者取消一条船或选手的报名，前提是该船或选手符合世界帆联规章20广告守则。

76.3　在世界和洲际锦标赛中，如未先获得有关世界帆联级别组织（或离岸赛理事会）或世界帆联的批准，则不应拒绝或取消规定额内的报名。

## 77　帆上识别标志

船应遵守附录G有关帆上的级别标识、国家代码和帆号的规定。

## 78 COMPLIANCE WITH CLASS RULES; CERTIFICATES

78.1 While a boat is *racing*, her owner and any other person in charge shall ensure that the boat is maintained to comply with her class rules and that her measurement or rating certificate, if any, remains valid. In addition, the boat shall also comply at other times specified in the class rules, the notice of race or the sailing instructions.

78.2 When a *rule* requires a valid certificate to be produced or its existence verified before a boat *races*, and this cannot be done, the boat may *race* provided that the race committee receives a statement signed by the person in charge that a valid certificate exists. The boat shall produce the certificate or arrange for its existence to be verified by the race committee. The penalty for breaking this rule is disqualification without a hearing from all races of the event.

## 79 CLASSIFICATION

If the notice of race or class rules state that some or all competitors must satisfy classification requirements, the classification shall be carried out as described in World Sailing Regulation 22, Sailor Classification Code.

## 80 ADVERTISING

A boat and her crew shall comply with World Sailing Regulation 20, Advertising Code.

## 81 RESCHEDULED EVENT

When an event is rescheduled to dates different from the dates stated in the notice of race, all boats entered shall be notified. The race committee may accept new entries that meet all the entry requirements except the original deadline for entries.

## 78　遵守级别规则；证书

78.1　当一条船参加*竞赛*，船东和其他负责人应保证该船始终符合其级别规则，如果有证书的话，应该保证其丈量和等级证书有效。此外，在其他时间，该船也应当始终符合级别规则、竞赛通知或航行细则的规定。

78.2　当*规则*要求船在*竞赛*前出示有效的证书或证实证书存在，而如果船未能这样做时，在竞赛委员会收到有负责人签字证明的关于有效证书确实存在的声明后，该船方可参加竞赛。该船应当出示证书或者安排由竞赛委员会验证其证书确实存在。违反本规则，可以给予该船在本赛事中所有轮次取消资格的判罚而无须审理。

## 79　分级

如果竞赛通知或者级别规则声明一些或者全部的选手必须符合分级的要求，就应根据世界帆联规章22，选手分级法规所描述的来进行分级。

## 80　广告

船及其船员应遵守世界帆联规章20，即广告守则的有关规定。

## 81　重新安排的赛事

当一场赛事被重新安排时，应通知所有参加原比赛的船。竞赛委员会可自行决定是否接受符合原报名条件的报名。

# PART 7 RACE ORGANIZATION

## 84 GOVERNING RULES

The organizing authority, race committee, technical committee, protest committee and other race officials shall be governed by the *rules* in the conduct and judging of races.

## 85 CHANGES TO RULES

**85.1** A change to a *rule* shall refer specifically to the *rule* and state the change. A change to a *rule* includes an addition to it or deletion of all or part of it.

**85.2** A change to one of the following types of *rules* may be made only as shown below.

| *Type of rule* | *Change only if permitted by* |
|---|---|
| Racing rule | Rule 86 |
| Rule in a World Sailing code | A rule in the code |
| National authority prescription | Rule 88.2 |
| Class rule | Rule 87 |
| Rule in the notice of race | Rule 89.2(b) |
| Rule in the sailing instructions | Rule 90.2(c) |
| Rule in any other document governing the event | A rule in the document itself |

## 86 CHANGES TO THE RACING RULES

**86.1** A racing rule shall not be changed unless permitted in the rule itself or as follows:

(a) Prescriptions of a national authority may change a racing rule, but not the Definitions; the Basic Principles; a rule in the Introduction; Part 1, 2 or 7; rule 42, 43, 63.4, 69, 70, 71, 75, 76.3, 79 or 80; a rule of an appendix that changes one of these rules; Appendix H or N; World Sailing Regulation 19, 20, 21, 22, 35 or 37.

# 第七章 竞赛组织

## 84 执行的规则

组织机构、竞赛委员会、技术委员会、抗议委员会和其他竞赛官员在竞赛实施和裁决时应执行*规则*。

## 85 规则的更改

85.1 对*规则*更改应特别指明某条*规则*并说明是如何更改的。对*规则*的更改包括对其进行全部或部分的增补或删除。

85.2 对以下类型的*规则*的更改只能按照下表显示的情况做出：

| *规则类型* | *只能按以下规则所允许的进行更改* |
| --- | --- |
| 竞赛规则 | 规则86 |
| 世界帆联守则中的规则 | 守则中的规则 |
| 国家管理机构的规定 | 规则88.2 |
| 级别规则 | 规则87 |
| 竞赛通知中的规则 | 规则89.2(b) |
| 航行细则中的规则 | 规则90.2(c) |
| 赛事执行的其他文件中的规则 | 该文件中的规则 |

## 86 竞赛规则的更改

86.1 不能更改竞赛规则，除非规则本身允许或有下列情况：

（a）国家管理机构的规定可更改某条竞赛规则，但不能更改：定义；基本原则；导言中某条规则；第一、二或七章；规则42、43、63.4、69、70、71、75、76.3、79和 80；附录中改变这些规则的某条规则；附录H或N；世界帆联规章19、20、21、22、35或37。

(b) The notice of race or sailing instructions may change a racing rule, but not rule 76.1 or 76.2, Appendix R, or a rule listed in rule 86.1(a).

(c) Class rules may change only racing rules 42, 49, 50, 51, 52, 53 and 54.

**86.2** In exception to rule 86.1, World Sailing may in limited circumstances (see World Sailing Regulation 28.1.3) authorize changes to the racing rules for a specific international event. The authorization shall be stated in a letter of approval to the event organizing authority and in the notice of race and sailing instructions, and the letter shall be posted on the event's official notice board.

**86.3** If a national authority so prescribes, the restrictions in rule 86.1 do not apply if rules are changed to develop or test proposed rules. The national authority may prescribe that its approval is required for such changes.

## 87 CHANGES TO CLASS RULES

The notice of race or sailing instructions may change a class rule only when the class rules permit the change, or when written permission of the class association for the change is displayed on the official notice board.

## 88 NATIONAL PRESCRIPTIONS

### 88.1 Prescriptions that Apply

The prescriptions that apply to an event are the prescriptions of the national authority with which the organizing authority is associated under rule 89.1. However, if boats will pass through the waters of more than one national authority while *racing*, the notice of race or sailing instructions shall identify the prescriptions that will apply and when they will apply.

### 88.2 Changes to Prescriptions

The notice of race or sailing instructions may change a prescription. However, a national authority may restrict changes to its prescriptions with a prescription to this rule, provided World Sailing approves its application to do so. The restricted prescriptions shall not be changed.

（b）竞赛通知或航行细则可对竞赛规则进行更改，但不能更改规则76.1、76.2、附录R或规则86.1(a)中所列的条款。

（c）级别规则只能对竞赛规则42、49、50、51、52、53 和54进行更改。

86.2 除规则86.1，世界帆联可在有限的条件下（参见世界帆联规章28.1.3）授权给特定的国际赛事更改规则。该授权将在给赛事组织机构的批准书中以及竞赛通知和航行细则中声明。该批准书应张贴在赛事官方公告栏上。

86.3 若国家管理机构有如此规定，如果规则的更改是为了发展或测试所建议的规则，那么规则86.1中的限制不适用。国家管理机构可以规定此类更改需经其批准。

## 87 级别规则的更改

只有当级别规则允许更改时，或者当级别协会在官方公告栏发布书面许可做出更改时，竞赛通知或航行细则才能够更改级别规则。

## 88 国家规定

### 88.1 适用的规定

适用于赛事的规定是根据规则89.1和组织机构相联系的国家管理机构的规定。然而如果船在竞赛中需要航越不止一个国家管理机构的水域时，竞赛通知或航行细则应该说明所适用的规定及其适用的时间。

### 88.2 规定的更改

竞赛通知或航行细则可以更改某一国家规定。然而，国家管理机构可对本规则进行规定以限制对其规定的更改，条件是世界帆联同意其这么做。航行细则不应对受限制的规定进行更改。

## 89 ORGANIZING AUTHORITY; NOTICE OF RACE; APPOINTMENT OF RACE OFFICIALS

### 89.1 Organizing Authority

Races shall be organized by an organizing authority, which shall be

(a) World Sailing;

(b) a member national authority of World Sailing;

(c) an affiliated club;

(d) an affiliated organization other than a club and, if so prescribed by the national authority, with the approval of the national authority or in conjunction with an affiliated club;

(e) an unaffiliated class association, either with the approval of the national authority or in conjunction with an affiliated club;

(f) two or more of the above organizations;

(g) an unaffiliated body in conjunction with an affiliated club where the body is owned and controlled by the club. The national authority of the club may prescribe that its approval is required for such an event; or

(h) if approved by World Sailing and the national authority of the club, an unaffiliated body in conjunction with an affiliated club where the body is not owned and controlled by the club.

In rule 89.1, an organization is affiliated if it is affiliated to the national authority of the venue; otherwise the organization is unaffiliated. However, if boats will pass through the waters of more than one national authority while *racing*, an organization is affiliated if it is affiliated to the national authority of one of the ports of call.

### 89.2 Notice of Race; Appointment of Race Officials

(a) The organizing authority shall publish a notice of race that conforms to rule J1.

(b) The notice of race may be changed provided adequate notice is given.

(c) The organizing authority shall appoint a race committee and, when appropriate, appoint a protest committee, a technical committee and umpires. However, the race committee, an international jury, a technical committee and umpires may be appointed by World Sailing as provided in its regulations.

## 89 组织机构；竞赛通知；竞赛官员的任命

### 89.1 组织机构

比赛应由下列组织机构来组织：

（a）世界帆船运动联合会；

（b）世界帆船运动联合会的一个会员国国家管理机构；

（c）隶属的俱乐部；

（d）如果国家管理机构这样规定的话，获得国家管理机构许可的或者与一个隶属俱乐部协力举办的一个隶属组织而不是俱乐部；

（e）经国家管理机构批准或与某隶属俱乐部协力举办的非隶属的级别协会；

（f）2个或2个以上上述组织；

（g）与某隶属俱乐部协力举办的某非隶属团体，该团体为俱乐部拥有和控制。该俱乐部所属的国家管理机构可说明此比赛应得到其批准；或

（h）如果获得了世界帆联和俱乐部所属的国家管理机构的允许，一个非隶属实体可与隶属俱乐部协力组织，该实体不被此俱乐部拥有和控制。

在规则89.1中，如果一个组织隶属于该场馆所在的国家管理机构，那么该机构就是隶属机构，否则就是非隶属机构。但是，如果竞赛中船将会航越一个以上国家管理机构的水域，当该组织隶属于船只停靠港口之一的国家管理机构时，该组织是隶属机构。

### 89.2 竞赛通知；竞赛官员的任命

（a）组织机构应按照规则J1发布竞赛通知。

（b）只要给予了适当的通知，竞赛通知可以被更改。

（c）组织机构应任命一个竞赛委员会并在适当时任命一个抗议委员会、一个技术委员会和现场裁判。但是根据世界帆联规章，世界帆联可任命竞赛委员会、国际仲裁、技术委员会和现场裁判。

## 90 RACE COMMITTEE; SAILING INSTRUCTIONS; SCORING

### 90.1 Race Committee

The race committee shall conduct races as directed by the organizing authority and as required by the *rules*.

### 90.2 Sailing Instructions

(a) The race committee shall publish written sailing instructions that conform to rule J2.

(b) When appropriate, for an event where entries from other countries are expected, the sailing instructions shall include, in English, the applicable national prescriptions.

(c) The sailing instructions may be changed provided the change is in writing and posted on the official notice board before the time stated in the sailing instructions or, on the water, communicated to each boat before her warning signal. Oral changes may be given only on the water, and only if the procedure is stated in the sailing instructions.

### 90.3 Scoring

(a) The race committee shall score a race or series as provided in Appendix A using the Low Point System, unless the notice of race or sailing instructions specify some other system. A race shall be scored if it is not *abandoned* and if one boat sails the course in compliance with rule 28 and *finishes* within the time limit, if any, even if she retires after *finishing* or is disqualified.

(b) When a scoring system provides for excluding one or more race scores, any score that is a Disqualification Not Excludable (DNE) shall be included in a boat's series score.

(c) When the race committee determines from its own records or observations that it has scored a boat incorrectly, it shall correct the error and make the corrected scores available to competitors.

## 90 竞赛委员会；航行细则；记分

### 90.1 竞赛委员会

竞赛委员会应在组织机构的指导下根据*规则*要求组织实施竞赛。

### 90.2 航行细则

（a）竞赛委员会应发布书面的符合规则J2的航行细则。

（b）合适时，当希望有其他国家报名参加赛事的时候，航行细则应包括英文的所适用的国家规定。

（c）可以更改航行细则，前提是更改应在航行细则规定的时间前以书面形式张贴在官方公告栏上，或在预告信号之前通知水上的每条船。口头的更改只能在水上进行通知，并事先在航行细则中注明口头通知的程序。

### 90.3 记分

（a）除非竞赛通知或航行细则中特别规定了某些其他方法，否则竞赛委员会应使用附录A中提供的低分记分法对一轮比赛或系列赛进行记分。如果一轮竞赛没有被*放弃*，一条船遵守规则28.1完成航线行驶并在规定的时限内*到达终点*，即使该船*到达终点*后退出了比赛或被取消了资格，该轮比赛也应记分。

（b）当记分方法规定取消一轮或多轮的分数，任何被记为取消资格且不能去掉（DNE）的分数都应带入船只系列赛总分。

（c）当竞赛委员会从自己的记录或者观察中确定某条船被记的分数不正确时，应当改正错误并将改正的得分告知选手。

**91 PROTEST COMMITTEE**

A protest committee shall be

(a) a committee appointed by the organizing authority or race committee;

(b) an international jury appointed by the organizing authority or as prescribed in the World Sailing Regulations. It shall be composed as required by rule N1 and have the authority and responsibilities stated in rule N2. A national authority may prescribe that its approval is required for the appointment of international juries for races within its jurisdiction, except World Sailing events or when international juries are appointed by World Sailing under rule 89.2(c); or

(c) a committee appointed by the national authority under rule 71.2.

**92 TECHNICAL COMMITTEE**

**92.1** A technical committee shall be a committee of at least one member and be appointed by the organizing authority or the race committee or as prescribed in the World Sailing Regulations.

**92.2** The technical committee shall conduct equipment inspection and event measurement as directed by the organizing authority and as required by the *rules*.

## 91 抗议委员会

抗议委员会应是

（a）由组织机构或竞赛委员委会任命的一个委员会；

（b）国际仲裁由组织机构或依照世界帆联规章的规定任命，国际仲裁的组成应当遵照规则N1的要求，并且享有规则N2所写明的权利和义务。国家管理机构对其权限内掌管的比赛可以做这样的规定：任命的国际仲裁需得到其批准，除非是世界帆联组织的赛事或国际仲裁是按照规则 89.2(c)由世界帆联任命的；或者

（c）根据规则71.2由国家管理机构任命的委员会。

## 92 技术委员会

92.1 技术委员会应为至少有一名成员的委员会，由国家管理机构或者竞赛委员会，或者按照世界帆联规章的规定任命。

92.2 技术委员会可以按照组织机构的指示和*规则*的要求进行器材检查和赛事丈量。

# APPENDIX A SCORING

*See rule 90.3.*

**A1 NUMBER OF RACES**

The number of races scheduled and the number required to be completed to constitute a series shall be stated in the notice of race or sailing instructions.

**A2 SERIES SCORES**

**A2.1** Each boat's series score shall, subject to rule 90.3(b), be the total of her race scores excluding her worst score. (The notice of race or sailing instructions may make a different arrangement by providing, for example, that no score will be excluded, that two or more scores will be excluded, or that a specified number of scores will be excluded if a specified number of races are completed. A race is completed if scored; see rule 90.3(a).) If a boat has two or more equal worst scores, the score(s) for the race(s) sailed earliest in the series shall be excluded. The boat with the lowest series score wins and others shall be ranked accordingly.

**A2.2** If a boat has entered any race in a series, she shall be scored for the whole series.

**A3 STARTING TIMES AND FINISHING PLACES**

The time of a boat's starting signal shall be her starting time, and the order in which boats *finish* a race shall determine their finishing places. However, when a handicap or rating system is used a boat's corrected time shall determine her finishing place.

**A4 LOW POINT SYSTEM**

*The Low Point System will apply unless the notice of race or sailing instructions specify another system; see rule 90.3(a).*

# 附录A 记分

*参见规则90.3。*

## A1 比赛轮次

在竞赛通知或航行细则中应注明比赛所安排的轮次及组成完整的系列赛所必须竞赛的轮次数目。

## A2 系列赛的记分

A2.1 依据规则90.3(b)，每条船参加系列赛的得分是去掉最差得分的全部比赛得分的总和。［竞赛通知或航行细则可以做出不同的规定，比如不去掉任何得分、去掉两轮或更多的得分，或者完成一定数量轮次的比赛将去掉一定的分数。如果有记分，该轮比赛就完成了；参见规则90.3(a)。］如果一条船有两个或两个以上的同样最坏的分数，将去掉最前面竞赛的分数。获得最低分数的船获胜，其他船排名依此类推。

A2.2 一旦一条船参加了系列赛中的一轮竞赛，其在该系列赛中的每一轮都将被记分。

## A3 起航时间和到达终点名次

一条船起航信号时间将作为该船的起航时间，按*到达终点*的顺序决定名次。但如果使用了让分制或分级制的记分法，记分按修正后的时间决定其到达终点的名次。

## A4 低分记分法

*使用低分记分方法，除非竞赛通知或航行细则中规定另外特定的记分方法；参见规则 90.3(a)。*

**A4.1** Each boat *starting* and *finishing* and not thereafter retiring, being penalized or given redress shall be scored points as follows:

| *Finishing place* | *Points* |
|---|---|
| First | 1 |
| Second | 2 |
| Third | 3 |
| Fourth | 4 |
| Fifth | 5 |
| Sixth | 6 |
| Seventh | 7 |
| Each place thereafter | Add 1 point |

**A4.2** A boat that did not *start*, did not *finish*, retired or was disqualified shall be scored points for the finishing place one more than the number of boats entered in the series. A boat that is penalized under rule 30.2 or that takes a penalty under rule 44.3(a) shall be scored points as provided in rule 44.3(c).

## A5 SCORES DETERMINED BY THE RACE COMMITTEE

A boat that did not *start* or *finish* or comply with rule 30.2, 30.3, 30.4 or 78.2, or that retires or takes a penalty under rule 44.3(a), shall be scored accordingly by the race committee without a hearing. Only the protest committee may take other scoring actions that worsen a boat's score.

## A6 CHANGES IN PLACES AND SCORES OF OTHER BOATS

**A6.1** If a boat is disqualified from a race or retires after *finishing*, each boat with a worse finishing place shall be moved up one place.

**A6.2** If the protest committee decides to give redress by adjusting a boat's score, the scores of other boats shall not be changed unless the protest committee decides otherwise.

A4.1 每条船在一轮竞赛中*起航*并*到达终点*，其后既没有退出比赛也没有被惩罚或给予补偿，她们的分数将按如下方法计算：

| *终点名次* | *记分* |
| --- | --- |
| 第一名 | 1 |
| 第二名 | 2 |
| 第三名 | 3 |
| 第四名 | 4 |
| 第五名 | 5 |
| 第六名 | 6 |
| 第七名 | 7 |
| 此后每名次 | 加1分 |

A4.2 一条船没有*起航*、没有*到达终点*、退出比赛或被取消资格，她的终点名次分数应是参加该轮比赛的船数加1分。根据规则30.2被处罚的船或根据规则44.3(a)接受惩罚的船应按规则44.3(c)记分。

## A5 竞赛委员会决定的分数

一条船没有按规则30.2、30.3、30.4或78.2*起航*或*到达终点*，或退出比赛或按规则44.3(a)接受惩罚，其分数将由竞赛委员会在不须审理的情况下进行相应记分。只有抗议委员会可采取其他记分方法来使其分数更差。

## A6 其他船的名次和分数的改变

A6.1 如果一条船在一轮比赛中被取消资格或在*到达终点*后退出比赛，其后面的每条船应向前移动一个名次。

A6.2 如果抗议委员会为给予一条船补偿而调整分数时，其他船的分数不改动，除非抗议委员会做出其他决定。

## A7 RACE TIES

If boats are tied at the finishing line or if a handicap or rating system is used and boats have equal corrected times, the points for the place for which the boats have tied and for the place(s) immediately below shall be added together and divided equally. Boats tied for a race prize shall share it or be given equal prizes.

## A8 SERIES TIES

**A8.1** If there is a series-score tie between two or more boats, each boat's race scores shall be listed in order of best to worst, and at the first point(s) where there is a difference the tie shall be broken in favour of the boat(s) with the best score(s). No excluded scores shall be used.

**A8.2** If a tie remains between two or more boats, they shall be ranked in order of their scores in the last race. Any remaining ties shall be broken by using the tied boats' scores in the next-to-last race and so on until all ties are broken. These scores shall be used even if some of them are excluded scores.

## A9 RACE SCORES IN A SERIES LONGER THAN A REGATTA

For a series that is held over a period of time longer than a regatta, a boat that came to the starting area but did not *start,* did not *finish*, retired or was disqualified shall be scored points for the finishing place one more than the number of boats that came to the starting area. A boat that did not come to the starting area shall be scored points for the finishing place one more than the number of boats entered in the series.

## A10 GUIDANCE ON REDRESS

If the protest committee decides to give redress by adjusting a boat's score for a race, it is advised to consider scoring her

(a) points equal to the average, to the nearest tenth of a point (0.05 to be rounded upward), of her points in all the races in the series except the race in question;

## A7 单轮竞赛中的平分

如果在到达终点线后船只分数出现平分或使用让分制记分方法时船只修正后的时间相同时，平分的船的名次得分应与下面紧连的名次得分相加并取其平均分。得分相同的船获奖时应共享或获得同等的奖品。

## A8 系列赛的平分

A8.1 如果在两条船或更多的船之间发生了系列赛的平分，每条船的各轮分数将按从最好到最差的顺序排列，在第一个出现差异的分数处，以分数好者列前来打破平分，不得使用被去掉的分数。

A8.2 如果两条船或更多船的分数仍然相同时，以最后一轮比赛中船的分数顺序来打破平分。如果有两条以上的船分数仍相同，将根据并列船的倒数第2轮的分数来打破并列，以此类推，直到并列被打破。即使是被去掉的分数也可以用来打破平分。

## A9 比一场赛事时间长的系列竞赛分

在一段时间举办的系列赛（时间长于一场赛事）中，一条船到达了起航区，但没有*起航*、没有*到达终点*、退出比赛或被取消资格，将按照到达起航区船只数目加1计算终点名次。未到达起航区的船将按报名参加系列赛船只数目加1 排列终点名次。

## A10 补偿指南

如果抗议委员会决定给予一条船补偿而调整一轮分数，建议考虑按如下方式记分：

（a）给予的分数等于系列赛中扣除其有问题的一轮比赛后所有轮次得分的平均数，该分数应四舍五入精确到小数点后面一位数；

(b) points equal to the average, to the nearest tenth of a point (0.05 to be rounded upward), of her points in all the races before the race in question; or

(c) points based on the position of the boat in the race at the time of the incident that justified redress.

## A11 SCORING ABBREVIATIONS

These scoring abbreviations shall be used for recording the circumstances described:

| | |
|---|---|
| DNC | Did not *start*; did not come to the starting area |
| DNS | Did not *start* (other than DNC and OCS) |
| OCS | Did not *start*; on the course side of the starting line at her starting signal and failed to *start*, or broke rule 30.1 |
| ZFP | 20% penalty under rule 30.2 |
| UFD | Disqualification under rule 30.3 |
| BFD | Disqualification under rule 30.4 |
| SCP | Scoring Penalty applied |
| DNF | Did not *finish* |
| RET | Retired |
| DSQ | Disqualification |
| DNE | Disqualification that is not excludable |
| RDG | Redress given |
| DPI | Discretionary penalty imposed |

（b）给予的分数等于有问题的这轮比赛之前的全部比赛得分的平均数，该分数应四舍五入精确到小数点后面一位数；或

（c）根据给予补偿的事件发生时船所在的位置给予名次。

## A11 记分缩写

须使用下列缩写记录下述情况：

DNC　*未起航*；未到达起航区

DNS　*未起航*（不同于 DNC 和 OCS）

OCS　*未起航*；竞赛信号发出后在起航线航线一侧并且*起航*失败，或违反规则 30.1

ZFP　根据规则30.2 执行的 20%惩罚

UFD　根据规则30.3被取消资格

BFD　根据规则30.4被取消资格

SCP　接受分数惩罚

DNF　*未到达终点*

RET　退出比赛

DSQ　取消资格

DNE　不得去掉的取消资格

RDG　给予补偿

DPI　可自定义的强制性惩罚

# APPENDIX B WINDSURFING COMPETITION RULES

*Windsurfing races shall be sailed under* The Racing Rules of Sailing *as changed by this appendix. The term 'boat' elsewhere in the racing rules means 'board' or 'boat' as appropriate. The term 'heat' means one elimination race, a 'round' consists of several heats, and an 'elimination series' consists of one or more rounds. However, in speed competition, a 'round' consists of one or more speed 'runs'.*

*A windsurfing event can include one or more of the following disciplines or their formats:*

| Discipline | Formats |
|---|---|
| *Racing* | *Course racing; Slalom; Marathon* |
| *Expression* | *Wave performance; Freestyle* |
| *Speed* | *Standard Offshore Speed Course; Speed Crossings; Alpha Speed Course* |

*In racing or expression competition, boards may compete in elimination series, and only a limited number of them may advance from round to round. A marathon race is a race scheduled to last more than one hour.*

*In expression competition a board's performance is judged on skill and variety rather than speed and is organized using elimination series. Either wave performance or freestyle competition is organized, depending on the wave conditions at the venue.*

*In speed competition a board's performance is based on her speed over a measured course. Boards take turns sailing runs over the course.*

## CHANGES TO THE DEFINITIONS

The definitions *Mark-Room*, and *Tack, Starboard* or *Port* are deleted and replaced by:

***Mark-Room*** *Mark-Room* for a board is *room* to sail her *proper course* to round or pass the *mark*. However, *mark-room* for a board

# 附录B 帆板竞赛规则

*帆板竞赛应遵守本附录更改过的帆船竞赛规则。在规则其他内容中术语“船”意为“板”，或恰当时为“船”。“预赛”意为一次淘汰赛，“一轮比赛”包括数次的预赛，一次“淘汰系列赛”包括1轮或1轮以上的比赛。然而，在竞速比赛中，“一轮比赛”包括1圈或1圈以上的速度“航程”。*

*一场帆板竞赛中可包括下列一个或更多竞赛类别或它们的模式：*

| 竞赛赛制 | 模式 |
|---|---|
| *竞赛* | *场地赛；障碍赛；马拉松（长距离）* |
| *表演赛* | *滑浪表演；自由滑* |
| *竞速赛* | *标准离岸场地竞速赛；竞速穿越赛；α型场地竞速赛* |

*竞赛或表演赛中，各板在淘汰系列赛中竞争，仅有限的人成功晋级后续的轮次。马拉松（长距离）比赛是计划航行1小时以上的竞赛。*

*技巧表演是根据选手操板表演的技术和做出的花样来评判成绩而不是看速度，使用淘汰法组织比赛。根据场地浪的条件而决定组织滑浪还是自由滑比赛。*

*在竞速赛中，选手的表现是基于其在既定距离航线上的速度。各板的选手在此航线上行驶数趟航程。*

**定义的更改**

*绕标空间*、*舷风*、*右舷*或*左舷*的定义被删除且替换为：

***绕标空间*** 一条帆板的*绕标空间*是指其行驶的*正当航线*绕标或通过标志的空间。然而，一条板的*绕标空间*不包括迎风转向的

does not include *room* to tack unless she is *overlapped* inside and to *windward* of the board required to give *mark-room* and she would be *fetching* the *mark* after her tack.

***Tack, Starboard*** **or** ***Port*** A board is on the *tack*, *starboard* or *port*, corresponding to the competitor's hand that would be nearer the mast if the competitor were in normal sailing position with both hands on the wishbone and arms not crossed. A board is on *starboard tack* when the competitor's right hand would be nearer the mast and is on *port tack* when the competitor's left hand would be nearer the mast.

The definition *Zone* is deleted.

Add the following definitions:

***Capsized*** A board is *capsized* when she is not under control because her sail or the competitor is in the water.

***Rounding or Passing*** A board is *rounding or passing* a *mark* from the time her *proper course* is to begin to manoeuvre to round or pass it, until the *mark* has been rounded or passed.

## B1 CHANGES TO THE RULES OF PART 1

*[No changes.]*

## B2 CHANGES TO THE RULES OF PART 2

### B2.13 WHILE TACKING

Rule 13 is changed to:

After a board passes head to wind, she shall *keep clear* of other boards until her sail has filled. During that time rules 10, 11 and 12 do not apply. If two boards are subject to this rule at the same time, the one on the other's port side or the one astern shall *keep clear*.

### B2.17 ON THE SAME TACK; PROPER COURSE

Rule 17 is changed to:

When, at the warning signal, the course to the first *mark* is approximately ninety degrees from the true wind, a board *overlapped* to *leeward* of another board on the same *tack* during the last 30 seconds before her starting signal shall not sail above the shortest course to the first *mark* while they

*空间*，除非她是从内侧建立*相联*并向上风板要求给予*绕标空间*，且将在完成转向后飞*弛*该标。

***舷风，右舷***或***左舷***　一条板在*右舷风*或*左舷风*时，相对应的选手的一只手将更接近桅杆，选手的身体在正常航行的位置双手握住帆杆且手臂没有交叉。一条板在*右舷风*时选手的右手将更接近桅杆，在*左舷风*时选手的左手将更接近桅杆。

***标区***的定义被删除。

增加以下定义：

***翻船***　由于一条板的帆或选手的身体在水中而板失去控制时称为*翻船*。

***绕标***或者***通过***　在*绕过*或*通过标志*时，一条板的*正当航线*是从她开始准备做动作去绕过或通过*标志*的那一刻开始，直到完全绕过或通过*标志*为止。

## B1　第一章规则的更改

*［无更改］*

## B2　第二章规则的更改

### B2.13 迎风换舷时

规则13更改为：

在一条板越过正顶风后，应*避让*其他的板至她的帆重新受风。这期间规则10、11和12不适用。如果两条板同时受本规则制约，在另一条板的左舷或其后方的板应予*避让*。

### B2.17 同舷风；正当航线

规则17更改为：

当预告信号发出，到第一个*标志*的航线大约与真风成90°时，在起航信号发出前的最后30秒内，与另一条同*舷风*的板*下风相联*的一条板，在*相联*没有打破的情况下，如果会导致另一条板需要采取行动来避免接触，那该板不得高于其至第

remain *overlapped* if as a result the other board would need to take action to avoid contact, unless in doing so she promptly sails astern of the other board.

### B2.18 MARK-ROOM

Rule 18 is changed as follows:

The first sentence of rule 18.1 is changed to:

Rule B2.18 applies between boards when they are required to leave a *mark* on the same side and at least one of them is *rounding or passing* it.

Rule 18.2(b) is changed to:

(b) If boards are *overlapped* when the first of them is *rounding or passing* the *mark*, the outside board at that moment shall thereafter give the inside board *mark-room*. If a board is *clear ahead* when she is *rounding or passing* the *mark*, the board *clear astern* at that moment shall thereafter give her *mark-room*.

Rule 18.2(c) is changed to:

(c) When a board is required to give *mark-room* by rule B2.18.2(b), she shall continue to do so even if later an *overlap* is broken or a new *overlap* begins. However, if the board entitled to *mark-room* passes head to wind, rule B2.18.2(b) ceases to apply.

### B2.18.4 Gybing or Bearing Away

Rule 18.4 is changed to:

When an inside *overlapped* right-of-way board must gybe or bear away at a *mark* to sail her *proper course*, until she gybes or bears away she shall sail no farther from the *mark* than needed to sail that course. Rule B2.18.4 does not apply at a gate *mark*.

### B2.23 CAPSIZED; AGROUND; RESCUING

Rule 23 is changed to:

**B2.23.1** If possible, a board shall avoid a board that is *capsized* or has not regained control after *capsizing*, is aground, or is trying to help a person or vessel in danger.

**B2.23.2** If possible, a board that is *capsized* or aground shall not interfere with another board.

一*标*的最短航线航行，除非其这样做时能迅速行驶到另一条板的后方。

**B2.18 绕标空间**

规则18 更改如下：

规则18.1 第一句更改为：

当各板被要求在同侧离开*标志*，并且其中至少一条板正在或已经*绕过*或*通过标志*时，规则B2.18适用。

规则18.2(b)更改为：

（b）如果各板*相联*，当其中的第一条板正在*绕过*或*通过标志*时，此时处于外侧的板随后应给予内侧板*绕标空间*。如果正在*绕过*或*通过标志*时一条板*明显在前*，那么此时*明显在后*的板随后应给予其*绕标空间*。

规则18.2(c)更改为：

（c）当根据规则B2.18.2(b)，一条板被要求给予*绕标空间*时，即使稍后*相联*被打破或建立起新的*相联*，她也应该继续这么做。然而，如果有权拥有*绕标空间*的板越过正顶风，规则B2.18.2(b)停止适用。

B2.18.4 顺风换舷或顺风偏转

规则18.4更改为：

如果一条内侧*相联*且拥有航行权的板必须顺风换舷或者在*标志*旁顺风偏转来行驶其*正当航线*，在其顺风换舷或顺风偏转以前，她驶离*标志*的距离不能远于行驶那条航线所需的距离。在门标处规则B2.18.4不适用。

**B2.23 翻船；搁浅；救援**

规则23更改为：

B2.23.1 如有可能，一条板应避让*翻船*的板或*翻船*后已失控或搁浅的板，或正努力帮助处于危险中的人员或船舶的板。

B2.23.2 如有可能，一条*翻船*或搁浅的板不得妨碍其他板。

### B2.24 INTERFERING WITH ANOTHER BOARD; SAIL OUT OF WATER

Add new rule B2.24.3:

**B2.24.3** In the last minute before her starting signal, a board shall have her sail out of the water and in a normal position, except when accidentally *capsized.*

### PART 2 RULES DELETED

Rule 18.3 is deleted.

## B3 CHANGES TO THE RULES OF PART 3

### B3.26 STARTING RACES

Rule 26 is changed to:

**B3.26.1 System 1**

Races shall be started by using the following signals. Times shall be taken from the visual signals; the absence of a sound signal shall be disregarded.

| *Minutes before starting signal* | *Visual signal* | *Sound signal* | *Means* |
|---|---|---|---|
| 5* | Class flag | One | Warning signal |
| 4 | P, I, Z, Z with I, U, or black flag | One | Preparatory signal |
| 1 | Preparatory flag removed | One long | One minute |
| 0 | Class flag removed | One | Starting signal |

*or as stated in the sailing instructions

The warning signal for each succeeding class shall be made with or after the starting signal of the preceding class.

**B3.26.2 System 2**

Races shall be started by using the following signals. Times shall be taken from the visual signals; the absence of a sound signal shall be disregarded.

**B2.24 妨碍另一条板；帆离开水面**

增加新规则 B2.24.3：

B2.24.3 在起航信号发出前的最后1分钟，一条板应使帆离开水面并处于正常位置，除非意外*翻船*。

**第二章删除的规则**

删除规则 18.3。

## B3 第三章规则的更改

**B3.26 竞赛起航**

规则 26更改为：

B3.26.1 **程序1**

使用以下信号来进行竞赛起航。时间以视觉信号为准，音响信号的缺失可不予理会。

| *起航信号前的时间* | *视觉信号* | *音响信号* | *含义* |
|---|---|---|---|
| 5* | 级别旗 | 一声 | 预告信号 |
| 4 | P、I、Z旗，或Z旗和I、U旗或黑旗 | 一声 | 准备信号 |
| 1 | 移除准备旗 | 一长声 | 1分钟 |
| 0 | 移除级别旗 | 一声 | 起航信号 |

*或者遵循航行细则中的规定

下个级别的预告信号应该在前一个级别起航信号发出时或之后发出。

B3.26.2 **程序2**

使用以下信号来进行比赛起航。时间以视觉信号为准，音响信号的缺失可不予理会。

| *Minutes before starting signal* | *Visual signal* | *Sound signal* | *Means* |
|---|---|---|---|
| 3 | Class flag or heat number | | Attention signal |
| 2 | Red flag; attention signal removed | One | Warning signal |
| 1 | Yellow flag; red flag removed | One | Preparatory signal |
| 1/2 | Yellow flag removed | | 30 seconds |
| 0 | Green flag | One | Starting signal |

**B3.26.3 System 3 (for Beach Starts)**

[Note：World Sailing has decided to move it to the website because this part is not used often. ]

### B3.31 TOUCHING A MARK

Rule 31 is changed to:

A board may touch a *mark* but shall not hold on to it.

## B4 CHANGES TO THE RULES OF PART 4

### B4.42 PROPULSION

Rule 42 is changed to:

A board shall be propelled only by the action of the wind on the sail, by the action of the water on the hull and by the unassisted actions of the competitor. However, significant progress shall not be made by paddling, swimming or walking.

### B4.43 COMPETITOR CLOTHING AND EQUIPMENT

Rule 43.1(a) is changed to:

Competitors shall not wear or carry clothing or equipment for the purpose of increasing their weight. However, a competitor may wear a drinking container that shall have a capacity of at least one litre and weigh no more than 1.5 kilograms when full.

### B4.44 PENALTIES AT THE TIME OF AN INCIDENT

Rule 44 is changed to:

| *起航信号前的时间* | *视觉信号* | *音响信号* | *含义* |
|---|---|---|---|
| 3 | 级别旗或预赛数字 | | 注意信号 |
| 2 | 红旗；移除注意信号 | 一声 | 预告信号 |
| 1 | 黄旗；移除红旗 | 一声 | 准备信号 |
| 1/2 | 移除黄旗 | | 30秒准备 |
| 0 | 绿旗 | 一声 | 起航信号 |

B23.6.3 **程序3（适用于沙滩起航）**

（译者注：由于是不常用到的规则，俗称“僵尸规则”，世界帆联已决定之后将本部分内容移至世界帆联网站。）

B3.31 **碰标**

规则31修改为：

帆板可以碰标，但是不能挂住它。

## B4 第四章规则的更改

B4.42 **推进**

规则42更改为：

帆板只能依靠风对帆、水对板体的作用和选手的非辅助性作用力作为推进力。然而，不能通过划水、游泳或是在板上行走使板获得大幅前进。

B4.43 **选手的服装和装备**

规则43.1(a)更改为：

选手不应穿着或携带专为增加自身体重的服装或装备。然而，选手可身背装有饮料的容器，该容器至少要有1升的容量，在装满时其重量不得超过 1.5公斤。

B4.44 **事件发生时的惩罚**

规则44更改为：

### B4.44.1 Taking a Penalty

A board may take a 360°-Turn Penalty when she may have broken one of more rules of Part 2 in an incident while *racing.* The sailing instructions may specify the use of some other penalty. However, if the board caused injury or serious damage or, despite taking a penalty, gained a significant advantage in the race or series by her breach, her penalty shall be to retire.

### B4.44.2 360°-Turn Penalty

After getting well clear of other boards as soon after the incident as possible, a board takes a 360°-Turn Penalty by promptly making a 360° turn with no requirement for a tack or a gybe. When a board takes the penalty at or near the finishing line, she shall sail completely to the course side of the line before *finishing.*

### PART 4 RULES DELETED

Rules 43.2, 44.3, 45, 47.2, 48.1, 49, 50, 51, 52 and 54 are deleted.

## B5 CHANGES TO THE RULES OF PART 5

### B5.60 RIGHT TO PROTEST; RIGHT TO REQUEST REDRESS OR RULE 69 ACTION

Rule 60.1(a) is changed by deleting 'or saw'.

### B5.61 PROTEST REQUIREMENTS

The first three sentences of rule 61.1(a) are changed to:

A board intending to protest shall inform the other board at the first reasonable opportunity. When her *protest* will concern an incident in the racing area that she was involved in or saw, she shall hail 'Protest'. She shall also inform the racc committee of her intention to protest as soon as practicable after she *finishes* or retires.

### B5.62 REDRESS

Rule 62.1(b) is changed to:

(b) injury, physical damage or *capsize* because of the action of

(1) a board that broke a rule of Part 2 and took the appropriate penalty or was penalized, or

(2) a vessel not *racing* that was required to keep clear.

**B4.44.1 解脱**

在竞赛中，当帆板违反了规则第二章的一条或多条规则时，她将进行自转360° 的解脱。航行细则可以说明其他惩罚的用法。然而，不管做没做解脱，若帆板造成了受伤或严重损坏，或因其犯规而在竞赛或系列赛中获得明显优势，则对她的惩罚应该是退出比赛。

**B4.44.2 360° 解脱**

事件发生后，做360° 解脱的帆板应尽快完全避让其他的帆板，即刻做出的360° 解脱，不要求做一个迎风换舷和一个顺风换舷。在终点线或终点线附近的板可以在*到达终点*前在终点线任意一侧做解脱。

**第四章删除的规则**

规则43.2、44.3、45、47.2、48.1、49、50、51、52和54被删除。

## B5 第五章规则的更改

**B5.60 抗议和要求补偿的权利或规则69的措施**

规则60.1(a)更改部分为删除“或目睹”。

**B5.61 对抗议的要求**

规则 61.1(a)的前3句话更改为：

一条有意提出抗议的板，应在最先出现的合理时机通知另外一条板。当其*抗议*关系到她在比赛水域中涉及或目睹的事件，应呼喊“Protest（抗议）”。在她*到达终点*或退出比赛后，还应立即通知竞赛委员会其抗议意图。

**B5.62 补偿**

规则 62.1(b)更改为：

（b）由于以下行为而导致的受伤、有形损坏或*翻船*：

（1）帆板违反了第二章的规则，做了适当的解脱或被判罚，或

（2）被要求避让的不在*竞赛*的船舶。

### B5.64 DECISIONS

Rule 64.3(b) is changed to:

(b) When the protest committee is in doubt about a matter concerning the measurement of a board, the meaning of a class rule, or damage to a board, it shall refer its questions, together with the relevant facts, to an authority responsible for interpreting the rule. In making its decision, the committee shall be bound by the reply of the authority.

## B6 CHANGES TO THE RULES OF PART 6

### B6.78 COMPLIANCE WITH CLASS RULES; CERTIFICATES

Add to rule 78.1: 'When so prescribed by World Sailing, a numbered and dated device on a board and her centreboard, fin and rig shall serve as her measurement certificate.'

## B7 CHANGES TO THE RULES OF PART 7

### B7.90 RACE COMMITTEE; SAILING INSTRUCTIONS; SCORING

The last sentence of rule 90.2(c) is changed to: 'Oral instructions may be given only if the procedure is stated in the sailing instructions.'

## B8 CHANGES TO APPENDIX A

### B8.A1 NUMBER OF RACES; OVERALL SCORES

Rule A1 is changed to:

The number of races scheduled and the number required to be completed to constitute a series shall be stated in the notice of race or sailing instructions. If an event includes more than one discipline or format, the notice of race or sailing instructions shall state how the overall scores are to be calculated.

### B8.A2.1 SERIES SCORES

Rule A2.1 is changed to:

Each board's series score shall, subject to rule 90.3(b), be the total of her race scores excluding her

(a) worst score when from 5 to 11 races have been completed, or

**B5.64 裁决**

规则 64.3(b)更改为：

（b）当抗议委员会对板的丈量问题、级别规则的含义或板体破损有疑问时，应将问题连同相关事实一起提交给负责解释规则的一个权威机构。抗议委员会应依据该权威机构的回复进行裁决。

## B6　第六章规则的更改

**B6.78 遵守级别规则；证书**

在规则78.1后添加：“当世界帆联这样规定：板及其稳向板、尾鳍和索具上被编号和标注日期的装置可作为其丈量证书。”

## B7　第七章规则的更改

**B7.90 竞赛委员会；航行细则；记分**

规则90.2(c)最后一句更改为：“只要航行细则中规定了相关流程，就可以给予口头指示。”

## B8　附录A的更改

**B8.A1 比赛轮次；总分**

规则A1更改为：

竞赛通知和航行细则应注明比赛计划的轮次及组成系列赛所需要完成的轮次数目。如果一个赛事包含了不止一种比赛类别或模式，竞赛通知或航行细则须说明如何计算总分。

**B8.A2.1 系列赛的记分**

规则A2.1更改为：

每条板参加系列赛的得分按照规则90.3(b)的规定，是其全部轮次得分的总和，去掉其

（a）第5轮至第11轮比赛完成时的最差得分，或

(b) two worst scores when 12 or more races have been completed.

(The notice of race or sailing instructions may make a different arrangement. A race is completed if scored; see rule 90.3(a).) If a board has two or more equal worst scores, the score(s) for the race(s) sailed earliest in the series shall be excluded. The board with the lowest series score wins and others shall be ranked accordingly.

**B8.A8 SERIES TIES**

Rule A8 is changed to:

**B8.A8.1** If there is a series-score tie between two or more boards, they shall be ranked in order of their best excluded race score.

**B8.A8.2** If a tie remains between two or more boards, each board's race scores, including excluded scores, shall be listed in order of best to worst, and at the first point(s) where there is a difference the tie shall be broken in favour of the board(s) with the best score(s). These scores shall be used even if some of them are excluded scores.

**B8.A8.3** If a tie still remains between two or more boards, they shall be ranked in order of their scores in the last race. Any remaining ties shall be broken by using the tied boards' scores in the next-to-last race and so on until all ties are broken. These scores shall be used even if some of them are excluded scores.

**B9 CHANGES TO APPENDIX G**

**B9.G1 WORLD SAILING CLASS BOARDS**

**B9.G1.3 Positioning**

Rule G1.3(a) is changed to:

(a) The class insignia shall be displayed once on each side of the sail in the area above a line projected at right angles from a point on the luff of the sail one-third of the distance from the head to the wishbone. The national letters and sail numbers shall be in the central third of that part of the sail above the wishbone, clearly separated from any advertising. They shall be black and applied back to back on an opaque white background. The background shall extend a minimum of 30 mm beyond the characters. There shall be a '–' between the national （b）当有12轮或更多轮次的比赛完成时的最差两轮得分。［竞赛通知或航行细则可以另有安排。如果有记分，该轮比赛就算完成，参见规则 90.3(a)］。如果一条板有两个或更多相同的最差分数，将去掉这条板系列赛最前面的最差分数。系列赛获得总分最低的板获胜，其他板的名次依次排列。

**B8.A8 系列赛的平分**

规则A8更改为：

B8.A8.1 如果两条板或多条板中产生了系列赛的平分，将按照去掉的最好竞赛分数排名。

B8.A8.2 如果两条板或多条板中仍有平分，各板的竞赛得分，包括去掉轮次的分数，将按从好到坏的顺序排列，在第一个出现差异的分数处，以最佳分数多者列前来打破平分。被去掉的分数也可用于打破平分。

B8.A8.3 如果两条板或多条板中依然还有平分，以最后一轮比赛中各板的分数顺序来打破平分。此时任何依然存在的平分，将根据存在平分的板的倒数第二轮的分数来打破平分，以此类推，直到所有平分被打破。即使是被去掉的分数也将用于打破平分。

## B9 附录G的更改

**B9.G1 世界帆联的帆板级别**

**B9.G13 位置**

规则G1.3(a)更改为：

（a）级别标识应在帆的每一面展示一个，在从帆杆至帆顶角的上三分之一处前缘做出的直角投影线上方区域。国家字母和帆号应在帆杆以上帆的中三分之一处，与广告明显地区别开。它们应为黑色并且背对背粘贴在不透明的白色背景上。背景至少比字母多出30mm的距

letters and the sail number, and the spacing between characters shall be adequate for legibility.

## APPENDIX G RULES DELETED

The first sentence of rule G1.3(b) is deleted. Rules G1.3(c), G1.3(d) and G1.3(e) are deleted.

## B10 CHANGES TO RULES FOR EVENTS THAT INCLUDE ELIMINATION SERIES

### B10.29 RECALLS

For a race of an elimination series that will qualify a board to compete in a later stage of an event, rule 29 is changed to:

(a) When at a board's starting signal any part of her hull, crew or equipment is on the course side of the starting line, the race committee shall signal a general recall.

(b) If the race committee acts under rule B10.29(a) and the board is identified, she shall be disqualified without a hearing, even if the race is *abandoned*. The race committee shall hail or display her sail number, and she shall leave the course area immediately. If the race is restarted or resailed, she shall not sail in it.

(c) If the race was completed but was later *abandoned* by the protest committee, and if the race is resailed, a board disqualified under rule B10.29(b) may sail in it.

### B10.37 ELIMINATION SERIES INCLUDING HEATS

Add new rule B10.37:

*Rule B10.37 applies in elimination series in which boards compete in heats.*

#### B10.37.1 Elimination Series Procedure

(a) Competition shall take the form of one or more elimination series. Each of them shall consist of either rounds in a single elimination series where only a number of the best scorers advance, or rounds in a double elimination series where boards have more than one opportunity to advance.

离。在国家代码和帆号间应有“-”号，字母间应有适当的距离，以便于辨认。

**附录G删除的规则**

规则G1.3(b)的第一句被删除。规则G1.3(c)、G1.3(d)和G1.3(e)被删除。

## B10 包括淘汰赛赛事的规则更改

### B10.29 召回

对于淘汰系列赛轮次，即确认能参加赛事后面阶段比赛的帆板，规则29更改为：

（a）帆板起航信号发出时，板体、选手或装备的任何部分处于起航线航线一侧时，竞赛委员会应发出全召信号。

（b）如果竞赛委员会按照规则B10.29(a)采取措施并识别了某条板，她将被取消资格而无需审理，即使该轮竞赛被*放弃*。竞赛委员会应呼喊或展示她的帆号，她应立即离开航线区域。如果该轮竞赛重新起航或重新竞赛，她也不应参加。

（c）如果该轮竞赛完成，但随后被抗议委员会*放弃*，并且如果该轮重新竞赛，根据规则B10.29(b)被取消资格的板可参加这轮竞赛。

### B10.37 包括预赛的淘汰系列赛

增加新规则B10.37：

*在进行帆板预赛的淘汰系列赛中，规则B10.37适用。*

### B10.37.1 淘汰程序

（a）比赛应采取一场或多场淘汰系列赛的形式。在单一淘汰系列赛中，只有少数最好成绩者可晋级，或者在双淘汰系列赛中选手会有多于一次的晋级机会。

(b) Boards shall sail one against another in pairs, or in groups determined by the elimination ladder. The selected form of competition shall not be changed while a round remains uncompleted.

**B10.37.2 Seeding and Ranking Lists**

(a) When a seeding or ranking list is used to establish the heats of the first round, places 1–8 (four heats) or 1–16 (eight heats) shall be distributed evenly among the heats.

(b) For a subsequent elimination series, if any, boards shall be reassigned to new heats according to the ranking in the previous elimination series.

(c) The organizing authority's seeding decisions are final and are not grounds for a request for redress.

**B10.37.3 Heat Schedule**

The schedule of heats shall be posted on the official notice board no later than 30 minutes before the starting signal for the first heat.

**B10.37.4 Advancement and Byes**

(a) In racing and expression competition, the boards in each heat to advance to the next round shall be announced by the race committee no later than 10 minutes before the starting signal for the first heat. The number advancing may be changed by the protest committee as a result of a redress decision.

(b) In expression competition, any first-round byes shall be assigned to the highest-seeded boards.

(c) In wave performance competition, only the winner of each heat shall advance to the next round.

(d) In freestyle competition, boards shall advance to the next round as follows: from an eight-board heat, the best four advance, and the winner will sail against the fourth and the second against the third; from a four-board heat, the best two advance and will sail against each other.

**B10.37.5 Finals**

(a) The final shall consist of a maximum of three races. The race committee shall announce the number of races to be sailed in the final no later than 5 minutes before the warning signal for the first final race.

（b）帆板应两两配对竞赛，或按照淘汰途径决定的分组竞赛。当一个循环未完成时，比赛形式不应改变。

B10.37.2 **种子选手和排名**

（a）当使用种子选手或排名名单安排预赛第一回合时，在预赛中应平均分配第1~8 名（4场预赛）或第1~16 名（8场预赛）。

（b）如果有随后的淘汰系列赛，将根据前一轮淘汰系列赛的排名重新安排新的预赛。

（c）组织管理机构所列的种子名单为最终名单，该名单不能作为提出补偿要求的理由。

B10.37.3 **预赛日程安排**

预赛日程安排应在不晚于第一场预赛起航信号前30分钟张贴于官方公告栏上。

B10.37.4 **晋级和轮空**

（a）在竞赛和表演赛中，竞赛委员会应在不晚于第一场预赛起航信号前10分钟公布每场预赛中进入下一回合的名单。作为给予补偿决定的结果，抗议委员会可改变进入下一回合预赛的板数。

（b）表演赛中任何第一回合轮空选手将安排给最高种子排名的板。

（c）在滑浪比赛中，只有每组预赛中的获胜者可进入下一回合。

（d）在自由滑比赛中，帆板应按下列程序进入下一轮：8条板预赛的前4名可晋级，第1名与第4名比赛，第2名与第3名比赛；4条板预赛的前2名晋级并彼此竞赛。

B10.37.5 **决赛**

（a）决赛最多包括3轮竞赛。竞赛委员会将在不晚于第1轮决赛的预告信号前5 分钟公布决赛进行的轮次数。

(b) A runners-up final may be sailed after the final. All boards in the semi-final heats that failed to qualify for the final may compete in it.

**B10.63 HEARINGS**

For a race of an elimination series that will qualify a board to compete in a later stage of an event, rules 61.2 and 65.2 are deleted and rule 63.6 is changed to:

**B10.63.6 Taking Evidence and Finding Facts**

*Protests* and requests for redress need not be in writing; they shall be made orally to a member of the protest committee as soon as reasonably possible following the race. The protest committee may take evidence in any way it considers appropriate and may communicate its decision orally.

**B10.70 APPEALS AND REQUESTS TO A NATIONAL AUTHORITY**

Add new rule B10.70.7:

**B10.70.7** Appeals are not permitted in disciplines and formats with elimination series.

**B10.A2.1 SERIES SCORES**

Rule A2.1 is changed to:

Each board's elimination series score shall, subject to rule 90.3(b), be the total of her race scores excluding her

(a) worst score when 3 or 4 races are completed,

(b) two worst scores when from 5 to 7 races are completed,

(c) three worst scores when 8 or more races are completed.

Each board's final series score shall be the total of her race scores excluding her worst score when 3 races are completed. (The notice of race or sailing instructions may make a different arrangement. A race is completed if scored; see rule 90.3(a).) If a board has two or more equal worst scores, the score(s) for the race(s) sailed earliest in the series shall be excluded. The board with the lowest series score wins and others shall be ranked accordingly.

**B10.A4 LOW POINT SYSTEM**

Add at the end of the first sentence of rule A4.2: 'or, in a race of an elimination series, the number of boards in that heat'.

（b）亚军争夺赛将在决赛后进行，所有在半决赛中未取得决赛资格的帆板可参加这场竞赛。

**B10.63 审理**

对于淘汰系列赛的轮次，将确认能参加赛事后续阶段比赛的帆板，规则61.2和65.2被删除，规则63.6更改为：

**B10.63.6 取证和认定事实**

抗议和要求补偿不必提交书面报告，应在接下来的轮次中尽可能早的合理时机口头通知抗议委员会的成员。抗议委员会将通过其认为合适的任何途径取证并口头公布裁决结果。

**B10.70 上诉及寻求国家管理机构的确认**

增加新规则B10.70.7：

B10.70.7 不能针对淘汰系列赛的竞赛赛制和模式提出上诉。

**B10.A2.1 系列赛记分**

规则A2.1更改为：

每条板的淘汰系列赛得分按照规则90.3(b)的要求，即其每轮得分的总和，去掉

（a）完成3或4轮后的最差成绩，

（b）完成5至7轮时的最差2轮成绩，

（c）完成8轮或更多轮次时最差的3轮成绩。

当决赛系列赛完成3轮时，每条板的决赛得分是其所有轮次总分减去最差一轮的得分。[竞赛通知或航行细则可以做出不同的安排，只要有记分，一轮比赛就算完成；见规则90.3(a)。]如果一条板有两个或两个以上同样差的成绩，则去掉系列赛中轮次在前的最差轮次成绩。最终得分最低的板胜出，其他板的排名依次类推。

**B10.A4 低分记分法**

在规则A4.2第一句末加入："或者，在淘汰系列赛轮次中，为该预赛中的板数"。

Add new rule B10.A4.3:

**B10.A4.3** When a heat cannot be completed, the points for the unscored places shall be added together and divided by the number of places in that heat. The resulting number of points, to the nearest tenth of a point (0.05 to be rounded upward), shall be given to each board entered in the heat.

## B11 CHANGES TO RULES FOR EXPRESSION COMPETITION

Add the following definitions:

***Coming In* and *Going Out*** A board sailing in the same direction as the incoming surf is *coming in*. A board sailing in the direction opposite to the incoming surf is *going out*.

***Jumping*** A board is *jumping* when she takes off at the top of a wave while *going out*.

***Overtaking*** A board is *overtaking* from the moment she gains an *overlap* from *clear astern* until the moment she is *clear ahead* of the *overtaken* board.

***Possession*** The first board sailing shoreward immediately in front of a wave has *possession* of that wave. However, when it is impossible to determine which board is first the *windward* board has *possession*.

***Recovering*** A board is *recovering* from the time her sail or, when water-starting, the competitor is out of the water until she has steerage way.

***Surfing*** A board is *surfing* when she is on or immediately in front of a wave while *coming in*.

***Transition*** A board changing *tacks*, or taking off while *coming in*, or one that is not *surfing*, *jumping*, *capsized* or *recovering* is in *transition*.

### B11.PART 2 – WHEN BOARDS MEET

The rules of Part 2 are deleted and replaced by:

(a) COMING IN AND GOING OUT

A board *coming in* shall *keep clear* of a board *going out*. When two boards are *going out* or *coming in* while on the same wave, or when neither is *going out* or *coming in*, a board on *port tack* shall *keep clear* of the one on *starboard tack*.

增加新规则B10.A4.3：

B10.A4.3不能完成时，未记分的名次的分数相加后除以该预赛板数。所得分数精确到小数点后一位（0.05分四舍五入后为0.1），该分数分别给予进入该预赛的每条板。

## B11 表演赛规则的更改

增加以下定义：

***顺浪**和**迎浪**：* 板在与来浪同一方向航行时称为*顺浪*。板在与来浪方向相对航行时称为*迎浪*。

***跳跃**：* *迎浪*航行时板在浪最高点处腾空称为*跳跃*。

***追赶**：* 一条板从*明显在后*开始与被追赶的板形成*相联*直到其*明显在前*称为*追赶*。

***拥有权**：* 第一条紧紧靠近浪前向岸边航行的板将具有那个浪的*拥有权*。然而在不可能判断哪条板是第一条板时，上风的板将得到*拥有权*。

***复位**：* 一条板从她的帆离开水面或在水中起航时，选手离开水面直到其开始操纵行驶为止称为*复位*。

***滑浪**：* 一条板*顺浪*航行在浪上或在浪前航行时称为*滑浪*。

***过渡**：* 一条板在换*舷*时或*顺浪*航行时腾空，或不是在*滑浪*、*跳跃*、*翻船*或*复位*时称为*过渡*。

## B11. 第二章——船只相遇时

规则第二章被删除且替换为：

（a）顺浪和迎浪

*顺浪*航行的板应*避让迎浪*航行的板。在同一浪中，当两条板都在*顺浪*或*迎浪*航行时或两条板都未*顺浪*或*迎浪*航行时，*左舷*航行板应*避让右舷*航行板。

(b) BOARDS ON THE SAME WAVE, COMING IN

When two or more boards are on a wave *coming in*, a board that does not have *possession* shall *keep clear*.

(c) CLEAR ASTERN, CLEAR AHEAD AND OVERTAKING

A board *clear astern* and not on a wave shall *keep clear* of a board *clear ahead*. An *overtaking* board that is not on a wave shall *keep clear*.

(d) TRANSITION

A board in *transition* shall *keep clear* of one that is not. When two boards are in *transition* at the same time, the one on the other's port side or the one astern shall *keep clear*.

(e) JUMPING

A board that is *jumping* shall *keep clear* of one that is not.

## B11.26 STARTING AND ENDING HEATS

Rule 26 is changed to:

Heats shall be started and ended by using the following signals:

(a) STARTING A HEAT

Each flag shall be removed when the next flag is displayed.

| *Minutes before starting signal* | *Visual signal* | *Sound signal* | *Means* |
|---|---|---|---|
| Beginning of transition period | Heat number with red flag | One | Warning |
| 1 | Yellow flag | One | Preparatory |
| 0 | Green flag | One | Starting signal |

(b) ENDING A HEAT

| *Minutes before ending signal* | *Visual signal* | *Sound signal* | *Means* |
|---|---|---|---|
| 1 | Green flag removed | One | End warning |
| 0 | Red flag | One | Ending signal |

（b）同一浪中的板，顺浪

当两条或两条以上的板同在一个浪上*顺浪*航行时，没有*拥有权*的板应*避让*。

（c）明显在后、明显在前和追赶

*明显在后*并不在浪上的板应*避让明显在前*的板。不处在浪上并正在*追赶*的板应*避让*。

（d）过渡

*过渡*过程中的板应*避让*没在这样做的板。如两条板同时在*过渡*中，在另外一条板左舷一侧或在后的板应*避让*。

（e）跳跃

正在*跳跃*的板必须*避让*没在这样做的板。

**B11.26 开始和结束预赛**

规则26更改为：

使用以下信号开始和结束预赛：

（a）预赛开始

下一个信号旗展示的同时上一个信号旗应被移除。

| *起航信号前时间（分钟）* | *视觉信号* | *音响信号* | *含义* |
|---|---|---|---|
| 过渡时段开始 | 预赛数字旗加红旗 | 一声 | 预告 |
| 1 | 黄旗 | 一声 | 准备 |
| 0 | 绿旗 | 一声 | 起航 |

（b）预赛结束

| *结束信号前时间（分钟）* | *视觉信号* | *音响信号* | *含义* |
|---|---|---|---|
| 1 | 移除绿旗 | 一声 | 结束预告信号 |
| 0 | 红旗 | 一声 | 结束 |

### B11.38 REGISTRATION; COURSE AREA; HEAT DURATION; ADVANCEMENT AND BYES

Add new rule B11.38:

(a) Boards shall register with the race committee the colours and other particulars of their sails, or their identification according to another method stated in the sailing instructions, no later than the starting signal for the heat two heats before their own.

(b) The course area shall be defined in the sailing instructions and posted on the official notice board no later than 10 minutes before the starting signal for the first heat. A board shall be scored only while sailing in the course area.

(c) Any change in heat duration shall be announced by the race committee no later than 15 minutes before the starting signal for the first heat in the next round.

(d) Rule B10.37.4 applies.

### B11.41 OUTSIDE HELP

Change the number of rule 41 to B11.41.1 and add new rule B11.41.2:

**B11.41.2** An assistant may provide replacement equipment to a board. The assistant shall not interfere with other competing boards. A board whose assistant interferes with another board may be penalized at the discretion of the protest committee.

### APPENDIX A – SCORING

The rules of Appendix A are deleted and replaced by:

### B11.A1 EXPRESSION COMPETITON SCORING

(a) Expression competition shall be scored by a panel of three judges. However, the panel may have a greater odd number of members, and there may be two such panels. Each judge shall give points for each manoeuvre based on the scale stated in the notice of race or sailing instructions.

(b) The criteria of scoring shall be decided by the race committee and announced on the official notice board no later than 30 minutes before the starting signal for the first heat.

**B11.38 注册；竞赛区域；预算持续时间；晋级和轮空**

增加新规则B11.38：

（a）帆板选手向竞赛委员会注册帆的颜色和其他特征，或者选手可参照航行细则注明的另外方法注册其特征，注册时间应不晚于自己所在预赛前两场的预赛起航信号发出时。

（b）比赛区域应在航行细则中注明，并于不晚于第一场预赛起航信号发出前10分钟张贴在官方公告栏上。只有在比赛区域里比赛的板方可计算成绩。

（c）任何有关预赛持续时间的改变将由竞赛委员会在不晚于下一回合第一次预赛前15分钟公布。

（d）规则B10.37.4适用。

**B11.41 外部援助**

规则41更改为B11.41.1，并增加新规则B11.41.2：

B11.41.2 助手可以向某条板提供替换器材，助手不得干扰其他正在竞赛的板。某条板的助手干扰到任何其他板的选手将受到抗议委员会给予的适当处罚。

**附录A——记分**

**B11.A1 表演赛记分**

（a）表演赛将由3人组成的裁判小组进行打分。但该裁判小组可以由更多的奇数个成员组成，也可以有两个这样的组。每位裁判根据竞赛通知或航行细则中说明的评判尺度对每个动作打分。

（b）记分标准由竞赛委员会决定，并在不晚于第一场预赛起航信号发出前的30 分钟张贴在官方公告栏上。

(c) A board's heat standing shall be determined by adding together the points given by each judge. The board with the highest score wins and others shall be ranked accordingly.

(d) Both semi-final heats shall have been sailed for an elimination series to be valid.

(e) Except for members of the race committee responsible for scoring the event, only competitors in the heat shall be allowed to see judges' score sheets for the heat. Each score sheet shall bear the full name of the judge.

(f) Scoring decisions of the judges shall not be grounds for a request for redress by a board.

**B11.A2 SERIES TIES**

(a) In a heat, if there is a tie in the total points given by one or more judges, it shall be broken in favour of the board with the higher single score in the priority category. If the categories are weighted equally, in wave performance competition the tie shall be broken in favour of the board with the higher single score in wave riding, and in freestyle competition in favour of the board with the higher score for overall impression. If a tie remains, in wave performance competition it shall be broken in favour of the board with the higher single score in the category without priority, and in freestyle competition it shall stand as the final result.

(b) If there is a tie in the series score, it shall be broken in favour of the board that scored better more times than the other board. All scores shall be used even if some of them are excluded scores.

(c) If a tie still remains, the heat shall be resailed. If this is not possible, the tie shall stand as the final result.

## B12 CHANGES TO RULES FOR SPEED COMPETITION

The rules of Part 2 are deleted and replaced by:

**B12.PART 2 – GENERAL RULES**

(a) WATER STARTING

A board shall not water start on the course or in the starting area, except to sail off the course to avoid boards that are making, or about to make, a run.

（c）选手的预赛排名取决于每位裁判打分的总和。最高分者为胜者，依此类推。

（d）两个半决赛预赛结束后，淘汰系列赛才有效。

（e）除竞赛委员会负责为赛事记分的人员，只允许预赛选手查阅裁判对该轮预赛记分的记分单。每张记分单都应注明裁判的全名。

（f）裁判的记分决定不应成为选手提出补偿的依据。

**B11.A2 系列赛平分**

（a）在预赛中，如果一个或更多的裁判给予的总分中出现平分，打破平分是以优先类目的单轮成绩更高者为胜者；如果类目权重相等，滑浪表演赛中，打破平分是以浪上滑行单轮成绩更高者为胜者；在自由滑比赛中，打破平分是以总印象单轮成绩更高者为胜者。如果平分仍未打破，滑浪赛中，打破平分是以不享有优先类目的单轮成绩更高者为胜者；在自由滑比赛中，应将其作为最后决赛分数。

（b）如果在系列赛中出现平分，打破平分是以比其他板具有更多次好分数者为胜。所有的分数都将被使用，即使一些分数已被去掉。

（c）如果平分仍未打破，将重新安排进行预赛。如果没有可能重新安排，平分成绩将作为最终成绩。

## B12　竞速赛规则的更改

第二章规则被删除和替换为：

**B12.第二章——总则**

（a）水中起航

帆板在航线区域或起航区域内不得进行水中起航，除非为避开正在起航或即将要起航的帆板驶离航线。

(b) LEAVING THE COURSE AREA

A board leaving the course area shall *keep clear* of boards making a run.

(c) COURSE CONTROL

When the race committee points an orange flag at a board, she is penalized and the run shall not be counted.

(d) RETURNING TO THE STARTING AREA

A board returning to the starting area shall keep clear of the course.

(e) MAXIMUM NUMBER OF RUNS FOR EACH BOARD

The maximum number of runs that may be made by each board in a round shall be announced by the race committee no later than 15 minutes before the starting signal for the first round.

(f) DURATION OF A ROUND

The duration of a round shall be announced by the race committee no later than 15 minutes before the starting signal for the next round.

(g) CONDITIONS FOR ESTABLISHING A RECORD

The minimum distance for a world record is 500 metres. Other records may be established over shorter distances. The course shall be defined by posts and transits ashore or by buoys afloat. Transits shall not converge.

(h) VERIFICATION RULES

(1) An observer appointed by the World Sailing Speed Record Council shall be present and verify run times and speeds at world record attempts. The race committee shall verify run times and speeds at other record attempts.

(2) A competitor shall not enter the timing control area or discuss any timing matter directly with the timing organization. Any timing question shall be directed to the race committee.

**B12.26 STARTING AND ENDING A ROUND**

Rule 26 is changed to:

Rounds shall be started and ended by using the following signals. Each flag shall be removed when the next flag is displayed.

（b）离开航线区域

正离开航线区域的板必须*避让*正处于比赛航程中的板。

（c）航线控制

当竞赛委员会用橙色旗指向某一条板时，该板选手被判罚且该航段不会被记分。

（d）返回起航区域

返回起航区域的板应避开航线。

（e）每条板的最多航程数

竞赛委员会应在不晚于第一回合起航信号前15分钟公布每条板每一回合最多的航程数目。

（f）一回合比赛持续的时间

竞赛委员会应在不晚于下一回合比赛起航信号前15分钟公布一回合的持续时间。

（g）创纪录的条件

世界纪录的距离至少为500米。其他纪录可在更短的距离创造。航线可由标杆和岸上参照物或漂在水中的浮标来划定。参照物不得集中在一点上。

（h）认证规则

（1）由世界帆联速度纪录理事会（WSSRC）指定的观察员将出席比赛并确认欲创造世界纪录的时间和速度。竞赛委员会应确认欲创造其他纪录的时间和速度。

（2）选手不得进入记时控制区或直接与记时组织商谈任何计时事宜。任何计时问题应直接交给竞赛委员会。

**B12.26 一个回合开始和结束**

规则26更改为：

使用下列信号开始和结束一回合比赛。展示下一面信号旗时应移除前一面信号旗。

(a) STARTING A ROUND

| *Signal* | *Flag* | *Means* |
|---|---|---|
| Stand-by | AP flag | Course closed. Races are *postponed* |
| Course closed | Red flag | Course closed; will open shortly |
| Preparatory | Red and yellow flag | Course will open in 5 minutes |
| Starting | Green flag | Course is open |

(b) ENDING A ROUND

| *Signal* | *Flag* | *Means* |
|---|---|---|
| End warning | Green and yellow flag | Course will be closed in 5 minutes |
| Extension | Yellow flag | Current round extended by 15 minutes |
| Round ended | Red flag | A new round will be started shortly |

**B12.64 DECISIONS**

Rule 64.1 is deleted and replaced by:

**B12.64.1 Penalties**

(a) If a board fails to comply with a rule, she may be warned. If a board is warned a second time during the same round, she shall be excluded by the race committee from the remainder of the round. A list of the sail numbers of boards that have received warnings or have been excluded shall be posted on a notice board near the finishing line.

(b) A board observed in the course area after having been excluded from a round shall be excluded from the competition without a hearing, and none of her previous times or results shall be valid.

(c) Any breach of the verification rules may result in exclusion from one or more rounds or from the competition.

（a）开始一个回合比赛

| *信号* | *旗帜* | *含义* |
|---|---|---|
| 等待 | AP旗 | 场地关闭。比赛*推迟* |
| 场地关闭 | 红旗 | 场地关闭；将很快打开 |
| 准备 | 红旗和黄旗 | 场地将在5分钟内打开 |
| 起航 | 绿旗 | 场地打开 |

（b）结束一个回合

| *信号* | *旗帜* | *含义* |
|---|---|---|
| 结束预告 | 绿旗和黄旗 | 场地将在5分钟内关闭 |
| 延长 | 绿旗 | 目前1个回合延长15分钟 |
| 结束 | 红旗 | 新一回合比赛很快开始 |

B12.64 **裁决**

规则64.1被删除并替换为：

B12.64.1惩罚

（a）如果一条板未遵守规则，她应被警告。如果一条板在同一回合中被警告第二次，该板将被竞赛委员会禁止继续参加该回合比赛。被警告及取消该回合比赛资格的帆号将被张贴在终点线附近的公告栏上。

（b）一回合中已被禁赛的板如果被发现仍在航线区域中，可直接取消其资格而无需审理，她之前的任何竞赛时间或成绩均无效。

（c）违反认证规则可能会导致禁止参加一个或多个回合的比赛，或者禁止参加整个赛事。

## APPENDIX A -- SCORING

The rules of Appendix A are deleted and replaced by:

### B12.A1 SPEED COMPETITON SCORING

(a) On Standard Offshore Speed Courses, the speeds of a board's fastest two runs in a round shall be averaged to determine her standing in that round. The board with the highest average wins and others shall be ranked accordingly. If boards are tied, the tie shall be broken in favour of the board with the fastest run in the round.

(b) On Speed Crossings and Alpha Speed Courses, boards shall be ranked based on their fastest run in the round.

(c) If there is a series-score tie between two or more boards, it shall be broken in favour of the board(s) with the fastest run during the competition. If a tie remains, it shall be broken by applying rules B8.A8.2 and B8.A8.3.

**附录A——记分**

规则附录A被删除并替换为：

**B12.A1 竞速赛记分**

（a）对于标准离岸场地竞速赛，按照该回合最快两个航程的平均速度决定她在该回合的排名。拥有最快平均速度的板胜出，其他板的成绩依此类推。如果出现平分，以该回合中最快的板的胜出来打破平分。

（b）对于竞速穿越赛和α型场地竞速赛，按照该回合中最快航程来排列名次。

（c）如果两条或多条板出现系列赛平分，将以比赛中最快航程的帆板来打破平分。如果仍存在平分，按照规则B8.A8.2和 B8.A8.3来打破平分。

# APPENDIX C MATCH RACING RULES

*Match races shall be sailed under* The Racing Rules of Sailing *as changed by this appendix. Matches shall be umpired unless the notice of race and sailing instructions state otherwise.*

*Note: A Standard Notice of Race, Standard Sailing Instructions, and Match Racing Rules for Blind Competitors are available at the World Sailing website.*

## C1 TERMINOLOGY

'Competitor' means the skipper, team or boat as appropriate for the event. 'Flight' means two or more matches started in the same starting sequence.

## C2 CHANGES TO THE DEFINITIONS AND THE RULES OF PARTS 1, 2, 3 AND 4

**C2.1** The definition *Finish* is changed to:

> ***Finish*** A boat *finishes* when any part of her hull crosses the finishing line in the direction of the course from the last *mark* after completing any penalties. However, when penalties are cancelled under rule C7.2(d) after one or both boats have *finished* each shall be recorded as *finished* when she crossed the line.

**C2.2** The definition *Mark-Room* is changed to:

> ***Mark-Room*** *Room* for a boat to sail her *proper course* to round or pass the *mark* on the required side.

**C2.3** Add to the definition *Proper Course*: 'A boat taking a penalty or manoeuvring to take a penalty is not sailing a *proper course*.'

**C2.4** In the definition *Zone* the distance is changed to two hull lengths.

# 附录C　对抗赛规则

*对抗赛应该根据本附录修改的《帆船竞赛规则》进行。除非竞赛通知和航行细则另行规定，否则对抗赛应进行现场裁决。*

*注意：标准版本的竞赛通知、航行细则，以及盲人选手的对抗赛规则可在世界帆联官网查看。*

## C1　术语

“选手”意为适合于本比赛的舵手、参赛队或船。“组”意为排在同一起航顺序起航的两个或两个以上的对抗赛。

## C2　对定义及第一、第二、第三和第四章规则的更改

C2.1　*到达终点*的定义更改为：

***到达终点***　船在完成了任何的惩罚后，当其船体的任何部分从上一个*标志*方向驶来的航线上越过终点线时，该船即为*到达终点*。但按照规则C7.2(d)在一条或两条船*到达终点*后惩罚被取消，每条船越过终点线时应记为*到达终点*。

C2.2　*绕标空间*的定义更改为：

***绕标空间***　一条船航行于*正当航线*上在被要求一侧绕过或通过*标志*时需要的*空间*。

C2.3　在*正当航线*定义中增加：“正在接受惩罚的船或正在操作准备做解脱的船不是航行在*正当航线*上”。

C2.4　定义*标区*中的距离被更改为2倍船长。

**C2.5** Add new rule 8 to Part 1:

**8 LAST POINT OF CERTAINTY**

The umpires will assume that the state of a boat, or her relationship to another boat, has not changed, until they are certain that it has changed.

**C2.6** Rule 13 is changed to:

**13 WHILE TACKING OR GYBING**

**13.1** After a boat passes head to wind, she shall *keep clear* of other boats until she is on a close-hauled course.

**13.2** After the foot of the mainsail of a boat sailing downwind crosses the centreline she shall *keep clear* of other boats until her mainsail has filled or she is no longer sailing downwind.

**13.3** While rule 13.1 or 13.2 applies, rules 10, 11 and 12 do not. However, if two boats are subject to rule 13.1 or 13.2 at the same time, the one on the other's port side or the one astern shall *keep clear*.

**C2.7** Rule 16.2 is deleted.

**C2.8** Rule 17 is deleted.

**C2.9** Rule 18 is changed to:

**18 MARK-ROOM**

**18.1 When Rule 18 Applies**

Rule 18 applies between boats when they are required to leave a *mark* on the same side and at least one of them is in the *zone*. However, it does not apply between a boat approaching a *mark* and one leaving it.

**18.2 Giving Mark-Room**

(a) When the first boat reaches the *zone*,

(1) if boats are *overlapped*, the outside boat at that moment shall thereafter give the inside boat *mark-room*.

(2) if boats are not *overlapped*, the boat that has not reached the *zone* shall thereafter give *mark-room*.

C2.5 在第一章中增加新的规则8：

**8 确定性的最后一点**

现场仲裁会假设某船的状态或者她与另一条船之间的关系没有发生改变，直到她们能确定这两条船的关系发生了改变。

C2.6 规则13更改为：

**13 迎风换舷或顺风换舷时**

13.1 在一条船越过正顶风后，该船应*避让*其他船，直至其处于近迎风的航线上。

13.2 在一条船顺风航行时主帆后角越过中线后，该船应*避让*其他船，直至其主帆为满帆或不再顺风航行。

13.3 当规则13.1或13.2适用时，规则10、11和12不适用。但如果两条船同时适用规则13.1或13.2，那条在另外一条船左舷的船或明显在后的船应*避让*。

C2.7 删除规则16.2。

C2.8 删除规则17。

C2.9 规则18更改为：

**18 绕标空间**

**18.1 规则18适用时**

当船被要求同侧离开*标志*，并且至少有一条船在*标区*内，此时规则18适用。然而，它并不适用于接近和离开*标志*的船之间。

**18.2 给予绕标空间**

（a）当第一条船到达*标区*时，

（1）如果船*相联*，此时外侧船此后应该给予内侧船*绕标空间*。

（2）如果船不*相联*，还没有进入该*标区*的船此后应该给予*绕标空间*。

(b) If the boat entitled to *mark-room* leaves the *zone*, the entitlement to *mark-room* ceases and rule 18.2(a) is applied again if required based on the relationship of the boats at the time rule 18.2(a) is re-applied.

(c) If a boat obtained an inside *overlap* and, from the time the *overlap* began, the outside boat is unable to give *mark-room*, she is not required to give it.

**18.3 Tacking or Gybing**

(a) If *mark-room* for a boat includes a change of *tack*, such tack or gybe shall be done no faster than a tack or gybe to sail her *proper course*.

(b) When an inside *overlapped* right-of-way boat must change *tack* at a *mark* to sail her *proper course*, until she changes *tack* she shall sail no farther from the *mark* than needed to sail that course. Rule 18.3(b) does not apply at a gate *mark* or a finishing *mark* and a boat shall not be penalized for breaking this rule unless the course of another boat was affected by the breach of this rule.

**C2.10** When rule 20 applies, the following arm signals by the helmsman are required in addition to the hails:

(a) for 'Room to tack', repeatedly and clearly pointing to windward; and

(b) for 'You tack', repeatedly and clearly pointing at the other boat and waving the arm to windward.

**C2.11** Rule 22.3 is deleted.

**C2.12** Rule 24.1 is changed to: 'If reasonably possible, a boat not *racing* shall not interfere with a boat that is *racing* or an umpire boat.'

**C2.13** Add new rule 24.3: 'When boats in different matches meet, any change of course by either boat shall be consistent with complying with a *rule* or trying to win her own match.'

（b）如果有权要求*绕标空间*的船离开*标区*，则享有*绕标空间*的权利终止。并且在规则18.2(a)再次适用下，基于船之间的关系，如果有需要的话，规则18.2(a)再次适用。

（c）如果一条船在内部建立*相联*，从*相联*建立的那一刻起，外侧船不能给予*绕标空间*，外侧船不被要求给予*绕标空间*。

18.3 迎风换舷或顺风换舷

（a）如果一条船的*绕标空间*包含换舷，不管是迎风换舷还是顺风换舷，该动作的速度不能快于其在*正当航线*上迎风换舷或顺风换舷的速度。

（b）如果一条内侧*相联*并拥有航行权的船在*标志*旁必须迎风换舷来行驶其*正当航线*，直到其换舷，她应行驶在距离*标志*不远于其需要行驶的航线。在门标或终点标时，规则18.3(b)不适用。除非其他船因为该条船违反了这条规则而受到影响，否则该船不会因为违反这条规则而受到惩罚。

C2.10 当规则20适用时，除呼喊外，舵手还被要求使用下列手臂信号：

（a）要求“迎风换舷的空间（Room to tack）”时反复而明显指向上风，

（b）表示“你迎风换舷（You tack）”时反复而明显指向另外一条船并向上风摆动上臂。

C2.11 删除规则22.3。

C2.12 规则24.1更改为：“如果可能，没有*竞赛*的船不得干扰正在*竞赛*的船或现场裁判船。”

C2.13 增加新的规则24.3：“当不参加同一对抗赛的船相遇时，任何一条船在改变航线时应始终遵守*规则*，并且其目的是赢得自己的对抗赛。”

**C2.14** Rule 31 is changed to:

**31 TOUCHING A MARK**

While *racing*, neither the crew nor any part of a boat's hull shall touch a starting *mark* before *starting*, a *mark* that begins, bounds or ends the leg of the course on which she is sailing, or a finishing *mark* after *finishing*. In addition, while *racing*, a boat shall not touch a race committee vessel that is also a *mark*.

**C2.15** Rule 42 shall also apply between the warning and preparatory signals.

**C2.16** Rule 42.2(d) is changed to: 'sculling: repeated movement of the helm to propel the boat forward;'.

## C3 RACE SIGNALS AND CHANGES TO RELATED RULES

### C3.1 Starting Signals

The signals for starting a match shall be as follows. Times shall be taken from the visual signals; the failure of a sound signal shall be disregarded. If more than one match will be sailed, the starting signal for one match shall be the warning signal for the next match.

| *Time in minutes* | *Visual signal* | *Sound signal* | *Means* |
|---|---|---|---|
| 10 | Flag F displayed | One | Attention signal |
| 6 | Flag F removed | None | |
| 5 | Numeral pennant displayed* | One | Warning signal |
| 4 | Flag P displayed | One | Preparatory signal |
| 2 | Blue or yellow flag or both displayed** | One** | End of pre-start entry time |
| 1 | Flag P removed | One long | |
| 0 | Warning signal removed | One | Starting signal |

*Within a flight, numeral pennant 1 means Match 1, pennant 2 means Match 2, etc., unless the sailing instructions state otherwise.

**These signals shall be made only if one or both boats fail to comply with rule C4.2. The flag(s) shall be displayed until the umpires have signalled a penalty or for one minute, whichever is earlier.

C2.14 规则31更改为：

**31　碰标**

*竞赛*时，不管是船员还是船体的任何一部分在*起航*前不允许碰起航*标志*，以及标示其正在航行的航线上某航段的起点、边界和末端的*标志*，*到达终点*后也不许碰撞终点*标志*。另外，*竞赛*时，船不能触碰竞赛委员会的船只，因为那也是一个*标志*。

C2.15 规则42也应该适用于预告信号和准备信号之间。

C2.16 规则42.2(d)更改为：“摇舵：舵的反复运动推动船向前行驶”。

## C3　竞赛信号和有关规则的更改

### C3.1　起航信号

对抗赛的起航信号应按如下内容发出。时间将以视觉信号为准计算，音响信号的缺失不必理会。如果将举行一个以上场次的对抗赛，前一场对抗赛的起航信号将是下一场对抗赛的预告信号。

| *时间* | *视觉信号* | *音响信号* | *含义* |
|---|---|---|---|
| 10分钟 | 展示F旗 | 一声 | 注意信号 |
| 6分钟 | 移除F旗 | 无 | |
| 5分钟 | 展示数字三角旗* | 一声 | 预告信号 |
| 4分钟 | 展示P旗 | 一声 | 准备信号 |
| 2分钟 | 展示蓝或黄旗，或两面旗都展示** | 一声** | 起航前的入场时间结束 |
| 1分钟 | 移除P旗 | 一长声 | |
| 0分钟 | 移除预告信号 | 一声 | 起航信号 |

*在一组中，数字三角旗1意为第一场，数字三角旗2意为第二场，以此类推，除非航行细则另有规定。

**只有在一条船或两条船都没有遵守规则C4.2时才使用这些信号。这些旗要一直展示到现场裁判发出惩罚信号或1分钟后，以在先的为准。

**C3.2 Changes to Related Rules**

(a) Rule 29.1 is changed to:

(1) When at a boat's starting signal any part of her hull, crew or equipment is on the course side of the starting line or one of its extensions, the race committee shall promptly display a blue or yellow flag identifying the boat with one sound. The flag shall be displayed until the boat is completely on the pre-start side of the starting line or one of its extensions or until two minutes after her starting signal, whichever is earlier.

(2) When after her starting signal a boat sails from the pre-start side to the course side of the starting line across an extension without having *started* correctly, the race committee shall promptly display a blue or yellow flag identifying the boat. The flag shall be displayed until the boat is completely on the pre-start side of the starting line or one of its extensions or until two minutes after her starting signal, whichever is earlier.

(b) In the race signal AP the last sentence is changed to: 'The attention signal will be made 1 minute after removal unless at that time the race is *postponed* again or *abandoned*.'

(c) In the race signal N the last sentence is changed to: 'The attention signal will be made 1 minute after removal unless at that time the race is *abandoned* again or *postponed*.'

**C3.3 Finishing Line Signals**

The race signal Blue flag or shape shall not be used.

**C4 REQUIREMENTS BEFORE THE START**

**C4.1** At her preparatory signal, each boat shall be outside the line that is at a 90° angle to the starting line through the starting *mark* at her assigned end. In the pairing list, the boat listed on the left-hand side is assigned the port end and shall display a blue flag at her stern while *racing*. The other boat is assigned the starboard end and shall display a yellow flag at her stern while *racing*.

**C4.2** Within the two-minute period following her preparatory signal, a boat shall cross and clear the starting line, the first time from the course side to the pre-start side.

## C3.2 有关规则的更改

（a）规则29.1更改为：

（1）在起航信号发出时，船的船体、船员或装备的任何一部分已处在起航线或其延伸部分的航线一侧时，竞赛委员会将尽快展示一面蓝旗或黄旗识别该船并伴随一声音响。该旗帜应展示至该船完全在起航线准备起航区一侧或直至起航信号发出后2分钟，以时间在先的为准。

（2）当起航信号发出后，一条船由于*起航*失误正从起航准备区一侧穿越延长线回到起航线准备区一侧时，竞赛委员会将尽快展示一面识别该船的蓝旗或黄旗。该旗帜应展示至该船完全回到起航线或其延长线的起航准备区一侧，或直至起航信号发出后2分钟，以时间在先的为准。

（b）竞赛信号AP的最后一句话更改为："在移除后1分钟发出注意信号，除非那时竞赛被再次*推迟*或*放弃*。"

（c）竞赛信号N的最后一句更改为："在移除后1分钟发出注意信号，除非那时竞赛被再次*推迟*或*放弃*。"

## C3.3 终点线信号

不应使用竞赛信号蓝色旗或蓝色物体。

# C4 起航前的要求

C4.1 准备信号发出时，每条船应在指定一侧起航标与起航线成90° 的连线外。在对阵表中，被列在左边的船应指定在左舷端点，在*竞赛*中应在船尾展示一面蓝旗。另外一条船被指定在右舷端点，*竞赛*中应在船尾展示一面黄旗。

C4.2 准备信号发出后的2分钟之内，船应第一次从航线一侧越过并离开起航线到达准备起航区一侧。

## C5 SIGNALS BY UMPIRES

**C5.1** A green and white flag with one long sound means 'No penalty'.

**C5.2** A blue or yellow flag identifying a boat with one long sound means 'The identified boat shall take a penalty by complying with rule C7.'

**C5.3** A red flag with or soon after a blue or yellow flag with one long sound means 'The identified boat shall take a penalty by complying with rule C7.3(d).'

**C5.4** A black flag with a blue or yellow flag and one long sound means 'The identified boat is disqualified, and the match is terminated and awarded to the other boat.'

**C5.5** One short sound means 'A penalty is now completed.'

**C5.6** Repetitive short sounds mean 'A boat is no longer taking a penalty and the penalty remains.'

**C5.7** A blue or yellow flag or shape displayed from an umpire boat means 'The identified boat has an outstanding penalty.'

## C6 PROTESTS AND REQUESTS FOR REDRESS BY BOATS

**C6.1** A boat may protest another boat

(a) under a rule of Part 2, except rule 14, by clearly displaying flag Y immediately after an incident in which she was involved;

(b) under any rule not listed in rule C6.1(a) or C6.2 by clearly displaying a red flag as soon as possible after the incident.

**C6.2** A boat may not protest another boat under

(a) rule 14, unless damage or injury results;

(b) a rule of Part 2, unless she was involved in the incident;

(c) rule 31 or 42; or

(d) rule C4 or C7.

**C6.3** A boat intending to request redress because of circumstances that arise before she *finishes* or retires shall clearly display a red flag as soon as possible after she becomes aware of those circumstances, but no later than two minutes after *finishing* or retiring.

## C5 现场裁判使用的信号

C5.1 一面绿白旗并伴随一声长音响，意为“没有惩罚”。

C5.2 识别一条船的一面蓝旗或黄旗并伴随一声长音响，意为“所识别的船应按规则C7接受惩罚”。

C5.3 在展示蓝旗或黄旗同时或之后展示红旗并伴随一声长音响，意为“所识别的船应按规则C7.3(d)接受惩罚”。

C5.4 在展示蓝旗或黄旗同时展示黑旗并伴随一声长音响，意为“所识别的船被取消资格，对抗赛终止，另外一条船获胜”。

C5.5 一声短音响意为“惩罚已完成”。

C5.6 重复短的音响意为“船不再接受惩罚，惩罚保留”。

C5.7 蓝旗或黄旗，或同颜色形状的物体在现场裁判船上展示，意为“所识别的船有一个未做的惩罚”。

## C6 船的抗议和要求补偿

C6.1 一条船抗议另一条船：

（a）依据规则第二章，除规则14外，在所涉及的事件发生后立即清楚地展示Y旗。

（b）依据未列入规则C6.1(a)或C6.2中的任何规则，在事件后尽快清楚地展示红旗。

C6.2 一条船不能依据下列规则抗议另外一条船：

（a）规则14，除非有损坏或损伤发生；

（b）规则第二章的某一条，除非该船涉及事件；

（c）规则31或42；或者

（d）规则C4或C7。

C6.3 因在*到达终点*或退出比赛之前所发生的情况想要求补偿的船，应在其意识到这些情况后，尽快清楚地展示红旗，但不能晚于*到达终点*或退出比赛后2分钟。

**C6.4** (a) A boat protesting under rule C6.1(a) shall remove flag Y before or as soon as possible after the umpires' signal.

(b) A boat protesting under rule C6.1(b) or requesting redress under rule C6.3 shall, for her *protest* or request to be valid, keep her red flag displayed until she has so informed the umpires after *finishing* or retiring. No written *protest* or request for redress is required.

**C6.5 Umpire Decisions**

(a) After flag Y is displayed, the umpires shall decide whether to penalize any boat. They shall signal their decision in compliance with rule C5.1, C5.2 or C5.3. However, when the umpires penalize a boat under rule C8.2 and in the same incident there is a flag Y from a boat, the umpires may disregard the flag Y.

(b) The red-flag penalty in rule C5.3 shall be used when a boat has gained a controlling position as a result of breaking a *rule*, but the umpires are not certain that the conditions for an additional umpire-initiated penalty have been fulfilled.

**C6.6 Protest Committee Decisions**

(a) The protest committee may take evidence in any way it considers appropriate and may communicate its decision orally.

(b) If the protest committee decides that a breach of a *rule* has had no significant effect on the outcome of the match, it may

(1) impose a penalty of one point or part of one point;

(2) order a resail; or

(3) make another arrangement it decides is equitable, which may be to impose no penalty.

(c) The penalty for breaking rule 14 when damage or injury results will be at the discretion of the protest committee, and may include exclusion from further races in the event.

**C6.7** Add new rule N1.10 to Appendix N:

**N1.10** In rule N.1, one International Umpire may be appointed to the jury, or a panel of it, in place of one International Judge.

C6.4 （a）按照规则C6.1(a)提出抗议的船应在现场裁判发出信号前或后，尽快移除Y旗。

（b）为使所提出的*抗议*或要求有效，按照规则C6.1(b)提出抗议或按照规则C6.3提出补偿要求的船，应将其红旗展示至*到达终点*或退出比赛后通知到现场裁判。不要求书面提出*抗议*或做出补偿要求。

**C6.5 现场裁判的裁决**

（a）Y旗展示后，现场裁判将决定是否判罚某条船，并根据规则C5.1、C5.2或C5.3 向其发出裁决的信号。但是，当现场裁判按规则C8.2判罚了一条船时，即便该船在该事件中展示了Y旗，现场裁判也可无视该Y旗。

（b）当某条船因违反*规则*而取得船位控制权时，应使用规则C5.3中的红旗惩罚，但现场裁判不确定其发出的额外判罚条件是否已经满足。

**C6.6 抗议委员会的裁决**

（a）抗议委员会可以按其认为恰当的任何方法去取得证据，并且可以口头传达其裁决。

（b）如果抗议委员会认定违反*规则*的行为对比赛的结果没有明显的影响时，它可以：

（1）实施1分或零点几分的惩罚；

（2）命令重新比赛；或

（3）做出它认为公平的其他安排，这种安排可能是不实施惩罚。

（c）违反规则14而发生了损坏和损伤情况的惩罚将由抗议委员会酌情处理，惩罚可以是取消参加后面比赛的资格。

C6.7 在附录N中增加新规则N1.10：

N1.10在规则N.1中，一名国际现场裁判可以被任命到仲裁委员会或仲裁小组，来代替一名国际裁判。

## C7 PENALTY SYSTEM

### C7.1 Deleted Rule

Rule 44 is deleted.

### C7.2 All Penalties

(a) A penalized boat may delay taking a penalty within the limitations of rule C7.3 and shall take it as follows:

(1) When on a leg of the course to a windward *mark*, she shall gybe and, as soon as reasonably possible, luff to a close-hauled course.

(2) When on a leg of the course to a leeward *mark* or the finishing line, she shall tack and, as soon as reasonably possible, bear away to a course that is more than ninety degrees from the true wind.

(b) Add to rule 2: 'When *racing*, a boat need not take a penalty unless signalled to do so by an umpire.'

(c) A boat completes a leg of the course when her bow crosses the extension of the line from the previous *mark* through the *mark* she is rounding, or on the last leg when she *finishes*.

(d) A penalized boat shall not be recorded as having *finished* until she takes her penalty and sails completely to the course side of the line and then *finishes*, unless the penalty is cancelled before or after she crosses the finishing line.

(e) If a boat has one or two outstanding penalties and the other boat in her match is penalized, one penalty for each boat shall be cancelled except that a red-flag penalty shall not cancel or be cancelled by another penalty.

(f) If a boat has more than two outstanding penalties, the umpires shall signal her disqualification under rule C5.4.

### C7.3 Penalty Limitations

(a) A boat taking a penalty that includes a tack shall have the spinnaker head below the main-boom gooseneck from the time she passes head to wind until she is on a close-hauled course.

(b) No part of a penalty may be taken inside the *zone* of a rounding *mark* that begins, bounds or ends the leg the boat is on.

## C7 惩罚系统

### C7.1 删除规则

删除规则44。

### C7.2 所有惩罚

（a）被惩罚的船可以在规则C7.3限制内延迟解脱，可按下列办法处理：

（1）在向上风*标志*行驶的航段上，她应顺风换舷并尽快迎风偏转至近迎风航线上。

（2）在向下风*标志*或终点线行驶的航段上，她应迎风换舷并尽早顺风偏转至一个超过真风 90° 的航线上。

（b）在规则2后增加："*竞赛*时，某船不需要解脱，除非现场裁判发出信号要求其这么做。"

（c）当一条船的船头越过前一个*标志*至她正在绕行的*标志*连线的延长线时，该船就完成了航线的某一航段，或当她*到达终点*时，是处于最后一个航段。

（d）被判罚的船直到其做了解脱并完全行驶到终点线航线一侧，然后再通过终点才应被记录为*到达终点*，除非她在通过终点线之前或之后惩罚被取消了。

（e）如果一条船有一或两个未完成的惩罚，而在同一对抗赛中的另一条船也被判罚，每条船可以取消一个惩罚，但红旗惩罚不能取消或因另一船的惩罚而取消。

（f）如果一条船有两个以上的未完成惩罚，现场裁判可依据规则C5.4 发出取消资格的信号。

### C7.3 惩罚限制

（a）一条船接受包括一个迎风换舷的惩罚时，自其越过正顶风直至处于近迎风航线上时，其球帆上角都应在主帆杆销之下。

（b）解脱的任何过程不得在船所在航段上的标示起点、边界和结束的需绕行*标志*的*标区*内进行。

(c) If a boat has one outstanding penalty, she may take the penalty any time after *starting* and before *finishing*. If a boat has two outstanding penalties, she shall take one of them as soon as reasonably possible, but not before *starting*.

(d) When the umpires display a red flag with or soon after a penalty flag, the penalized boat shall take a penalty as soon as reasonably possible, but not before *starting*.

**C7.4 Taking and Completing Penalties**

(a) When a boat with an outstanding penalty is on a leg to a windward *mark* and gybes, or is on a leg to a leeward *mark* or the finishing line and passes head to wind, she is taking a penalty.

(b) When a boat taking a penalty either does not take the penalty correctly or does not complete the penalty as soon as reasonably possible, she is no longer taking a penalty. The umpires shall signal this as required by rule C5.6.

(c) The umpire boat for each match shall display blue or yellow flags or shapes, each flag or shape indicating one outstanding penalty. When a boat has taken a penalty, or a penalty has been cancelled, one flag or shape shall be removed, with the appropriate sound signal. Failure of the umpires to signal correctly shall not change the number of penalties outstanding.

## C8 PENALTIES INITIATED BY UMPIRES

**C8.1 Rule Changes**

(a) Rules 60.2(a) and 60.3(a) do not apply to *rules* for which penalties may be imposed by umpires.

(b) Rule 64.1(a) is changed so that the provision for exonerating a boat may be applied by the umpires without a hearing, and it takes precedence over any conflicting rule of this appendix.

（c）如果一条船有一个未做的惩罚，她可在*起航*后和*到达终点*前的任何时间去解脱。如果一条船有两个未做的惩罚，她应在合适的机会尽早去完成其中的一个解脱，但不能在*起航*前进行。

（d）当现场裁判在举起惩罚旗同时或之后很快展示了红旗，被罚的船应尽早完成该惩罚，但不能在*起航*前进行。

C7.4 **接受和完成惩罚**

（a）带有一个未做的惩罚的船在驶向上风标志的航段上航行并顺风换舷，或者在向下风标志或终点线航行的航段上航行并越过正顶风将被视为正在解脱。

（b）当某条船不是按照正确的方法解脱或未尽早完成解脱动作时，该船被视为已不再做解脱的动作。现场裁判可按规则C5.6的要求发出信号。

（c）每一场对抗赛现场裁判船上应展示蓝色或黄色旗帜或物体，每一次旗或物体代表一个未完成的惩罚。当船已解脱或已被取消了一个惩罚时，应移除该旗或物体。现场裁判没有正确发出信号不应改变未做惩罚的次数。

## C8 现场裁判给予的惩罚

C8.1 **规则的更改**

（a）规则60.2(a)和60.3(a)不适用于现场裁判采用惩罚的*规则*。

（b）规则64.1(c)被更改，以使裁判在不审理的情况下可采用免除对一条船的惩罚的规定，它可优先于与本附录中任何相冲突的规则。

**C8.2** When the umpires decide that a boat has broken rule 31, 42, C4, C7.3(c) or C7.3(d) she shall be penalized by signalling her under rule C5.2 or C5.3. However, if a boat is penalized for breaking a rule of Part 2 and if she in the same incident breaks rule 31, she shall not be penalized for breaking rule 31. Furthermore, a boat that displays an incorrect flag or does not display the correct flag shall be warned orally and given an opportunity to correct the error before being penalized.

**C8.3** When the umpires decide that a boat has

(a) gained an advantage by breaking a *rule* after allowing for a penalty,

(b) deliberately broken a *rule*, or

(c) committed a breach of sportsmanship,

she shall be penalized under rule C5.2, C5.3 or C5.4.

**C8.4** If the umpires or protest committee members decide that a boat may have broken a *rule* other than those listed in rules C6.1(a) and C6.2, they shall so inform the protest committee for its action under rule 60.3 and rule C6.6 when appropriate.

**C8.5** When, after one boat has *started*, the umpires are satisfied that the other boat will not *start*, they may signal under rule C5.4 that the boat that did not *start* is disqualified and the match is terminated.

**C8.6** When the match umpires, together with at least one other umpire, decide that a boat has broken rule 14 and damage resulted, they may impose a points-penalty without a hearing. The competitor shall be informed of the penalty as soon as practicable and, at the time of being so informed, may request a hearing. The protest committee shall then proceed under rule C6.6. Any penalty decided by the protest committee may be more than the penalty imposed by the umpires. When the umpires decide that a penalty greater than one point is appropriate, they shall act under rule C8.4.

## C9 REQUESTS FOR REDRESS OR REOPENING; APPEALS; OTHER PROCEEDINGS

**C9.1** There shall be no request for redress or an appeal from a decision made under rule C5, C6, C7 or C8. In rule 66 the third sentence is changed to: 'A *party* to the hearing may not ask for a reopening.'

C8.2 当现场裁判判定一条船违反了规则31、42、C4、C7.3(c)或C7.3(d)时，应按照规则C5.2或C5.3对其发出惩罚信号。然而，一条船因为违反规则第二章被惩罚，并且如果她在同一事件中违反规则31，她不应因违反规则31而被惩罚。此外，如果一条船展示了错误的旗或没有展示正确的旗时应被口头警告，在受到惩罚前可得到改正错误的机会。

C8.3 当现场裁判判定一条船

（a）在接受惩罚后仍因违反*规则*而获得优势时；

（b）故意违反*规则*，或

（c）违反了体育道德，

她应根据规则C5.2、C5.3 或 C5.4受到惩罚。

C8.4 如果现场裁判或抗议委员会成员判定一条船违反了除规则C6.1(a)和C6.2中所列以外的*规则*时，他们应在适当时候通知抗议委员会根据规则60.3和C6.6采取措施。

C8.5 当一条船*起航*后，现场裁判都认为另外一条船将不会参加*起航*，他们可根据规则C5.4发出信号，通知未*起航*的船被取消资格，比赛终止。

C8.6 当对抗赛的现场裁判和至少一名其他的现场裁判同时判定一条船违反了规则14并且造成了损坏，他们可以不通过审理给予加分惩罚。只要可行的话，选手应立即被告知受到惩罚，并且在被告知的同时可以要求审理。抗议委员会应根据规则C6.6进行审理，任何由抗议委员会决定的惩罚应多于裁判的罚分。当现场裁判认为多于1分的惩罚是合适的，他们应根据规则C8.4采取措施。

## C9 补偿或重新审理的要求；上诉；其他程序

C9.1 根据规则C5、C6、C7或C8所做的裁决不能要求补偿或上诉。规则66中第三句话更改为：“审理的一方不可要求重新审理。”

**C9.2** A competitor may not base a request for redress on a claim that an action by an official boat was improper. The protest committee may decide to consider giving redress in such circumstances but only if it believes that an official boat, including an umpire boat, may have seriously interfered with a competing boat.

**C9.3** No proceedings of any kind may be taken in relation to any action or non-action by the umpires, except as permitted in rule C9.2.

## C10 SCORING

**C10.1** The winning competitor of each match scores one point (half a point each for a dead heat); the loser scores no points.

**C10.2** When a competitor withdraws from part of an event the scores of all completed races shall stand.

**C10.3** When a single round robin is terminated before completion, or a multiple round robin is terminated during the first round robin, a competitor's score shall be the average points scored per match sailed by the competitor. However, if any of the competitors have completed less than one third of the scheduled matches, the entire round robin shall be disregarded and, if necessary, the event declared void. For the purposes of tie-breaking in rule C11.1(a), a competitor's score shall be the average points scored per match between the tied competitors.

**C10.4** When a multiple round robin is terminated with an incomplete round robin, only one point shall be available for all the matches sailed between any two competitors, as follows:

| *Number of matches completed between any two competitors* | *Points for each win* |
|---|---|
| 1 | One point |
| 2 | Half a point |
| 3 | A third of a point |
| (etc.) | |

**C10.5** In a round-robin series,

(a) competitors shall be placed in order of their total scores, highest score first;

C9.2 选手不得以一条官员船不恰当的行动为理由提出补偿。在这种情况下，抗议委员会只能在确认官员船包括裁判船可能已严重干扰了正在比赛的船后方可考虑给予补偿。

C9.3 与现场裁判采取的任何措施或未采取的措施有关的任何形式的诉讼均不予采用，除非是规则C9.2准许的情况。

## C10 记分

C10.1 每场对抗赛的胜者记1分（平局时每人得半分）；负者得零分。

C10.2 当选手退出部分比赛时，所赛完的成绩依然有效。

C10.3 当单循环赛在结束循环前中止，或多次循环赛在第一个单循环赛就中止时，选手的成绩记为她所参加轮次的平均得分。但是，如果选手完成的轮次少于对阵表三分之一的轮次时，应无视整个循环赛，如果需要，该赛事可宣布无效。根据规则C11.1(a)，为了打破平分，成绩可记为平分的选手之间每轮比赛得分的平均分。

C10.4 当多次循环赛以一个未完成的循环赛结束时，任何两名选手之间的所有比赛以下列方式记分：

| *任何两名选手间完成的比赛轮次* | *每位胜者得分* |
|---|---|
| 1 | 1分 |
| 2 | 半分 |
| 3 | 1/3分 |
| （等） | |

C10.5 在一个循环系列赛中，

（a）选手应根据总分排列名次，总分最高者为第一名；

(b) a competitor who has won a match but is disqualified for breaking a *rule* against a competitor in another match shall lose the point for that match (but the losing competitor shall not be awarded the point); and

(c) the overall position between competitors who have sailed in different groups shall be decided by the highest score.

**C10.6** In a knockout series the sailing instructions shall state the minimum number of points required to win a series between two competitors. When a knockout series is terminated it shall be decided in favour of the competitor with the higher score.

## C11 TIES

### C11.1 Round-Robin Series

*In a round-robin series competitors are assigned to one or more groups and scheduled to sail against all other competitors in their group one or more times. Each separate stage identified in the event format shall be a separate round-robin series irrespective of the number of times each competitor sails against each other competitor in that stage.*

Ties between two or more competitors in a round-robin series shall be broken by the following methods, in order, until all ties are broken. When one or more ties are only partially broken, rules C11.1(a) to C11.1(e) shall be reapplied to them. Ties shall be decided in favour of the competitor(s) who

(a) placed in order, has the highest score in the matches between the tied competitors;

(b) when the tie is between two competitors in a multiple round robin, has won the last match between the two competitors;

(c) has the most points against the competitor placed highest in the round-robin series or, if necessary, second highest, and so on until the tie is broken. When two separate ties have to be resolved but the resolution of each depends upon resolving the other, the following principles shall be used in the rule C11.1(c) procedure:

(1) the higher-place tie shall be resolved before the lower-place tie, and

(2) all the competitors in the lower-place tie shall be treated as a single competitor for the purposes of rule C11.1(c);

（b）一场比赛中获胜的选手在对另外一场比赛的选手因违反了*规则*而被取消资格时，应失去那轮比赛的分数（但负者不应获得此分数）；和

（c）在不同组别参加比赛的选手的总排列名次应由分数高低决定。

C10.6 淘汰赛的航行细则将说明两名选手间赢得系列赛所要求的最小分数值。当淘汰系列赛完成时，细则也应说明获得高分的选手胜出。

## C11 平分

### C11.1 循环系列赛

*在循环系列赛中，选手被分配到一个或更多的组中并被安排和其所在组中的其他选手进行一次或者多次竞赛。每次比赛形式分不同阶段，皆为独立的循环系列赛，不考虑选手之间在那个阶段的相互对抗的次数。*

在循环系列赛中，两个或几个选手得分平分时将使用如下方法按顺序直到所有平分打破，当一个或一个以上的平分仅有部分被打破时，规则C11.1(a)至C11.1(e)将重新适用。下列选手胜出：

（a）按顺序排列，在对抗赛中平分选手中得分最高者；

（b）在多次循环赛中两个选手平分，最后一场比赛中的获胜者；

（c）在循环系列赛中对阵排名最高者，或如果有必要，对阵排名第二高者，以此类推，直到平分被打破。当不得不解决两个不同并列，且两个并列的解决相互依赖时，将根据规则C11.1(c)的程序运用下列原则：

（1）排名高的平分者先于排名低的平分者，以及

（2）为达到规则C11.1(c)的目的，所有低排名平分选手将被视为单个选手；

(d) after applying rule C10.5(c), has the highest place in the different groups, irrespective of the number of competitors in each group;

(e) has the highest place in the most recent stage of the event (fleet race, round robin, etc.).

**C11.2 Knockout Series**

Ties (including 0–0) between competitors in a knockout series shall be broken by the following methods, in order, until the tie is broken. The tie shall be decided in favour of the competitor who

(a) has the highest place in the most recent round-robin series, applying rule C11.1 if necessary;

(b) has won the most recent match in the event between the tied competitors.

**C11.3 Remaining Ties**

When rule C11.1 or C11.2 does not resolve a tie,

(a) if the tie needs to be resolved for a later stage of the event (or another event for which the event is a direct qualifier), the tie shall be broken by a sail-off when practicable. When the race committee decides that a sail-off is not practicable, the tie shall be decided in favour of the competitor who has the highest score in the round-robin series after eliminating the score for the first race for each tied competitor or, should this fail to break the tie, the second race for each tied competitor and so on until the tie is broken. When a tie is partially resolved, the remaining tie shall be broken by reapplying rule C11.1 or C11.2.

(b) to decide the winner of an event that is not a direct qualifier for another event, or the overall position between competitors eliminated in one round of a knockout series, a sail-off may be used (but not a draw).

(c) when a tie is not broken any monetary prizes or ranking points for tied places shall be added together and divided equally among the tied competitors.

（d）在规则C10.5(c)适用后，在不同组中排名最高者，不考虑每组选手的数量；

（e）在比赛最近阶段排名最高者（群发赛、循环赛等）。

**C11.2 淘汰系列赛**

两个选手在淘汰系列赛中平分（包括0-0的平分），将按照下列方法打破平分。下列选手胜出：

（a）在最近的循环系列赛中排名最高者，如有必要可采用规则C11.1；

（b）平分选手中在本赛事最近比赛中的获胜者。

**C11.3 仍未打破的平分**

当规则C11.1或C11.2不能解决平分时，

（a）如果平分需要在本赛事的后阶段（或另外赛事，而本赛事是其直接资格赛）解决，可行的话，可以由一场加赛来打破平分。当竞赛委员会认定加赛不可行时，在循环系列赛中去掉每个并列选手第一轮竞赛分数后有最高分数的选手获胜，或者，如果仍不能打破平分，则去掉每个并列选手的第二轮成绩后来打破平分，以此类推，直到平分被打破。当一个平分部分被解决，依然保持的平分应通过重新适用规则C11.1或C11.2来打破。

（b）要决定一个不是另一个赛事的直接资格赛的赛事的胜者，或要决定在淘汰系列赛的一轮中被淘汰的选手之间的总排名，可以使用一轮加赛（但不使用抽签方式）。

（c）当平分未能打破时，给予所并列名次的任何奖金或总排名分数应加起来并平等分给平分选手。

# APPENDIX D TEAM RACING RULES

*Team races shall be sailed under* The Racing Rules of Sailing *as changed by this appendix.*

## D1 CHANGES TO THE RACING RULES

### D1.1 Definitions and the Rules of Parts 2 and 4

(a) In the definition *Zone* the distance is changed to two hull lengths.

(b) Rule 18.2(b) is changed to:

If boats are *overlapped* when the first of them reaches the *zone*, the outside boat at that moment shall thereafter give the inside boat *mark-room*. If a boat is *clear ahead* when she reaches the *zone*, or she later becomes *clear ahead* when another boat passes head to wind, the boat *clear astern* at that moment shall thereafter give her *mark-room*.

(c) Rule 18.4 is deleted.

(d) When rule 20 applies the following arm signals by the helmsman are required in addition to the hails:

(1) for 'Room to tack', repeatedly and clearly pointing to windward; and

(2) for 'You tack', repeatedly and clearly pointing at the other boat and waving the arm to windward.

Sailing instructions may delete this requirement.

(e) Rule 24.1 is changed to: 'If reasonably possible, a boat not *racing* shall not interfere with a boat that is *racing*, and a boat that has *finished* shall not act to interfere with a boat that has not *finished*.'

(f) Add new rule 24.3: 'When boats in different races meet, any change of course by either boat shall be consistent with complying with a *rule* or trying to win her own race.'

(g) Add to rule 41:

# 附录D　队赛规则

*队赛应执行本附录所更改的《帆船竞赛规则》。*

## D1　竞赛规则的更改

### D1.1　定义及规则第二章和第四章

（a）在定义*标区*中，距离更改为2倍船长。

（b）规则18.2(b)更改为：

当*相联*船中的第一条船进入*标区*时，处于外侧的船随后必须给予内侧船*绕标空间*。当一条船到达*标区*时*明显在前*，或当另一条船越过正顶风时，该船变成*明显在前*，*明显在后*的船此后应当给予她*绕标空间*。

（c）删除规则18.4。

（d）当规则20适用时，除了呼喊，舵手还应做出下列手臂动作：

（1）呼喊"转向空间（Room to tack）"时，重复且明确地指向上风；以及

（2）呼喊"你转向（You tack）"时，重复且明确地指向另一条船并往上风挥动手臂。

（e）规则24.1更改为："在合理且可能的情况下，未*竞赛*的船不得干扰正在*竞赛*的船，已*到达终点*的船不得干扰未*到达终点*的船。"

（f）增加新规则24.3："当不同竞赛组别的船相遇时，任何一条船所做的航线的任何改变始终应遵守*规则*或要尽力赢得自己的比赛。"

（g）在规则41后增加：

(e) help from another boat on her team provided electronic communication is not used.

(h) Rule 45 is deleted.

**D1.2 Protests and Requests for Redress**

(a) Rule 60.1 is changed to:

A boat may

(a) protest another boat, but not for an alleged breach of a rule of Part 2 unless she was involved in the incident or the incident involved contact between members of the other team; or

(b) request redress.

(b) Rule 61.1(a) is changed so that a boat may remove her red flag after it has been conspicuously displayed.

(c) A boat intending to request redress for an incident in the racing area shall display a red flag at the first reasonable opportunity after the incident. She shall display the red flag until it is acknowledged by the race committee or by an umpire.

(d) The race committee or protest committee shall not protest a boat for breaking a rule of Part 2 or rule 31 or 42 except

(1) based on evidence in a report from an umpire after a black and white flag has been displayed; or

(2) under rule 14 upon receipt of a report from any source alleging damage or injury.

(e) *Protests* and requests for redress need not be in writing. The protest committee may take evidence in any way it considers appropriate and may communicate its decision orally.

(f) A boat is not entitled to redress based on damage or injury caused by another boat on her team.

(g) When a supplied boat suffers a breakdown, rule D5 applies.

**D1.3 Penalties**

(a) Rule 44.1 is changed to:

A boat may take a One-Turn Penalty when she may have broken one or more rules of Part 2, or rule 31 or 42, in an （e）船可以接受来自同队的另一条船的帮助，但不可以使用电子通信手段。

（h）删除规则45。

**D1.2 抗议和要求补偿**

（a）规则60.1更改为：

一条船可以

（a）抗议另外一条船，但对违反规则第二章的抗议只有当其涉及该事件，或该事件牵涉到其他船队的成员间的接触时才可以提出；或

（b）要求补偿。

（b）规则61.1(a)更改为一条船可以在其明显地展示红旗后将旗收回。

（c）一条在比赛区域中的船在事件发生后想要求补偿时，必须在事件发生后的第一合理时间内展示红旗。红旗要展示至被竞赛委员会或现场裁判看到。

（d）竞赛委员会或抗议委员会不得因一条船违反规则第二章、规则31或规则42而抗议她，除非

（1）出示一面黑白旗后有现场裁判记录的报告为证据；或者

（2）根据规则14，收到了任何来源的报告宣称出现损坏或受伤。

（e）*抗议*和补偿要求无需书面提出。抗议委员会可以按照任何其认为合理的方式收集证据，并口头宣布裁决结果。

（f）因队友的船导致损坏或受伤的船无权要求补偿。

（g）统一提供的船遭遇故障时，规则D5适用。

**D1.3 判罚**

（a）规则44.1更改为：

当一条竞赛中的船在一个事件中违反了规则第二章的一条或多条，或者规则31或规则42时，她将做一圈解

incident while *racing*. However, when she may have broken a rule of Part 2 and rule 31 in the same incident she need not take the penalty for breaking rule 31.

(b) A boat may take a penalty by retiring, in which case she shall notify the race committee as soon as possible and 6 points shall be added to her score.

(c) There shall be no penalty for breaking a rule of Part 2 when the incident is between boats on the same team and there is no contact.

**D2 UMPIRED RACES**

**D2.1 When Rule D2 Applies**

Rule D2 applies to umpired races. Races to be umpired shall be identified either in the sailing instructions or by the display of flag J no later than the warning signal.

**D2.2 Protests by Boats**

When a boat protests under a rule of Part 2 or under rule 31 or 42 for an incident in the racing area, she is not entitled to a hearing and the following applies:

(a) She shall hail 'Protest' and conspicuously display a red flag at the first reasonable opportunity for each.

(b) The boats shall be given time to respond. A boat involved in the incident may respond by promptly taking an appropriate penalty or clearly indicating that she will do so as soon as possible.

(c) If no boat takes a penalty, an umpire shall decide whether to penalize any boat.

(d) If more than one boat broke a rule and was not exonerated, an umpire may penalize any boat that broke a rule and did not take an appropriate penalty.

(e) An umpire shall signal a decision in compliance with rule D2.4.

(f) A boat penalized by an umpire shall take a Two-Turns Penalty.

脱。但是，当在同一事件中违反了规则第二章和规则31时，她将不必为违反规则31做解脱。

（b）一条船可以退赛接受惩罚，她需立即通知竞赛委员会，并在其成绩上加6分。

（c）当事件涉及同队船并且船之间没有接触时，无须因违反规则第二章做出判罚。

D2 **现场判罚的竞赛**

D2.1 **当规则D2适用时**

规则D2适用于有现场裁判的比赛。凡需要现场裁判的竞赛应在航行细则中说明或不迟于预告信号发出前通过展示J旗来通知。

D2.2 **船的抗议**

当船因竞赛区域的一个事件，依据规则第二章的某条规则或规则31或42提出抗议时，该船无权要求审理，以下规则适用：

（a）她将呼喊“Protest（抗议）”并在第一合理时间内清楚地展示红旗。

（b）应给予船只反应的时间。涉及该事件的船可尽快通过做出一个适当的解脱来做出反应，或者清楚地表示将尽快进行解脱。

（c）如果没有船做解脱，裁判将决定是否给予某船惩罚。

（d）如果一条以上的船违反规则且没有解脱时，裁判可判罚任意一条违反规则且没有接受适当惩罚的船。

（e）现场裁判将按照规则D2.4发出裁决信号。

（f）被现场裁判判罚的船必须进行两圈解脱。

**D2.3 Penalties Initiated by an Umpire**

An umpire may penalize a boat without a *protest* by another boat, or report the incident to the protest committee, or both, when the boat

(a) breaks rule 31 or 42 and does not take a penalty;

(b) breaks a rule of Part 2 and makes contact with another boat on her team or with a boat in another race, and no boat takes a penalty;

(c) breaks a *rule* and her team gains an advantage despite her, or another boat on her team, taking a penalty;

(d) breaks rule 14 and there is damage or injury;

(e) clearly indicates that she will take a One-Turn Penalty, and then fails to do so;

(f) fails to take a penalty signalled by an umpire;

(g) commits a breach of sportsmanship.

The umpire shall signal a decision in compliance with rule D2.4. A boat penalized by an umpire shall take a Two-Turns Penalty except that, when an umpire hails a number of turns, the boat shall take that number of One-Turn Penalties.

**D2.4 Signals by an Umpire**

An umpire shall signal a decision with one long sound and the display of a flag as follows:

(a) For no penalty, a green and white flag.

(b) To penalize one or more boats, a red flag. The umpire shall hail or signal to identify each boat penalized.

(c) To report the incident to the protest committee, a black and white flag.

**D2.5 Two-Flag Protest Procedure**

[Note: This rule is not used often and it will be deleted in 2020.]

**D2.3 现场裁判员做出的判罚**

当下列情况发生时，现场裁判可以无需另一条船提出*抗议*而判罚某船，或将该事件通告抗议委员会，或者两种都去做：

（a）违反规则31或规则42，且没有做解脱；

（b）违反第二章中的某条规则，并与其同队的另一条船接触，或与另一场比赛的船接触，并且没有船进行解脱；

（c）违反*规则*后该船或队友船做了解脱但该船队仍然获益；

（d）违反规则14，并造成损坏和损伤；

（e）清楚地表示她将进行一圈解脱，但随后并没有这么做；

（f）未接受现场裁判的判罚；

（g）违反体育精神。

现场裁判将根据规则D2.4发出裁决信号。被裁判判罚的船应进行两圈解脱，除非现场裁判呼喊了解脱的圈数，该船应按照该圈数做解脱。

**D2.4 现场裁决信号**

现场裁判应发出裁决信号，伴随一声长的音响信号并展示一面旗，具体如下：

（a）一面绿白旗意为不做惩罚。

（b）红旗意为判罚一条或多条船，现场裁判应呼喊或发出信号来确定每条被判罚的船。

（c）黑白旗意为将事件通告给抗议委员会。

**D2.5 双旗抗议程序**

［译者注：因是不常用到的规则，俗称“僵尸规则”，世界帆联将于2020年后删除本部分内容。］

**D2.6 Limited Umpiring**

[Note: This rule is not used often and it will be deleted in 2020.]

**D2.7 Limitations on Other Proceedings**

A decision, action or non-action of an umpire shall not be

(a) grounds for redress,

(b) subject to an appeal under rule 70, or

(c) grounds for *abandoning* a race after it has started.

The protest committee may decide to consider giving redress when it believes that an official boat, including an umpire boat, may have seriously interfered with a competing boat.

**D3 SCORING A RACE**

**D3.1** (a) Each boat *finishing* a race shall be scored points equal to her finishing place. All other boats shall be scored points equal to the number of boats entitled to *race*.

(b) When a boat is scored OCS, 10 points shall be added to her score unless she retired as soon as possible after the starting signal.

(c) When a boat fails to take a penalty imposed by an umpire at or near the finishing line, she shall be scored points for last place and other scores shall be adjusted accordingly.

(d) When a protest committee decides that a boat that is a *party* to a protest hearing has broken a *rule* and is not exonerated,

(1) if the boat has not taken a penalty, 6 points shall be added to her score;

(2) if the boat's team has gained an advantage despite any penalty taken or imposed, the boat's score may be increased;

(3) when the boat has broken rule 1 or 2, rule 14 when she has caused damage or injury, or a *rule* when not *racing*, half or more race wins may be deducted from her team, or no penalty may be imposed. Race wins deducted shall not be awarded to any other team.

D2.6 **有限制的现场裁决**

［同D2.5译者注。］

D2.7 **其他程序的限制**

现场裁判进行裁决、采取措施或不采取措施时都不得

（a）作为补偿的理由，

（b）根据规则70上诉，或者

（c）成为*放弃*一轮已起航的竞赛的理由。

当抗议委员会认为一条官方船，包括现场裁判船，可能已严重干扰了一条参赛船时可以决定考虑给予补偿。

## D3 比赛记分

D3.1（a）每条*到达终点*的船应被记为等于其终点名次的分数。其他船的分数等于有资格参加*竞赛*的所有船数。

（b）当船被记为OCS后，将在其成绩上加10分，除非其在起航信号发出后尽快地退出了比赛。

（c）当船在终点线上或附近没有接受现场裁判的判罚时，她应按最后一名被记分，其他船的得分应据此进行调整。

（d）当抗议委员会认为作为抗议审理一方的某船已违反*规则*而且未免责时，

（1）如果该船没有做解脱，在其成绩上加6分；

（2）尽管某船接受了惩罚或被施加了惩罚，但该船队仍然获益时，可以增加该船的分数；

（3）当某船违反了规则1或2、规则14，已导致损坏或损伤，或在没有*竞赛*时违反了某一*规则*，可以减去该船所在队一半或一半以上的获胜场次，或可不加以判罚。被减去的获胜场次不得奖给其他船队。

**D3.2** When all boats on one team have *finished*, retired or failed to *start*, the other team's boats *racing* at that time shall be scored the points they would have received had they *finished*.

**D3.3** The team with the lower total points wins the race. If the totals are equal, the team that does not have first place wins.

## D4 SCORING A STAGE

### D4.1 Terminology

(a) The racing format at an event will consist of one or more stages.

(b) In a round-robin stage teams are assigned to one or more groups and scheduled to sail one or more round-robins. A round robin is a schedule of races in which each team sails once against each other team in the same group.

(c) In a knock-out stage teams are scheduled to sail in matches. A match is one or more races between two teams.

(d) The notice of race or sailing instructions may specify other formats and scoring methods.

### D4.2 Terminating a Stage

(a) The race committee may terminate a stage at any reasonable time taking into account the entries, weather, time constraints and other relevant factors.

(b) When a round-robin stage is terminated, any round-robin in the stage in which 80% or more of the full schedule of races has been completed shall be scored as complete; if fewer races have been completed, the round-robin shall not be scored, but may be used to break ties.

### D4.3 Scoring a Round-Robin Stage

(a) In a round-robin stage the teams shall be ranked in order of number of race wins, highest number first. If the teams have not completed an equal number of races, they shall be ranked in order of the percentage of races won, highest number first.

D3.2 当一个船队的所有船*到达终点*、退出或没有成功*起航*，在那一时刻参加*竞赛*的另一船队的船应被记为假设她们已经*到达终点*所应取得的分数。

D3.3 获得总分最低的船队在本轮中获胜。如果总分并列，没有第一名终点名次的那支船队胜出。

## D4 阶段记分

### D4.1 术语

（a）一个赛事的竞赛模式将包含一个或多个阶段。

（b）在一个循环赛阶段中，船队被分成一个或一个以上的组别，按照计划航行一个或多个循环。循环赛的比赛日程是循环赛中每一支队伍都要与同组的其他队伍进行一轮竞赛。

（c）在淘汰赛阶段，各船队按计划日程进行对抗，每场对抗的两队之间进行一轮或多轮比赛。

（d）竞赛通知或航行细则可以指定其他的竞赛模式和记分方法。

### D4.2 终止一个阶段

（a）竞赛委员会考虑到参赛人员、天气、时间限制以及其他相关因素时，可以在任意合理的时间终止一个阶段。

（b）当一个循环赛阶段被终止时，就算该阶段整个循环赛只进行了全部场次的80%或更多，也将记为完成比赛。如果完成场次较少，该循环赛将不被记分，但是可能被用于打破平分。

### D4.3 循环赛阶段的记分

（a）在一个循环赛阶段中，船队应按获胜的场次数量排列名次，获胜场次多者胜。如果循环赛同组船队没有完成同等数量的场次时，船队应按获胜场次的百分比排列名次，获胜百分比高者胜。

(b) If a round-robin in the stage is not completed, teams shall be ranked according to the results from all completed round-robins in the stage.

**D4.4 Ties in a Completed Round-Robin Stage**

Ties in a completed round-robin stage shall be broken by using, in the following order, only results in the stage,

(a) the highest number of race wins in all races between the tied teams;

(b) the lowest total points scored in all races between the tied teams;

(c) if two teams remain tied, the winner of the last race between them;

(d) the lowest average points scored in all races against common opponents;

(e) a sail-off if possible, otherwise a game of chance.

If a tie is partially broken by one of these, the remaining tie shall be broken by starting again at rule D4.4(a).

**D4.5 Ties in an Incomplete Round-Robin Stage**

Ties in an incomplete round-robin stage shall be broken whenever possible using the results from races between the tied teams in any incomplete round-robin. Other ties shall be broken in accordance with rule D4.4.

**D4.6 Scoring a Knock-Out Stage**

The winner of a match is the first team to score the number of race wins stated in the sailing instructions.

**D4.7 Incomplete Knock-Out Stage**

If a match in a knock-out stage is not completed (including 0-0), the result of the match shall be determined using, in order,

(a) the higher number of race wins in the incomplete match;

(b) the higher number of race wins in all races in the event between the tied teams;

(c) the higher place in the most recent stage, applying rule D4.4(a) if necessary;

(d) the winner of the most recent race between the teams.

If this rule fails to determine a result, the stage shall be tied unless the sailing instructions provide for some other result.

（b）如果一个阶段的循环赛没有完成，船队应该按照已经完成的循环赛的结果来排名。

**D4.4 循环赛阶段完成时的平分**

已完成的循环赛阶段的平分应只使用本阶段成绩按下列顺序打破：

（a）平分船队之间比赛的获胜轮次数目高者胜；

（b）平分船队之间比赛所得总分低者胜；

（c）如果两队仍然平分，两队之间的最后一轮比赛赢者胜；

（d）与其共同对手竞赛的所有轮次总分的平均分低者胜；

（e）如有可能可加赛一场，否则只能抽签决定。

如果平分靠以上的某种方法得以部分打破，则仍未打破的平分应从规则D4.4(a)开始打破。

**D4.5 循环赛阶段未完成时的平分**

未完成循环赛的阶段的平分尽可能按照平分船队之间未完成的循环赛的成绩来打破。其他平分应按规则D4.4来打破。

**D4.6 淘汰赛阶段的记分**

一场对抗中的胜者是按照航行细则的规定获胜轮次分第一名的队伍。

**D4.7 未完成的淘汰赛阶段**

如果淘汰赛阶段中的一场对抗未完成（包括0-0）时，按照以下顺序决定成绩：

（a）未完成的对抗中获胜轮次多者胜；

（b）出现平分的两支队伍在赛事中完成的所有轮次中获胜轮次多者胜；

（c）如果需要，按照规则D4.4(a)，在最近的阶段赛中排名高者胜；

（d）在两队最近的比赛轮次中获胜者胜出。

如果该规则仍不能决出胜者，该阶段记为平分，除非航行细则规定一些其他的记分方法。

**D5 BREAKDOWNS WHEN BOATS ARE SUPPLIED BY THE ORGANIZING AUTHORITY**

**D5.1** Rule D5 applies when boats are supplied by the organizing authority.

**D5.2** When a boat suffers a breakdown in the racing area, she may request a score change by displaying a red flag at the first reasonable opportunity after the breakdown until it is acknowledged by the race committee or by an umpire. If possible, she shall continue *racing*.

**D5.3** The race committee shall decide requests for a score change in accordance with rules D5.4 and D5.5. It may take evidence in any way it considers appropriate and may communicate its decision orally.

**D5.4** When the race committee decides that the team's finishing position was made significantly worse, that the breakdown was through no fault of the crew, and that in the same circumstances a reasonably competent crew would not have been able to avoid the breakdown, it shall make as equitable a decision as possible. This may be to *abandon* and resail the race or, when the boat's finishing position was predictable, award her points for that position. Any doubt about a boat's position when she broke down shall be resolved against her.

**D5.5** A breakdown caused by defective supplied equipment or a breach of a *rule* by an opponent shall not normally be determined to be the fault of the crew, but one caused by careless handling, capsizing or a breach by a boat on the same team shall be. If there is doubt, it shall be presumed that the crew are not at fault.

## D5 当组织机构提供的船发生损坏时

D5.1 当组织机构提供参赛船时，规则D5适用。

D5.2 当船在竞赛区域遭到损坏，可以要求分数更改并在损坏后的第一合理的时间展示一面红旗直至被竞赛委员会或现场裁判看到，并且如果可能应继续参加*竞赛*。

D5.3 竞赛委员会应根据规则D5.4和D5.5对更改分数的要求做出裁决。委员会可通过其认为合适的任意途径来收集证据，并口头宣布裁决。

D5.4 当竞赛委员会决定该船队的到达终点名次明显变差，船的损坏不是船员的过失，而且在这种情况下，任何有相应能力的船员都无法避免这种损坏时，委员会应做出尽可能公平的裁决。这一裁决可能是要求*放弃*该轮竞赛并重赛，或当该船的终点名次可以预见时，给予她该名次相对应的分数。当有损坏发生时，任何对该船的名次的质疑将采纳不利于该船的解决方案。

D5.5 由于所提供器材有缺陷或由于对手违反某条*规则*所造成的损坏通常不应被认为是船员的过失，但由于粗心驾驶、翻船或同队船犯规造成的损坏则被认为是该船的过失。如果有怀疑，将假定有关船员没有过失。

# APPENDIX E
# RADIO SAILING RACING RULES

*Radio sailing races shall be sailed under* The Racing Rules of Sailing *as changed by this appendix.*

## E1 CHANGES TO THE DEFINITIONS, TERMINOLOGY AND THE RULES OF PARTS 1, 2 AND 7

### E1.1 Definitions

Add to the definition *Conflict of Interest*:

> However, an observer does not have a *conflict of interest* solely by being a competitor.

In the definition *Zone* the distance is changed to four hull lengths.

Add new definition:

> ***Disabled*** A boat is *disabled* while she is unable to continue in the heat.

### E1.2 Terminology

The Terminology paragraph of the Introduction is changed so that:

(a) 'Boat' means a sailboat controlled by radio signals and having no crew. However, in the rules of Part 1 and Part 5, rule E6 and the definitions *Party* and *Protest*, 'boat' includes the competitor controlling her.

(b) 'Competitor' means the person designated to control a boat using radio signals.

(c) In the racing rules, but not in its appendices, replace the noun 'race' with 'heat'. In Appendix E a race consists of one or more heats and is completed when the last heat in the race is completed.

### E1.3 Rules of Parts 1, 2 and 7

(a) Rule 1.2 is deleted.

(b) In rule 20, hails and replies shall be made by the competitor controlling the boat.

# 附录E　无线电帆船竞赛规则

*无线电帆船竞赛应遵照本附录更改后的《帆船竞赛规则》执行。*

## E1　关于定义、术语以及规则第一章、第二章和第七章的更改

### E1.1　定义

*利益冲突*的定义后增加：但是，观察员不会因为是选手就有了*利益冲突*。

在*标区*的定义中，距离更改为4倍船长。

新增定义：

***失能***　当船只不能继续当前组别的竞赛时称为*失能*。

### E1.2　术语

引言中术语段落的内容被更改，因此：

（a）“船”是指无船员驾驶的由无线电信号操控的帆船。但是，在规则第一章和第五章，规则E6以及*一方*和*抗议*的定义中，“船”包括操控她的选手。

（b）“选手”是指特定的通过无线电信号操控船的人。

（c）在竞赛规则而非其附录中，将名词“轮次”替换为“组别”。在附录E中一轮竞赛由一个或多个组别构成，并且当轮次中最后一组竞赛完成时该轮竞赛即为完成。

### E1.3　规则第一章、第二章和第七章

（a）删除规则1.2。

（b）在规则20中，呼喊和回应应当由操控船的选手进行。

(c) Rule 23 is changed to: 'If possible, a boat shall avoid a boatthat is *disabled*.'

(d) Rule 90.2(c) is changed to:

Changes to the sailing instructions may be communicated orally to all affected competitors before the warning signal of the relevant race or heat. When appropriate, changes shall be confirmed in writing.

## E2 ADDITIONAL RULES WHEN RACING

*Rule E2 applies only while boats are* ***racing****.*

### E2.1 Hailing Requirements

(a) A hail shall be made so that the competitors to whom the hail is directed might reasonably be expected to hear it.

(b) The individual digits of a boat's sail number shall be hailed; for example 'one five', not 'fifteen'.

### E2.2 Giving Advice

A competitor shall not give tactical or strategic advice to a competitor controlling a boat that is *racing*.

### E2.3 Boat Out of Radio Control

A competitor who loses radio control of his boat shall promptly hail and repeat '(The boat's sail number) out of control' and the boat shall retire.

### E2.4 Transmitter Aerials

If a transmitter aerial is longer than 200mm when extended, the extremity shall be adequately protected.

### E2.5 Radio Interference

Transmission of radio signals that cause interference with the control of other boats is prohibited. A competitor that has broken this rule shall not *race* again until permitted to do so by the race committee.

## E3 CONDUCT OF A RACE

### E3.1 Control Area

The sailing instructions may specify a control area; if not specified, it shall be unrestricted. Competitors shall be in this area when （c）规则23更改为：“如果可能的话，一条船应当避让一条失能的船。”

（d）规则90.2(c)更改为：

航行细则的更改可在相应轮次或组别预告信号发出之前，通过口头形式通知到所有相关选手。在合适的时候，更改内容应由书面形式进行确认。

## E2 竞赛时的附加规则

*规则E2仅在船只竞赛时适用。*

### E2.1 呼喊要求

（a）发出的呼喊应当使被呼喊的选手完全有理由地听到。

（b）应当呼喊船只帆号的每一位数字；例如“一五”，而不是“十五”。

### E2.2 给予建议

选手不应给另一名正在操控竞赛船的选手提供战术或战略建议。

### E2.3 失控船只

失去对船只无线电操控的选手应立即呼喊并重复“（船只帆号）失控”，且该船只应当退赛。

### E2.4 发射器天线

如果发射器天线展开长度超过200毫米，其末端应被妥善保护。

### E2.5 无线电干扰

严禁通过发射无线电信号干扰其他船的操控。违反此条规则的选手在未得到竞赛委员会允许前应被禁止竞赛。

## E3 竞赛组织

### E3.1 控制区

航行细则可指定控制区；如果没有指定，则此项不受限制。当操控船只竞赛时，选手应在此区域中，短暂地拿取然后放

controlling boats that are *racing*, except briefly to handle and then release or relaunch the boat.

**E3.2 Launching Area**

The sailing instructions may specify a launching area and its use; if not specified it shall be unrestricted.

**E3.3 Course Board**

The sailing instructions may require the course to be displayed on a board and, if so, the board shall be located in or adjacent to the control area.

**E3.4 Starting and Finishing**

(a) Rule 26 is changed to:

Heats shall be started using warning, preparatory and starting signals at one-minute intervals. During the minute before the starting signal, additional sound or oral signals shall be made at ten-second intervals, and during the final ten seconds at one-second intervals. Each signal shall be timed from the beginning of its sound.

(b) The starting and finishing lines shall be between the course sides of the starting and finishing *marks*.

**E3.5 Individual Recall**

Rule 29.1 is changed to:

When at a boat's starting signal any part of the boat is on the course side of the starting line or when she must comply with rule 30.1, the race committee shall promptly hail 'Recall (sail numbers)' and repeat the hail as appropriate. If rule 30.3 or 30.4 applies this rule does not.

**E3.6 General Recall**

Rule 29.2 is changed to:

When at the starting signal the race committee is unable to identify boats that are on the course side of the starting line or to which rule 30 applies, or there has been an error in the starting procedure, the race committee may hail and repeat as appropriate 'General recall' and make two loud sounds. The warning signal for a new start will normally be made shortly thereafter.

开或者让船只重新下水不受此限制。

E3.2 **下水区**

航行细则可指定下水区及其用途；如果没有指定，则此项不受限制。

E3.3 **航线公告板**

航行细则可要求在公告板上展示竞赛航线，在这种情况下，公告板应位于控制区内或临近位置。

E3.4 **起航和终点**

（a）规则26更改为：

组别起航应以1分钟作为时间间隔，发出预告、准备以及起航信号。在起航信号发出之前的1分钟内，每10秒应附加音响或口头信号，在最后10秒内，每1秒应附加音响或口头信号。每个信号应在其发出音响时开始计时。

（b）起航线和终点线应当位于起航及终点标志的航线一侧之间。

E3.5 **个别召回**

规则29.1更改为：

当起航信号发出时，船的任何部分位于起航线的航线一侧，或者当她必须执行规则30.1时，竞赛委员会应呼喊“召回（帆号）”并适当重复该呼喊。若此时规则30.3或30.4生效，则本条规则不适用。

E3.6 **全部召回**

规则29.2更改为：

当起航信号发出时，竞赛委员会不能识别位于起航线的航线一侧的船或者规则30的适用对象，或者起航过程出现错误时，竞赛委员会可呼喊并适当重复“全部召回”，并发出两声响亮音响。通常在不久之后，会发出新的起航预告信号。

**E3.7 U Flag and Black Flag Rules**

When the race committee informs a boat that she has broken rule 30.3 or 30.4, the boat shall immediately leave the course area.

**E3.8 Other Changes to the Rules of Part 3**

(a) Rules 30.2 and 33 are deleted.

(b) All race committee signals shall be made orally or by other sounds. No visual signals are required unless specified in the sailing instructions.

(c) Courses shall not be shortened.

(d) Rule 32.1(a) is changed to: 'because of foul weather or thunderstorms,'.

**E3.9 Disabled Competitors**

To enable a disabled competitor to compete on equal terms, the race committee shall make as fair an arrangement as possible.

## E4 RULES OF PART 4

**E4.1 Deleted Rules in Part 4**

Rules 40, 43, 44.3, 45, 47, 48, 49, 50, 52 and 54 are deleted.

**E4.2 Outside Help**

Rule 41 is changed to:

A boat or the competitor controlling her shall not receive help from any outside source, except

(a) help needed as a direct result of a competitor becoming ill, injured or in danger;

(b) when the boat is entangled with another boat, help from the other competitor;

(c) when the boat is entangled, or she is aground or in danger, help from a race committee vessel;

(d) help in the form of information freely available to all competitors;

(e) unsolicited information from a disinterested source. A competitor is not a disinterested source unless acting as an observer.

**E3.7 U旗和黑旗规则**

当竞赛委员会通知一条船已经违反规则30.3或30.4，则这条船应立刻驶离航线区域。

**E3.8 其他有关规则第三章的更改**

（a）删除规则30.2和33。

（b）所有竞赛委员会的信号应口头或者由其他声响发出。除航行细则的规定外，无需视觉信号。

（c）不允许缩短航线。

（d）规则32.1(a)更改为："由于恶劣天气或雷暴"。

**E3.9 残疾人选手**

为了使残疾人选手能在同等条件下完成竞赛，竞赛委员会应当做出尽可能公平的安排。

**E4 规则第四章**

**E4.1 第四章中删除的规则**

删除规则40、43、44.3、45、47、48、49、50、52以及54。

**E4.2 外部援助**

规则41更改为：

船或者操控船的选手不允许接收任何来自场外的帮助信息，下列情形除外：

（a）由于选手生病、受伤或者处于危险情形所直接导致的必要的帮助信息；

（b）当一条船与另一条船缠绕时，来自另一名选手的帮助信息；

（c）当船只被缠绕或搁浅，或处于危险情形时，来自竞赛委员会工作艇的帮助；

（d）对所有选手普遍适用的帮助信息；

（e）非利益方主动提供的信息。选手不是非利益方，除非他是观察员。

However, a boat that gains a significant advantage in the heat or race from help received under rule 41 may be protested and penalized; any penalty may be less than disqualification.

**E4.3 Taking a Penalty**

Rule 44.1 is changed to:

A boat may take a One-Turn Penalty when she may have broken one or more rules of Part 2, or rule 31, in an incident while *racing*. However,

(a) when she may have broken a rule of Part 2 and rule 31 in the same incident she need not take the penalty for breaking rule 31;

(b) if the boat gained a significant advantage in the heat or race by her breach despite taking a penalty, her penalty shall be an additional One-Turn Penalty;

(c) if the boat caused serious damage, or as a result of breaking a rule of Part 2 she caused another boat to become *disabled* and retire, her penalty shall be to retire.

**E4.4 Person in Charge**

Rule 46 is changed to: 'The member or organization that entered the boat shall designate the competitor. See rule 75.'

## E5 RACING WITH OBSERVERS AND UMPIRES

**E5.1 Observers**

(a) The race committee may appoint observers, who may be competitors.

(b) Observers shall hail the sail numbers of boats that make contact with a *mark* or another boat and shall repeat the hail as appropriate.

(c) At the end of a heat, observers shall report to the race committee all unresolved incidents, and any failure to sail the course as required by rule 28.

**E5.2 Umpired Races**

The International Radio Sailing Association Addendum Q shall apply to umpired races. Races to be umpired may be identified in the sailing instructions or orally before the warning signal.

*Note: The addendum is available at the website:* ***radiosailing.org****.*

但是，一条船依据规则41接受的帮助使其在组别或轮次中取得明显优势，可能会被抗议和受到惩罚；可以是任何轻于取消资格的处罚。

**E4.3 解脱**

规则44.1更改为：

当一条船在竞赛中发生事件，违反了一条或多条第二章规则，或违反规则31时，可转一圈解脱。但是

（a）当她在同一个事件中违反了第二章的某一条规则以及规则31时，不必再因违反规则31接受惩罚；

（b）若该船尽管已解脱，但仍因违反规则在其组别或轮次中获得明显优势，她应当接受追加一圈的惩罚；

（c）若该船导致严重损坏，或因违反规则第二章导致另一条船*失能*并退赛，她应接受退赛惩罚。

**E4.4 负责人**

规则46更改为："报名登记船只的成员或者组织应当指定选手。详见规则75。"

## E5 有观察员和现场裁判的竞赛

**E5.1 观察员**

（a）竞赛委员会可委派观察员，观察员可以是选手。

（b）当有船与标志或者另一条船发生接触时，观察员应呼喊该船的帆号，并适时重复呼喊。

（c）在组别竞赛结束时，观察员应向竞赛委员会报告所有未解决的事件，以及任何未按规则28要求行驶航线的事件。

**E5.2 现场判罚的竞赛**

国际无线电帆船运动协会附录Q应适用于现场判罚的竞赛。现场判罚的轮次应在航行细则中指出或在预告信号发出前口头说明。

*注：附录内容可通过网址radiosailing.org查询。*

**E5.3 Rules for Observers and Umpires**

Observers and umpires shall be located in the control area. They shall not use any aid or device that gives them a visual advantage over competitors.

## E6 PROTESTS AND REQUESTS FOR REDRESS

**E6.1 Right to Protest**

Rule 60.1 is changed to:

A boat may

(a) protest another boat, but not for an alleged breach of a rule of Part 2, 3 or 4 unless she was scheduled to sail in that heat; or

(b) request redress.

However, a boat or competitor may not protest for an alleged breach of rules E2 or E3.7.

**E6.2 Protest for a Rule Broken by a Competitor**

When a race committee or protest committee learns that a competitor may have broken a *rule*, it may protest the boat controlled by that competitor.

**E6.3 Informing the Protestee**

Rule 61.1(a) is changed to:

A boat intending to protest shall inform the other boat at the first reasonable opportunity. When her *protest* concerns an incident in the racing area that she was involved in or saw, she shall hail twice '(Her own sail number) protest (the sail number of the other boat)'.

**E6.4 Informing the Race Committee**

A boat intending to protest or request redress about an incident in the racing area or control area shall inform the race officer as soon as reasonably possible after *finishing* or retiring.

**E6.5 Time Limits**

A *protest*, request for redress or request for reopening shall be delivered to the race officer no later than ten minutes after the last boat in the heat *finishes* or after the relevant incident, whichever is later.

**E5.3 观察员和现场裁判的规则**

观察员和现场裁判应位于控制区内。他们不应使用任何辅助工具或设备来获得优于选手的视觉优势。

**E6 抗议和要求补偿**

**E6.1 抗议的权利**

规则60.1更改为：

一条船可以

（a）抗议另一条船，但只有她在编入相同组别时才可提出涉嫌违反规则第二章、第三章或第四章的抗议；或者

（b）要求补偿。

但是，一条船或选手不可提出涉嫌违反规则E2或者E3.7的抗议。

**E6.2 抗议选手违反某条规则**

当竞赛委员会或者抗议委员会得知有选手违反了某条规则，他们可以抗议该选手操控的船。

**E6.3 通知被抗议人**

规则61.1(a)更改为：

一条有意提出抗议的船应当在第一个合理的时机通知另一条船。当她的*抗议*是与她有关的或她看到的竞赛区域的事件，她应当呼喊两次“（她自己的帆号）抗议（Protest）（另一条船的帆号）”。

**E6.4 通知竞赛委员会**

一条有意对竞赛区域或控制区域的事件提出抗议或请求补偿的船应当在*到达终点*或退出竞赛后尽可能快地通知竞赛官。

**E6.5 时限**

*抗议*、补偿请求或重赛请求应当在同组别最后一条船*到达终点*或者相关事件发生后10分钟内提交给竞赛官，以较迟者为准。

**E6.6 Redress**

Add to rule 62.1:

(e) external radio interference acknowledged by the race committee, or

(f) becoming *disabled* because of the action of a boat that was breaking a rule of Part 2 or of a vessel not *racing* that was required to keep clear.

**E6.7 Right to Be Present**

In rule 63.3(a) 'the representatives of boats shall have been on board' is changed to 'the representative of each boat shall be the competitor designated to control her'.

**E6.8 Taking Evidence and Finding Facts**

Add to rule 63.6:

When the *protest* concerns an alleged breach of a rule of Part 2, 3 or 4, any witness shall have been in the control area at the time of the incident. If the witness is a competitor who was not acting as an observer, he shall also have been scheduled to race in the relevant heat.

**E6.9 Decisions on Redress**

Add to rule 64.2:

If a boat is given redress because she was damaged, her redress shall include reasonable time, but not more than 30 minutes, to make repairs before her next heat.

**E7 PENALTIES**

When a protest committee decides that a boat that is a *party* to a protest hearing has broken a *rule* other than a rule of Part 2, 3 or 4, it shall either

(a) disqualify her or add any number of points (including zero and fractions of points) to her score. The penalty shall be applied, if possible, to the heat or race in which the *rule* was broken; otherwise it shall be applied to the next heat or race for that boat. When points are added, the scores of other boats shall not be changed; or

### E6.6 补偿

规则62.1后增加：

（e）竞赛委员会证实的外部无线电干扰，或者

（f）由于一条违反规则第二章的船或者一条不参加*竞赛*被要求避让的船的行为而导致*失能*。

### E6.7 出席的权利

规则63.3(a)中“船的代表应在事件发生时在船上”更改为“每一条船的代表应当是被指定操控她的选手”。

### E6.8 取证和认定事实

规则63.6后增加：

当*抗议*与涉嫌违反规则第二章、第三章或第四章有关时，任何目击者应在事件发生时位于控制区内。如果目击者是一名不担任观察员的选手，他也应当被编入相关组别参与过竞赛。

### E6.9 补偿的决定

规则64.2后增加：

如果一条船因为受损获得补偿，补偿应当包括一段合理的时间，但不超过30分钟，来进行下一组别前的修复工作。

## E7 惩罚

当抗议委员会认定某条船作为参加抗议审理的一方违反了除规则第二章、第三章或第四章之外的某条*规则*时，抗议委员会应当

（a）取消其资格或者在其成绩上增加任何数量的分值（包括零和小数分值）。如果可能的话，惩罚应当适用于违反*规则*的组别或轮次；否则惩罚应当适用于该船只的下一个组别或轮次。当增加分值时，其他船的分数不应被变更；或者

(b) require her to take one or more One-Turn Penalties that shall be taken as soon as possible after the starting signal of her next heat that is started and not subsequently recalled or *abandoned.*

However, if the boat has broken a rule in Appendix G or rule E8, the protest committee shall act in accordance with rule G4.

**E8 CHANGES TO APPENDIX G, IDENTIFICATION ON SAILS**

Rule G1, except the table of National Sail Letters, is changed to:

**G1 WORLD SAILING AND IRSA CLASS BOATS**

*This rule applies to every boat of a class administered or recognised by World Sailing or by the International Radio Sailing Association (IRSA).*

**G1.1 Identification**

(a) A boat of a World Sailing or IRSA Class shall display her class insignia, national letters and sail number as specified in rule G1, unless her class rules state otherwise.

(b) At world and continental championships, sails shall comply with these rules. At other events they shall comply with these rules or the rules applicable at the time of their initial certification.

**G1.2 National Letters**

At all international events, a boat shall display national letters in accordance with the table of National Sail Letters denoting:

(a) when entered under rule 75.1(a), the national authority of the nationality, place of residence, or affiliation of the owner or the member.

(b) when entered under rule 75.1(b), the national authority of the organisation which entered her.

For the purposes of this rule, international events are world and continental championships and events described as international events in their notices of race and sailing instructions.

*Note: An up-to-date version of the National Sail Letters table is available on the World Sailing website.*

（b）要求她在下一组别未发生召回或放弃时，在起航信号发出之后立即做一个或更多圈的解脱。

但是，如果该船违反附录G的某条规则或者规则E8，抗议委员会应按照规则G4采取措施。

## E8 附录G的更改，帆上标识

规则G1，除国家帆号代码表之外，更改为：

### G1 世界帆联和国际无线电帆船运动协会级别船只

*本规则适用于世界帆联或者国际无线电帆船运动协会（IRSA）管理或认证级别的每一条船。*

#### G1.1 识别标志

（a）世界帆联或国际无线电帆船运动协会级别的船只应按照规则G1的说明展示其级别标识、国家代码以及帆号，除非其级别规则另有规定。

（b）在世界及洲际锦标赛中，船帆应符合这些规则。在其他赛事中，船帆应符合这些规则或者船只初始认证时适用的规则。

#### G1.2 国家代码

在所有国际赛事中，一条船应展示与国家帆号代码表相一致的国家代码，用以表明：

（a）当按照规则75.1(a)报名登记时，所属国的国家管理机构、居住地，或者船东或成员的隶属关系。

（b）当按照规则75.1(b)报名登记时，给其报名的组织所属的国家管理机构。

本规则所说的国际赛事是指世界和洲际锦标赛，以及在竞赛规程和航行细则中被描述为国际赛事的竞赛。

*注：在世界帆联网站上有国家帆号代码表的实时更新版本。*

### G1.3 Sail numbers

(a) The sail number shall be the last two digits of the boat's registration number or the competitor's or owner's personal number, allotted by the relevant issuing authority.

(b) When there is conflict between sail numbers, or when a sail number may be misread, the race committee shall require that the sail numbers of one or more boats be changed to numeric alternatives.

### G1.4 Specifications

(a) National letters and sail numbers shall be in capital letters and Arabic numerals, clearly legible and of the same colour. Commercially available typefaces giving the same or better legibility than Helvetica are acceptable.

(b) The height and spacing of letters and numbers shall be as follows:

| *Dimension* | *Minimum* | *Maximum* |
|---|---|---|
| Height of sail numbers | 100 mm | 110 mm |
| Spacing of adjacent sail numbers | 20 mm | 30 mm |
| Height of national letters | 60 mm | 70 mm |
| Spacing of adjacent national letters | 13 mm | 23 mm |

### G1.5 Positioning

(a) Class insignia, sail numbers and national letters shall be positioned

(1) on both sides of the sail;

(2) with those on the starboard side uppermost;

(3) approximately horizontally;

(4) with no less than 40 mm vertical spacing between numbers and letters on opposite sides of the sail;

(5) with no less than 20 mm vertical spacing between class insignia on opposite sides of the sail.

However, symmetrical or reversed class insignia may be positioned back to back.

### G1.3 帆号

（a）帆号应为船的注册编码或者选手或船东的个人编码的最后两位，由相关事项的管理机构分配。

（b）当帆号间出现冲突，或者帆号可能会被错误识别时，竞赛委员会应要求一条或多条船替换其帆号中的数字。

### G1.4 规格

（a）国家代码和帆号应是大写字母和阿拉伯数字，清晰可辨而且颜色相同。可以接受商业上可用的跟“Helvetica”字体有同样或更好的清晰度的字体。

（b）字母和数字的高度和间距如下表所示：

| *尺寸* | *最小* | *最大* |
|---|---|---|
| 帆号高度 | 100mm | 110mm |
| 帆号数字间距 | 20mm | 30mm |
| 国家代码高度 | 60mm | 70mm |
| 国家代码字母间距 | 13mm | 23mm |

### G1.5 位置

（a）级别标识、帆号以及国家代码应当

（1）位于帆的两面；

（2）在右舷一侧的位置更高；

（3）近似水平；

（4）与帆上两面的数字和字母的竖直间距不小于40毫米；

（5）与帆上两面的级别标识的竖直间距不小于20毫米。

但是，可对称或反转的级别标识在位置上可以背靠背。

(b) On a mainsail, sail numbers shall be positioned

   (1) below class insignia;

   (2) above the line perpendicular to the luff through the quarter leech point;

   (3) above national letters;

   (4) with sufficient space in front of the sail number for a prefix '1'.

**G1.6 Exceptions**

(a) Where the size of the sail prevents compliance with rule G1.2, National Letters, then exceptions to rules G1.2, G1.4, and G1.5 shall be made in the following order of precedence. National letters shall

   (1) be spaced vertically below sail numbers by less an 30 mm, but no less than 20 mm;

   (2) be spaced on opposite sides of the sail by less than 30 mm, but no less than 20 mm;

   (3) be reduced in height to less than 45 mm, but no less than 40 mm;

   (4) be omitted.

(b) Where the size of the sail prevents compliance with rule G1.3, Sail Numbers, then exceptions to rules G1.4 and G1.5 shall be made in the following order of precedence. Sail numbers shall

   (1) extend below the specified line;

   (2) be spaced on opposite sides of the sail by less than 30 mm, but no less than 20 mm apart;

   (3) be reduced in height to less than 90 mm, but no less than 80 mm;

   (4) be omitted on all except the largest sail;

   (5) be reduced in height until they do fit on the largest sail.

（b）主帆上帆号的位置应当

（1）低于级别标识；

（2）高于通过帆后缘1/4点且与帆前缘垂直的线；

（3）高于国家代码；

（4）在帆号前为前缀“1”留有足够的空间。

G1.6 **例外**

（a）当帆的尺寸与规则G1.2不相符时，国家代码以及规则G1.2、G1.4和G1.5的例外规定应按下列优先级顺序执行。国家代码应当

（1）在竖直方向上与帆号的间距小于30毫米，但不小于20毫米；

（2）与帆对面的间距小于30毫米，但不小于20毫米；

（3）缩减高度到小于45毫米，但不小于40毫米；

（4）被省略。

（b）当帆的尺寸与规则G1.3不相符时，帆号以及规则G1.4和G1.5的例外规定应按下列优先级顺序执行。帆号应当

（1）延伸低于指定参考线；

（2）与帆对面的分散间距小于30毫米，但不小于20毫米；

（3）缩减高度到小于90毫米，但不小于80毫米；

（4）除最大的帆之外，被省略；

（5）缩减高度直到它确实与最大的帆相称。

# APPENDIX F KITEBOARD RACING RULES

*Kiteboard course races shall be sailed under* The Racing Rules of Sailing *as changed by this appendix. The term 'boat' elsewhere in the racing rules means 'kiteboard' or 'boat' as appropriate.*

*Note: Rules for other kiteboard racing formats (such as Short Track, Kitecross, Slalom, Boarder X) or other kiteboard competitions (such as Freestyle, Wave, Big Air, Speed) are not included in this appendix. Links to current versions of these rules can be found on the World Sailing website.*

## CHANGES TO THE DEFINITIONS

The definitions *Clear Astern* and *Clear Ahead*; *Overlap*, *Finish*, *Keep Clear*, *Leeward* and *Windward*, *Mark-Room*, *Obstruction*, *Start*, *Tack*, *Starboard* or *Port* and *Zone* are changed to:

***Clear Astern* and *Clear Ahead*; *Overlap*** One kiteboard is *clear astern* of another when her hull is behind a line abeam from the aftermost point of the other kiteboard's hull. The other kiteboard is *clear ahead*. They *overlap* when neither is *clear astern*. However, they also *overlap* when a kiteboard between them *overlaps* both. These terms always apply to kiteboards on the same *tack*. They do not apply to kiteboards on opposite *tacks* unless both kiteboards are sailing more than ninety degrees from the true wind.

***Finish*** A kiteboard *finishes* when, while the competitor is in contact with the hull, any part of her hull, or the competitor in normal position, crosses the finishing line from the course side. However, she has not *finished* if after crossing the finishing line she

# 附录F　风筝板竞赛规则

*风筝板场地赛应受此附录更改后的《帆船竞赛规则》制约。竞赛规则中的术语“船”依不同语境表示“风筝板”或者“船”。*

*注：其他形式的风筝板比赛［如：短航线，Kitecross（译者注：障碍滑的一种），障碍滑，Boarder X（译者注：Boarder X是指青奥会采用的一种竞赛模式，航线为带有障碍物的顺风障碍滑，具体可参考世界帆联网站《帆船竞赛规则》附录Fs）］。或其他的风筝板比赛（如：自由式、浪上表演赛、空中特技、竞速）的规则不包含在此附录内。这些规则最新版本的链接可以在世界帆联网站上找到。*

## 定义的更改

*明显在后*和*明显在前*、*相联*、*到达终点*、*避让*、*下风*和*上风*、*绕标空间*、*障碍物*、*起航*，以及*舷风*、*右舷*或*左舷*、*标区*的定义更改为：

***明显在后*和*明显在前*；*相联***　当一条风筝板的板体处于另一条风筝板板体的最后一点的正横线之后，则该风筝板为*明显在后*，另一条风筝板为*明显在前*。当没有任何一条板为*明显在后*时即为*相联*。但是，当她们中间有条板与两者均*相联*时，她们仍为*相联*。这些术语总是适用于相同*舷风*的风筝板。除非两条板均同真风风向的角度大于90°，否则这些术语不适用于处于相对*舷风*的风筝板。

***到达终点***　当选手接触板体、板体的任何部分或者处于其正常位置从航线一侧越过终点线即为*到达终点*。但是，如果在

(a) takes a penalty under rule 44.2,

(b) corrects an error under rule 28.2 made at the line, or

(c) continues to sail the course.

***Keep Clear*** A kiteboard *keeps clear* of a right-of-way kiteboard

(a) if the right-of-way kiteboard can sail her course with no need to take avoiding action and,

(b) when the kiteboards are *overlapped*, if the right-of-way kiteboard can also, without immediately making contact, change course in both directions or move her kite in any direction.

***Leeward* and *Windward*** A kiteboard's *leeward* side is the side that is or, when she is head to wind, was away from the wind. However, when sailing by the lee or directly downwind, her *leeward* side is the side on which her kite lies. The other side is her *windward* side. When two kiteboards on the same *tack overlap*, the one whose hull is on the *leeward* side of the other's hull is the *leeward* kiteboard. The other is the *windward* kiteboard.

***Mark-Room*** *Room* for a kiteboard to sail her *proper course* to round or pass the *mark* on the required side.

***Obstruction*** An object that a kiteboard could not pass without changing course substantially, if she were sailing directly towards it and 10 metres from it. An object that can be safely passed on only one side and an area so designated by the sailing instructions are also *obstructions*. However, a kiteboard *racing* is not an *obstruction* to other kiteboards unless they are required to *keep clear* of her or, if rule 23 applies, avoid her. A vessel under way, including a kiteboard *racing*, is never a continuing *obstruction*.

***Start*** A kiteboard *starts* when, her hull and the competitor having been entirely on the pre-start side of the starting line at or after her starting signal, and having complied with rule 30.1 if it applies, any part of her hull, or the competitor crosses the starting line in the direction of the first *mark*.

越过终点线后她有如下情况，则为没有*到达终点*：

（a）根据规则44.2做解脱，

（b）根据规则28.2改正在终点线上犯的错误，或者

（c）继续行驶航线。

***避让*** 如果符合下面条件，一条风筝板就*避让*了另一条有航行权的风筝板

（a）有航行权的风筝板不需要做出避让动作就可以航行在其航线上，同时

（b）当风筝板*相联*时，有航行权的风筝板在两个方向上都能改变航线或者可以向任意方向移动她的风筝而不会立刻造成接触。

***下风***和***上风*** 风筝板的*下风*边是离开风的那一边，或当其正顶风行驶时刚刚离开风的那一边。但当背风航行或正顺风航行时，她的*下风*边就是其风筝所在的一边。另外一边为其*上风*边。当两条风筝板同*舷风相联*时，处在一条风筝板板体的*下风*边的是*下风*风筝板，这条板是*上风*风筝板。

***绕标空间*** 风筝板行驶其*正当航线*从要求的一侧绕过或通过*标志*的*空间*。

***障碍物*** 当风筝板正直接驶向一个物体并距离其10米时，若她不明显改变航线就不能通过的物体。只能从一侧安全通过的物体和航行细则中特指的区域也可作为*障碍物*。但是，正在*竞赛*的风筝板对其他风筝板不构成*障碍物*，除非这些风筝板应该*避让*她，若规则23适用，躲避她。正在行驶的各种船舶，包括正在*竞赛*的风筝板，永远不是连续*障碍物*。

***起航*** 在起航信号发出时或发出后，风筝板的板体和选手完全位于起航线准备区一侧，并且遵守了规则30.1（如果采用该规则），其板体的任何部分或选手向第一个*标志*方向越过起航线即为*起航*。

***Tack, Starboard* or *Port*** A kiteboard is on the *tack*, *starboard* or *port*, corresponding to the competitor's hand that would be forward if the competitor were in normal riding position (riding heel side with both hands on the control bar and arms not crossed). A kiteboard is on *starboard tack* when the competitor's right hand would be forward and is on the *port tack* when the competitor's left hand would be forward.

***Zone*** The area around a *mark* within a distance of 30 metres. A kiteboard is in the *zone* when any part of her hull is in the *zone*.

Add the following definitions:

***Capsized*** A kiteboard is *capsized* if

(a) her kite is in the water,

(b) her lines are tangled with another kiteboard's lines, or

(c) the competitor has, clearly by accident and for a significant period of time,

(1) fallen into the water or

(2) become disconnected from the hull.

***Jumping*** A kiteboard is *jumping* when her hull, its appendages and the competitor are clear of the water.

***Recovering*** A kiteboard is *recovering* from the time her kite is out of the water until she has steerage way.

## F1 CHANGES TO THE RULES OF PART 1

*[No changes.]*

## F2 CHANGES TO THE RULES OF PART 2

### PART 2 - PREAMBLE

In the second sentence of the preamble, 'injury or serious damage' is changed to 'injury, serious damage or a tangle'.

### 13 WHILE TACKING

Rule 13 is deleted.

### 14 AVOIDING CONTACT

Rule 14(b) is changed to:

***舷风、右舷*或*左舷*　风筝板的*舷风*边、*右舷*或*左舷*是与选手处于正常操板位置（脚站立的一侧，双手都放在控制杆上且手臂没有交叉）时在前的那只手一致的。选手的右手在前，则风筝板为*右舷风*，选手的左手在前，则风筝板为*左舷风*。

***标区***　距离标志30米的区域。当板体的任何部分在此*标区*内即为该风筝板在此*标区*内。

增加以下定义：

***翻船***　若出现下列情况，则风筝板为*翻船*

（a）其风筝处于水中，

（b）其操控绳和其他风筝板的操控绳缠绕在一起，或者

（c）很明确是由意外造成的，选手已处于下列状态并明显持续了一段时间

（1）落入水中或

（2）与板体分离。

***跳跃***　当风筝板的板体、附属物及选手脱离水面即为*跳跃*。

***复位***　风筝板的风筝脱离水面那一刻直到其操纵行驶称为*复位*。

## F1　对规则第一章的更改

*［没有更改。］*

## F2　对规则第二章的更改

第二章——前言

前言中的第二句，“受伤或严重损坏”更改为“受伤、严重损坏或缠绕”。

### 13　迎风换舷时

删除规则13。

### 14　避免接触

规则14(b)更改为：

(b) shall be exonerated if she breaks this rule and the contact does not cause damage, injury or a tangle.

**16 CHANGING COURSE OR KITE POSITION**

Rule 16 is changed to:

**16.1** When a right-of-way kiteboard changes course or the position of her kite, she shall give the other kiteboard *room* to *keep clear*.

**16.2** In addition, when after the starting signal a *port-tack* kiteboard is *keeping clear* by sailing to pass astern of a *starboard-tack* kiteboard, the *starboard-tack* kiteboard shall not change course or the position of her kite if as a result the *port-tack* kiteboard would immediately need to change course or the position of her kite to continue *keeping clear*.

**17 ON THE SAME TACK; PROPER COURSE**

Rule 17 is deleted.

**18 MARK-ROOM**

Rule 18 is changed to:

**18.1 When Rule 18 Applies**

Rule 18 applies between kiteboards when they are required to leave a *mark* on the same side and at least one of them is in the *zone*. However, it does not apply

(a) between a kiteboard approaching a *mark* and one leaving it, or

(b) between kiteboards on opposite *tacks*.

**18.2 Giving Mark-Room**

(a) When the first kiteboard reaches the *zone*,

(1) if kiteboards are *overlapped*, the outside kiteboard at that moment shall thereafter give the inside kiteboard *mark-room*.

(2) if kiteboards are not *overlapped*, the kiteboard that has not reached the *zone* shall thereafter give *mark-room*.

(b) If the kiteboard entitled to *mark-room* leaves the *zone*, the entitlement to *mark-room* ceases and rule 18.2(a) is applied again if required based on the relationship of the （b）如果她违反了本条规则，并没有造成损坏、受伤或缠绕，应被免责。

**16　改变航线或风筝位置**

规则16更改为：

16.1 当有航行权的风筝板改变航线或其风筝的位置时，她应给予另外一条风筝板*空间*去避让。

16.2 另外，起航信号后，一条*左舷*风筝板以从*右舷*风筝板板尾通过的方式*避让*时，如果*右舷*风筝板改变航线或其风筝的位置会造成*左舷*风筝板需要马上改变航线或其风筝的位置继续*避让*，*右舷*风筝板就不应改变航线或其风筝的位置。

**17　同舷风；正当航线**

删除规则17。

**18　绕标空间**

规则18更改为：

**18.1 规则18适用时**

在被要求同侧离开*标志*且至少其中一条风筝板处于*标区*内的风筝板之间，规则18适用。然而，不适用于

（a）在一条正接近*标志*的风筝板和一条正离开*标志*的风筝板之间，或者

（b）在以相对*舷风*行驶的风筝板之间。

**18.2 给予绕标空间**

（a）当第一条风筝板到达*标区*时，

（1）如果风筝板*相联*，此时外侧的风筝板之后应给予内侧风筝板*绕标空间*。

（2）如果风筝板不*相联*，没有到达*标区*的风筝板之后应给予*绕标空间*。

（b）如果有权要求*绕标空间*的风筝板离开了*标区*，要求*绕标空间*的权利随即终止，必要时根据风筝板

kiteboards at the time rule 18.2(a) is re-applied.

(c) If a kiteboard obtained an inside *overlap* and, from the time the *overlap* began, the outside kiteboard is unable to give *mark-room*, she is not required to give it.

**18.3 Tacking and Gybing**

When an inside *overlapped* right-of-way kiteboard must change *tack* at a *mark* to sail her *proper course*, until she changes *tack* she shall sail no farther from the *mark* than needed to sail that course. Rule 18.3 does not apply at a gate *mark* or a finishing *mark* and a kitebaord shall not be penalized for breaking this rule unless the course of another kiteboard was affected by the breach of this rule.

**20 ROOM TO TACK AT AN OBSTRUCTION**

Add new rule 20.4:

**20.4 Arm Signals**

The following arm signals are required in addition to the hails

(a) for 'Room to tack', repeatedly and clearly circling one hand over the head; and

(b) for 'You tack', repeatedly and clearly pointing at the other kiteboard and waving the arm to windward.

**22 STARTING ERRORS; TAKING PENALTIES; JUMPING**

Rule 22.3 is changed and new rule 22.4 is added:

**22.3** During the last minute before her starting signal, a kiteboard that stops, slows down significantly, or one that is not making significant forward progress shall *keep clear* of all others unless she is accidentally *capsized.*

**22.4** A kiteboard that is *jumping* shall *keep clear* of one that is not.

**23 CAPSIZED; RECOVERING; AGROUND; RESCUING**

Rule 23 is changed to:

**23.1** If possible, a kiteboard shall avoid a kiteboard that is *capsized* or has not regained control after *capsizing*, is aground, or is trying to help a person or vessel in danger.

之间的关系，规则18.2(a)会再次适用。

（c）如果一条风筝板建立内侧*相联*，*相联*开始的时候，外侧风筝板已经不能给予*绕标空间*，她就不必给予*绕标空间*。

18.3 迎风换舷和顺风换舷

当一条内侧*相联*有航行权的风筝板必须在*标志*旁换*舷*以行驶其*正当航线*时，直到换*舷*前她离*标志*的距离不得远于行驶那个航线所需要的距离。规则18.3不适用于门标或终点*标志*，且违反本条规则的风筝板不应被惩罚，除非另一条风筝板因其违反规则而受到了影响。

**20 障碍物旁迎风换舷的空间**

增加新规则20.4：

20.4 手臂信号

呼喊时要求配有如下手臂信号

（a）呼喊“迎风换舷的空间（Room to tack）”时，明显地重复用一只手在头顶画圈；和

（b）呼喊“你迎风换舷（You tack）”时，明显地重复指向另外一条风筝板并向上风摆动手臂。

**22 起航失误；解脱；跳跃**

更改规则22.3并增加新规则22.4：

22.3 在起航信号前的最后1分钟，除意外*翻船*，明显停止、减速或没有明显前进趋势的风筝板应*避让*其他所有风筝板。

22.4 *跳跃*的风筝板应*避让*没有在这样做的风筝板。

**23 翻船；复位；搁浅；救援**

更改规则23：

23.1 如有可能一条风筝板应躲避*翻船*的或在*翻船*后还未重新获得操纵能力的，以及搁浅的或正在帮助处于危险中的人或船舶的风筝板。

**23.2** A kiteboard that is *recovering* shall *keep clear* of a kiteboard that is not.

## F3 CHANGES TO THE RULES OF PART 3

### 29 RECALLS

In rule 29.1 'crew or equipment' is changed to 'competitor'.

### 30 STARTING PENALTIES

In rules 30.1, 30.2, 30.3 and 30.4, 'crew or equipment' is changed to 'or competitor'.

In rule 30.4, 'sail number' is changed to 'competitor number'.

### 31 TOUCHING A MARK

Rule 31 is changed to:

While *racing*, a kiteboard shall not touch a windward *mark*.

### 36 RACES RESTARTED OR RESAILED

Rule 36(b) is changed to:

(b) cause a kiteboard to be penalized except under rule 30.2, 30.4 or 69 or under rule 14 when she has caused injury, serious damage or a tangle.

## F4 CHANGES TO THE RULES OF PART 4

### 41 OUTSIDE HELP

Add new rules 41(e) and 41(f):

(e) help from another competitor in the same race to assist a relaunch;

(f) help to change equipment, but only in the launching area.

### 42 PROPULSION

Rule 42 is changed to:

A kiteboard shall be propelled only by the action of the wind on the kite, by the action of the water on the hull and by the unassisted actions of the competitor. However, the competitor shall not make significant progress by paddling, swimming or walking.

23.2 正在*复位*的风筝板应*避让*没有在这样做的风筝板。

## F3 对规则第三章的更改

### 29 召回

规则29.1中的“船员或装备”更改为“选手”。

### 30 起航惩罚

规则30.1、30.2、30.3和30.4中的“船员或装备”更改为“选手”。

规则30.4中的“帆号”更改为“选手号码”。

### 31 碰标

规则31更改为：

*竞赛*时，风筝板不允许触碰上风标。

### 36 重新起航或重新竞赛

规则36(b)更改为：

（b）导致一条风筝板被判罚，除非她违反了规则30.2、30.4、69，或规则14当她造成了损伤、严重损坏或缠绕。

## F4 对规则第四章的更改

### 41 外部援助

增加新规则41(e)和41(f)：

（e）来自于参加同一轮竞赛的其他选手的重新下水的帮助；

（f）帮助更换器材，但仅限于下水区域。

### 42 推进

规则42更改为：

风筝板只能依靠风对风筝的作用、水对板体的作用、选手的非辅助性作用作为推进力。但是，选手不应通过划桨、游泳或行走来使风筝板获得大幅前进。

## 43 COMPETITOR CLOTHING AND EQUIPMENT

Rule 43.1(a) is changed to:

(a) Competitors shall not wear or carry clothing or equipment for the purpose of increasing their weight. However, a competitor may wear a drinking container that shall have a capacity of at least one litre and weigh no more than 1.5 kilograms when full.

## 44 PENALTIES AT THE TIME OF AN INCIDENT

Rules 44.1 and 44.2 are changed to:

### 44.1 Taking a Penalty

A kiteboard may take a One-Turn Penalty when she may have broken one or more rules of Part 2 or rule 31 in an incident while *racing*. Alternatively, the notice of race or sailing instructions may specify the use of the Scoring Penalty or some other penalty, in which case the specified penalty shall replace the One-Turn Penalty. However,

(a) when a kiteboard may have broken a rule of Part 2 and rule 31 in the same incident she need not take the penalty for breaking rule 31; and

(b) if the kiteboard caused injury, damage or a tangle or, despite taking a penalty, gained a significant advantage in the race or series by her breach, her penalty shall be to retire.

### 44.2 One-Turn Penalty

After getting well clear of other kiteboards as soon after the incident as possible, a kiteboard takes a One-Turn Penalty by promptly making one turn with her hull in the water. The turn shall include one completed tack and one completed gybe. Forward motion shall be established between the tack and the gybe (or vice versa) with the competitor on the correct side of the hull in normal sailing position. When a kiteboard takes the penalty at or near the finishing line, she shall sail completely to the course side of the line before *finishing*.

## PART 4 RULES DELETED

Rules 43.2, 45, 47, 48.1, 49, 50, 51, 52 and 54 are deleted.

## 43 选手的服装与装备

规则43.1(a)更改为：

（a）选手不应穿着或携带专为增加他们体重的服装和装备。但是，选手可身背装有饮料的容器，该容器至少要有1升的容量，在装满时其重量不得超过1.5公斤。

## 44 事件发生时的惩罚

规则44.1和44.2更改为：

### 44.1 解脱

在*竞赛*中，当风筝板违反了第二章的一条或多条规则，或在某一事件中违反了规则31，她将做一圈解脱。或者，竞赛通知或航行细则可详细说明分数惩罚和其他惩罚的用法，在这种情况下，特别规定的惩罚办法将替换一圈解脱。但是，

（a）当一条风筝板在同一事件中违反了规则第二章和规则31时，她不必接受违反规则31的惩罚；同时

（b）如果风筝板造成了损伤、损坏或缠绕，或尽快做了解脱，但由于她在该轮竞赛或系列赛中因犯规而获得了明显优势，对她的惩罚应该是退出比赛。

### 44.2 一圈解脱

在事件发生后风筝板尽快完全避让其他风筝板后做一圈解脱，立即使板体在水中转一圈。这一圈包括一个完整的迎风换舷和一个完整的顺风换舷。前进动作应建立在选手处于正常航行位置的板体的正确一侧的迎风换舷和顺风换舷之间（反之亦然）。在终点线或终点线附近做解脱的风筝板，应该在*到达终点*前完全回到终点线的航线一侧。

## 删除的第四章规则

删除规则43.2、45、47、48.1、49、50、51、52和54。

## F5 CHANGES TO THE RULES OF PART 5

### 61 PROTEST REQUIREMENTS

Rule 61.1(a) is changed to:

(a) A kiteboard intending to protest shall inform the other kiteboard at the first reasonable opportunity. When her *protest* will concern an incident in the racing area that she was involved in or saw, she shall hail 'Protest' at the first reasonable opportunity. However,

(1) if the other kiteboard is beyond hailing distance, the protesting kiteboard need not hail but she shall inform the other kiteboard at the first reasonable opportunity;

(2) no red flag need be displayed;

(3) if the incident was an error by the other kiteboard in sailing the course, she need not hail but she shall inform the other kiteboard before that kiteboard *finishes* or at the first reasonable opportunity after she *finishes*;

(4) if as a result of the incident either competitor is in danger, or there is injury, serious damage or a tangle that is obvious to the kiteboard intending to protest, the requirements of this rule do not apply to her, but she shall attempt to inform the other kiteboard within the time limit of rule 61.3.

### 62 REDRESS

Rule 62.1(b) is changed to:

(b) injury, physical damage or a tangle because of the action of a kiteboard that was breaking a rule of Part 2 or of a vessel not *racing* that was required to keep clear;

## F5 对规则第五章的更改

### 61 对抗议的要求

规则61.1(a)更改为：

（a）一条有意提出抗议的风筝板应在最先出现的合理时机通知另外一条风筝板。当她的*抗议*是在竞赛区域中涉及她或她所看到的事件，她应在最先出现的合理时机呼喊“Protest（抗议）”。但是，

（1）如果另外一条风筝板远于可呼喊距离，抗议的风筝板无需呼喊，但需在最先出现的合理时机通知那条风筝板；

（2）无需展示红旗；

（3）如果该事件是另一条风筝板所犯的行驶航线错误，她不需要呼喊，但是应在该风筝板*到达终点*前或在其*到达终点*后最先出现的合理时机告知她；

（4）如果事件结果造成任一选手处于危险中，或打算提出抗议的风筝板有明显的损伤、严重损坏或缠绕，那么此条规则的要求对她不适用，但是她应尽力在规则63.1规定的时限内通知另外那条风筝板。

### 62 补偿

规则62.1(b)更改为：

（b）由另外一条风筝板违反规则第二章或一条应避让的不参加竞赛的船舶的行为而造成的损伤、有形损坏或缠绕；

## 63 HEARINGS

For a race of an elimination series that will qualify a kiteboard to compete in a later stage of an event, rules 61.2 and 65.2 are deleted and rule 63.6 is changed to:

**63.6** *Protests* and requests for redress need not be in writing; they shall be made orally to a member of the protest committee as soon as reasonably possible following the race. The protest committee may take evidence in any way it considers appropriate and may communicate its decision orally.

## 64 DECISIONS

Add new rule 64.1(d):

(d) when a kiteboard has broken a rule of Part 2 and, as a result, caused a tangle for which redress was given, she shall be scored RCT if she retired or DCT if she was disqualified. When she does this a second or subsequent time in the series, her penalty shall be DNE.

Rules 64.3(a) and 64.3(b) are changed to:

(a) When the protest committee finds that deviations in excess of acceptable manufacturing tolerances were caused by damage or normal wear and do not improve the performance of the kiteboard, it shall not penalize her. However, the kiteboard shall not *race* again until the deviations have been corrected, except when the protest committee decides there is or has been no reasonable opportunity to do so.

(b) When the protest committee is in doubt about any matter concerning the measurement of a kiteboard, the interpretation of a class rule, or a matter involving damage to a kiteboard, it shall refer its questions, together with the relevant facts, to an authority responsible for interpreting the rule. In making its decision, the committee shall be bound by the reply of the authority.

63　**审理**

对于将决出参加下一阶段比赛的风筝板的淘汰系列赛，删除规则61.2和65.2，规则63.6更改为：

63.6 *抗议*和补偿要求无需以书面形式提交；可以在竞赛过程中以口头通知的形式在最先出现的合理时机告知抗议委员会的一名成员。抗议委员会可以就其认为合适的任何方式取证并可以口头通知的形式告知裁决。

64　**裁决**

增加新规则64.1(d)：

(d) 当一条风筝板由于违反了规则第二章导致缠绕，需要给予补偿时，如果她退出比赛，应记为“RCT”，如果是被取消资格，应记为“DCT”。当她在系列赛中第二次或接下来又这样做时，其惩罚应为“DNE”。

规则64.3(a)和64.3(b)更改为：

(a) 当抗议委员会发现由于受损或正常磨损而使误差超过可接受的建造公差，但并不会提高该风筝板的性能时，不应对她做出惩罚。但是，该风筝板在修正误差之前将不允许再参加竞赛，除非抗议委员会认为该风筝板没有合理的机会进行修正。

(b) 当抗议委员会对一条风筝板的丈量相关事项、级别规则的解释或有关风筝板损坏的相关问题有疑问时，它应将问题连同有关事实一起提交给负责解释规则的一个管理机构。抗议委员会应依据管理机构的回复进行裁决。

### 70 APPEALS AND REQUESTS TO A NATIONAL AUTHORITY

Add new rule 70.7:

**70.7** Appeals are not permitted in disciplines and formats with elimination series.

## F6 CHANGES TO THE RULES OF PART 6

*[No changes.]*

## F7 CHANGES TO THE RULES OF PART 7

### 90 RACE COMMITTEE; SAILING INSTRUCTIONS; SCORING

The last sentence of rule 90.2(c) is changed to: 'Oral instructions may be given only if the procedure is stated in the sailing instructions.'

## F8 CHANGES TO APPENDIX A

### A1 NUMBER OF RACES; OVERALL SCORES

Rule A1 is changed to:

The number of races scheduled and the number required to be completed to constitute a series shall be stated in the notice of race or sailing instructions. If an event includes more than one discipline or format, the notice of race or sailing instructions shall state how the overall scores are to be calculated.

### A4 LOW POINT SYSTEM

Rule A4.2 is changed to:

**A4.2** A kiteboard that did not *start*, did not *finish*, retired or was disqualified shall be scored points for the finishing place one more than the number of kiteboards entered in the series or, in a race of an elimination series, the number of kiteboards in that heat. A kiteboard that is penalized under rule 30.2 shall be scored points as provided in rule 44.3(c).

### A11 SCORING ABBREVIATIONS

Add to Rule A11:

DCT Disqualified after causing a tangle in an incident
RCT Retired after causing a tangle

**70　上诉及寻求国家管理机构的确认**

增加新规则70.7：

70.7 在淘汰赛中，不允许针对类别和模式进行上诉。

## F6　对规则第六章的更改

*［没有更改。］*

## F7　对规则第七章的更改

**90　竞赛委员会；航行细则；记分**

规则90.2(c)最后一句话更改为：“只有在航行细则中有关于此程序的陈述时才可以给予口头指示。”

## F8　对附录A的更改

**A1　比赛轮次；总分**

规则A1更改为：

竞赛通知或航行细则中应注明比赛所安排的轮次及组成完整的系列赛所必须竞赛的轮次数目。如果一场赛事包含一种以上的类别或模式，竞赛通知或航行细则应注明总分的计算方式。

**A4　低分记分法**

规则A4.2更改为：

A4.2 一条风筝板没有*起航*、没有*到达终点*，退出比赛或被取消资格，其终点名次分数应是参加该系列赛的风筝板总数加1分，或者是在淘汰赛的一轮竞赛中，分数为那一轮预赛的风筝板总数加1分。根据规则30.2被惩罚的风筝板应根据规则44.3(c)记分。

**A11　记分缩写**

规则A11后增加：

DCT　因在事件中造成缠绕而被取消资格

RCT　在造成缠绕后退出比赛

**F9 CHANGES TO APPENDIX G**

Appendix G is changed to:

## Appendix G – Identification on Competitors

**G1** Every kiteboard shall be identified as follows:

(a) Each competitor shall be provided with and wear a shirt with a personal competition number of no more than three digits.

(b) The numbers shall be displayed on the front and back of the shirts and be at least 15 cm high.

(c) The numbers shall be Arabic numerals, all of the same solid colour, clearly legible and in a commercially available typeface giving the same or better legibility as Helvetica. The colour of the numbers shall contrast with the colour of the shirt.

## F9　对附录G的更改

附录G更改为：

**附录——选手标识**

G1　每条风筝板都应按照如下要求标识：

（a）每位选手都应被提供并穿着带有不多于三位数的个人号码背心。

（b）这些号码应在背心的前后均有展示，且高度至少为15厘米。

（c）这些号码应为阿拉伯数字，颜色相同，清晰可辨，可以接受商业上可用的与“Helvetica”字体有同样或更好的清晰度的字体。号码的颜色应为背心颜色的反差色。

# APPENDIX G IDENTIFICATION ON SAILS

*See rule 77.*

## G1 WORLD SAILING CLASS BOATS

### G1.1 Identification

Every boat of a World Sailing Class shall carry on her mainsail and, as provided in rules G1.3(d) and G1.3(e) for letters and numbers only, on her spinnaker and headsail

(a) the insignia denoting her class;

(b) at all international events, except when the boats are provided to all competitors, national letters denoting her national authority from the table below. For the purposes of this rule, international events are World Sailing events, world and continental championships, and events described as international events in their notices of race and sailing instructions; and

(c) a sail number of no more than four digits allotted by her national authority or, when so required by the class rules, by the class association. The four-digit limitation does not apply to classes whose World Sailing membership or recognition took effect before 1 April 1997. Alternatively, if permitted in the class rules, an owner may be allotted a personal sail number by the relevant issuing authority, which may be used on all his boats in that class.

Sails measured before 31 March 1999 shall comply with rule G1.1 or with the rules applicable at the time of measurement.

*Note: An up-to-date version of the table below is available on the World Sailing website.*

# 附录G　帆上标识

*参见规则77。*

## G1　世界帆联级别的帆船

### G1.1 识别标记

世界帆联级别或其认证级别的每条帆船应在其主帆上携有，并按照规则G1.3(d)和G1.3(e)的字母和号码规定在球帆和前帆上携有：

（a）代表该级别的标识；

（b）在所有国际赛事中，除了向所有选手提供帆船外，代表国家管理机构的国家代码应按下表内容展示。针对本规则而言，国际赛事是指世界帆联赛事、世界和洲际锦标赛，以及在竞赛通知和航行细则中注明为国际赛事的比赛；以及

（c）由国家管理机构分配的，或者级别规则或级别协会这样要求的不多于四位数字的帆号。这四位数字的限制不适用于在1997年4月1日前获得世界帆联成员资格或承认的级别。或者，如果级别规则允许，船东可以由相应的认证协会分配一个个人帆号，可以用于该级别中他所有的帆船。

1999年3月31日前丈量的帆应符合规则G1.1或符合其丈量时所适用的规则。

*注：世界帆联网站上可以查询到下表的实时更新版本。*

**NATIONAL SAIL LETTERS**

| *National authority* | *Letters* |
|---|---|
| Algeria | ALG |
| American Samoa | ASA |
| Andorra | AND |
| Angola | ANG |
| Antigua | ANT |
| Argentina | ARG |
| Armenia | ARM |
| Aruba | ARU |
| Australia | AUS |
| Austria | AUT |
| Azerbaijan | AZE |
| Bahamas | BAH |
| Bahrain | BRN |
| Barbados | BAR |
| Belarus | BLR |
| Belgium | BEL |
| Belize | BIZ |
| Bermuda | BER |
| Brazil | BRA |
| British Virgin Islands | IVB |
| Brunei Darussalam | BRU |
| Bulgaria | BUL |
| Canada | CAN |
| Cambodia | CAM |
| Cayman Islands | CAY |
| Chile | CHI |
| China, PR | CHN |
| Chinese Taipei | TPE |
| Colombia | COL |
| Cook Islands | COK |

| *National authority* | *Letters* |
|---|---|
| Ecuador | ECU |
| Egypt | EGY |
| El Salvador | ESA |
| Estonia | EST |
| Fiji | FIJ |
| Finland | FIN |
| France | FRA |
| Georgia | GEO |
| Germany | GER |
| Great Britain | GBR |
| Greece | GRE |
| Grenada | GRN |
| Guam | GUM |
| Guatemala | GUA |
| Hong Kong | HKG |
| Hungary | HUN |
| Iceland | ISL |
| India | IND |
| Indonesia | INA |
| Iraq | IRQ |
| Ireland | IRL |
| Israel | ISR |
| Italy | ITA |
| Jamaica | JAM |
| Japan | JPN |
| Kazakhstan | KAZ |
| Kenya | KEN |
| Korea, DPR | PRK |
| Korea, Republic of | KOR |
| Kosovo | KOS |

**帆上国家代码**

| 国家管理机构 | 字母代码 |
|---|---|
| 阿尔及利亚 | ALG |
| 美属萨摩亚 | ASA |
| 安道尔 | AND |
| 安哥拉 | ANG |
| 安提瓜 | ANT |
| 阿根廷 | ARG |
| 亚美尼亚 | ARM |
| 阿鲁巴岛 | ARU |
| 澳大利亚 | AUS |
| 奥地利 | AUT |
| 阿塞拜疆 | AZE |
| 巴哈马 | BAH |
| 巴林 | BRN |
| 巴巴多斯 | BAR |
| 白俄罗斯 | BLR |
| 比利时 | BEL |
| 伯利兹 | BIZ |
| 百慕大 | BER |
| 巴西 | BRA |
| 文莱达鲁萨兰国 | BRU |
| 英属维尔京群岛 | IVB |
| 保加利亚 | BUL |
| 加拿大 | CAN |
| 开曼群岛 | CAY |
| 柬埔寨 | CAM |
| 智利 | CHI |
| 中华人民共和国 | CHN |
| 中华台北 | TPE |
| 哥伦比亚 | COL |
| 库克群岛 | COK |

| 国家管理机构 | 字母代码 |
|---|---|
| 厄瓜多尔 | ECU |
| 埃及 | EGY |
| 艾萨瓦尔多 | ESA |
| 爱沙尼亚 | EST |
| 斐济 | FIJ |
| 芬兰 | FIN |
| 法国 | FRA |
| 格鲁吉亚 | GEO |
| 德国 | GER |
| 英国 | GBR |
| 希腊 | GRE |
| 格林纳达 | GRN |
| 关岛 | GUM |
| 危地马拉 | GUA |
| 中国香港 | HKG |
| 匈牙利 | HUN |
| 冰岛 | ISL |
| 印度 | IND |
| 印度尼西亚 | INA |
| 伊拉克 | IRQ |
| 爱尔兰 | IRL |
| 以色列 | ISR |
| 意大利 | ITA |
| 牙买加 | JAM |
| 日本 | JPN |
| 哈萨克斯坦 | KAZ |
| 肯尼亚 | KEN |
| 朝鲜 | PRK |
| 韩国 | KOR |
| 科索沃 | KOS |

| *National authority* | *Letters* |
|---|---|
| Croatia | CRO |
| Cuba | CUB |
| Cyprus | CYP |
| Czech Republic | CZE |
| Denmark | DEN |
| Djibouti | DJI |
| Dominican Republic | DOM |
| Lithuania | LTU |
| Luxembourg | LUX |
| Macedonia (FYRO) | MKD |
| Madagascar | MAD |
| Malaysia | MAS |
| Malta | MLT |
| Mauritius | MRI |
| Mexico | MEX |
| Moldova | MDA |
| Monaco | MON |
| Montenegro | MNE |
| Morocco | MAR |
| Mozambique | MOZ |
| Myanmar | MYA |
| Namibia | NAM |
| Netherlands | NED |
| Netherlands Antilles | AHO |
| New Zealand | NZL |
| Nicaragua | NCA |
| Nigeria | NGR |
| Norway | NOR |
| Oman | OMA |
| Pakistan | PAK |
| Palestine | PLE |

| *National authority* | *Letters* |
|---|---|
| Kuwait | KUW |
| Kyrgyzstan | KGZ |
| Latvia | LAT |
| Lebanon | LIB |
| Libya | LBA |
| Liechtenstein | LIE |
| | |
| Samoa | SAM |
| San Marino | SMR |
| Saudi Arabia | KSA |
| Senegal | SEN |
| Serbia | SRB |
| Seychelles | SEY |
| Singapore | SGP |
| Slovak Republic | SVK |
| Slovenia | SLO |
| South Africa | RSA |
| Spain | ESP |
| Sri Lanka | SRI |
| St Lucia | LCA |
| St Vincent & Grenadines | VIN |
| Sudan | SUD |
| Sweden | SWE |
| Switzerland | SUI |
| Tahiti | TAH |
| Tanzania | TAN |
| Thailand | THA |
| Timore Leste | TLS |
| Trinidad & Tobago | TTO |
| Tunisia | TUN |
| Turkey | TUR |

| *国家管理机构* | *字母代码* |
| --- | --- |
| 克罗地亚 | CRO |
| 古巴 | CUB |
| 塞浦路斯 | CYP |
| 捷克共和国 | CZE |
| 丹麦 | DEN |
| 吉布提 | DJI |
| 多米尼加共和国 | DOM |
| 立陶宛 | LTU |
| 卢森堡 | LUX |
| 马其顿（FYRO） | MKD |
| 马达加斯加 | MAD |
| 马来西亚 | MAS |
| 马耳他 | MLT |
| 毛里求斯 | MRI |
| 墨西哥 | MEX |
| 摩尔多瓦 | MDA |
| 摩纳哥 | MON |
| 黑山共和国 | MNE |
| 摩洛哥 | MAR |
| 莫桑比克 | MOZ |
| 缅甸 | MYA |
| 纳米比亚 | NAM |
| 荷兰 | NED |
| 荷属安的列斯 | AHO |
| 新西兰 | NZL |
| 尼加拉瓜 | NCA |
| 尼日利亚 | NGR |
| 挪威 | NOR |
| 阿曼 | OMA |
| 巴基斯坦 | PAK |
| 巴勒斯坦 | PLE |

| *国家管理机构* | *字母代码* |
| --- | --- |
| 科威特 | KUW |
| 吉尔吉斯斯坦 | KGZ |
| 拉脱维亚 | LAT |
| 黎巴嫩 | LIB |
| 利比亚 | LBA |
| 列支敦士登 | LIE |
| 萨摩亚 | SAM |
| 圣马力诺 | SMR |
| 沙特阿拉伯 | KSA |
| 塞内加尔 | SEN |
| 塞尔维亚 | SRB |
| 塞舌尔 | SEY |
| 新加坡 | SGP |
| 斯洛伐克共和国 | SVK |
| 斯洛文尼亚 | SLO |
| 南非 | RSA |
| 西班牙 | ESP |
| 斯里兰卡 | SRI |
| 圣卢西亚 | LCA |
| 圣文森特和格林纳丁斯 | VIN |
| 苏丹 | SUD |
| 瑞典 | SWE |
| 瑞士 | SUI |
| 法属波利尼西亚 | TAH |
| 坦桑尼亚 | TAN |
| 泰国 | THA |
| 帝汶岛 | TLS |
| 特立尼达和多巴哥 | TTO |
| 突尼斯 | TUN |
| 土耳其 | TUR |

| *National authority* | *Letters* |
| --- | --- |
| Panama | PAN |
| Papua New Guinea | PNG |
| Paraguay | PAR |
| Peru | PER |
| Philippines | PHI |
| Poland | POL |
| Portugal | POR |
| Puerto Rico | PUR |
| Qatar | QAT |
| Romania | ROU |
| Russia | RUS |

| *National authority* | *Letters* |
| --- | --- |
| Uganda | UGA |
| Ukraine | UKR |
| United Arab Emirates | UAE |
| United States of America | USA |
| Uruguay | URU |
| US Virgin Islands | ISV |
| Vanuatu | VAN |
| Venezuela | VEN |
| Vietnam | VIE |
| Zimbabwe | ZIM |

**G1.2 Specifications**

(a) National letters and sail numbers shall be in capital letters and Arabic numerals, clearly legible and of the same colour. Commercially available typefaces giving the same or better legibility than Helvetica are acceptable.

(b) The height of characters and space between adjoining characters on the same and opposite sides of the sail shall be related to the boat's overall length as follows:

| *Overall length* | *Minimum height* | *Minimum space between characters and from edge of sail* |
| --- | --- | --- |
| Under 3.5 m | 230 mm | 45 mm |
| 3.5 m – 8.5 m | 300 mm | 60 mm |
| 8.5 m – 11 m | 375 mm | 75 mm |
| Over 11 m | 450 mm | 90 mm |

| *国家管理机构* | *字母代码* |
|---|---|
| 巴拿马 | PAN |
| 巴布亚新几内亚 | PNG |
| 巴拉圭 | PAR |
| 秘鲁 | PER |
| 菲律宾 | PHI |
| 波兰 | POL |
| 葡萄牙 | POR |
| 波多黎各 | PUR |
| 卡塔尔 | QAT |
| 罗马尼亚 | ROU |
| 俄罗斯 | RUS |

| *国家管理机构* | *字母代码* |
|---|---|
| 乌干达 | UGA |
| 乌克兰 | UKR |
| 阿拉伯联合酋长国 | UAE |
| 美利坚合众国 | USA |
| 乌拉圭 | URU |
| 美属维尔京群岛 | ISV |
| 瓦努阿图 | VAN |
| 委内瑞拉 | VEN |
| 越南 | VIE |
| 津巴布韦 | ZIM |

### G1.2 规格

(a) 国家代码和帆号应为大写字母和阿拉伯数字，清晰可辨而且颜色相同。可以接受商业上可用的跟“Helvetica”字体有同样或更好清晰度的字体。

(b) 字符的高度和在帆的同一面或反面相邻字符的距离与船的总长关系如下：

| *总长* | *最小高度* | *字符之间与帆边的最小间隔* |
|---|---|---|
| 3.5m以下 | 230mm | 45mm |
| 3.5m ~ 8.5m | 300mm | 60mm |
| 8.5m ~ 11m | 375mm | 75mm |
| 11m以上 | 450mm | 90mm |

**G1.3 Positioning**

Class insignia, national letters and sail numbers shall be positioned as follows:

(a) Except as provided in rules G1.3(d) and G1.3(e), class insignia, national letters and sail numbers shall, if possible, be wholly above an arc whose centre is the head point and whose radius is 60% of the leech length. They shall be placed at different heights on the two sides of the sail, those on the starboard side being uppermost.

(b) The class insignia shall be placed above the national letters. If the class insignia is of such a design that two of them coincide when placed back to back on both sides of the sail, they may be so placed.

(c) National letters shall be placed above the sail number.

(d) The national letters and sail number shall be displayed on the front side of a spinnaker but may be placed on both sides. They shall be displayed wholly below an arc whose centre is the head point and whose radius is 40% of the foot median and, if possible, wholly above an arc whose radius is 60% of the foot median.

(e) The national letters and sail number shall be displayed on both sides of a headsail whose clew can extend behind the mast 30% or more of the mainsail foot length. They shall be displayed wholly below an arc whose centre is the head point and whose radius is half the luff length and, if possible, wholly above an arc whose radius is 75% of the luff length.

## G2 OTHER BOATS

Other boats shall comply with the rules of their national authority or class association in regard to the allotment, carrying and size of insignia, letters and numbers. Such rules shall, when practicable, conform to the above requirements.

### G1.3 位置

级别标识、国家代码和帆号的位置要求如下：

（a）除规则G1.3(d)和G1.3(e)的规定外，在可能的情况下，级别标识、国家代码和帆号应当完全位于以帆顶为圆心、以帆后缘的60%为半径画出的圆弧线的上方。应在帆的两面将它们放置在不同的高度，位于右舷帆面的标识为高。

（b）级别标识应位于国家代码之上。如果级别标识的图形背靠背放置于帆的两面时是重合的，就可以如此放置。

（c）国家代码应位于帆号之上。

（d）国家代码和帆号应放置于球形帆的前侧，但也可放在球帆两侧。它们应完全位于以帆顶为圆心、以帆底边中线的40%为半径画出的弧线的下方，如果可能的话，可以完全放置于以帆底边中线60%为半径画出的弧线的上方。

（e）在前帆后下角可以延伸至桅杆后面的量为主帆底边长度的30%或更多的情况下，国家代码和帆号应在前帆两面展示。它们应完全位于以帆顶为圆心、以前缘长度的一半为半径画出的弧线的下方；如果可能的话，它们应完全位于以前缘长度的75%为半径画出的弧线的上方。

## G2 其他帆船

其他帆船在标志、字母和数字的分配、携有和尺寸方面应遵守其国家管理机构或级别协会的规则。这些规则在实施时应与上述规则一致。

## G3 CHARTERED OR LOANED BOATS

When so stated in the notice of race or sailing instructions, a boat chartered or loaned for an event may carry national letters or a sail number in contravention of her class rules.

## G4 WARNINGS AND PENALTIES

When a protest committee finds that a boat has broken a rule of this appendix, it shall either warn her and give her time to comply or penalize her.

## G5 CHANGES BY CLASS RULES

World Sailing Classes may change the rules of this appendix provided the changes have first been approved by World Sailing.

## G3 租借的船

当竞赛通知或航行细则中有规定时，为参加某一赛事租借的帆船可以携有违背其级别规则的国家代码或帆号。

## G4 警告和惩罚

当抗议委员会发现帆船违反了本附录的规则时，应警告该船并给其时间改正或对其进行惩罚。

## G5 级别规则所做的更改

世界帆联级别组织可以更改本附录的规则，条件是首先要得到世界帆联的同意。

# APPENDIX H WEIGHING CLOTHING AND EQUIPMENT

*See rule 43. This appendix shall not be changed by sailing instructions or prescriptions of national authorities.*

**H1** Items of clothing and equipment to be weighed shall be arranged on a rack. After being saturated in water the items shall be allowed to drain freely for one minute before being weighed. The rack must allow the items to hang as they would hang from clothes hangers, so as to allow the water to drain freely. Pockets that have drain-holes that cannot be closed shall be empty, but pockets or items that can hold water shall be full.

**H2** When the weight recorded exceeds the amount permitted, the competitor may rearrange the items on the rack and the member of the technical committee in charge shall again soak and weigh them. This procedure may be repeated a second time if the weight still exceeds the amount permitted.

**H3** A competitor wearing a dry suit may choose an alternative means of weighing the items.

(a) The dry suit and items of clothing and equipment that are worn outside the dry suit shall be weighed as described above.

(b) Clothing worn underneath the dry suit shall be weighed as worn while *racing*, without draining.

(c) The two weights shall be added together.

# 附录H 服装和装备的称重

*参见规则43。本附录不得因航行细则或国家管理机构的规定而更改。*

H1 需要被称重的服装和装备应放置在架子上。在水中浸过的物品在称重前有1分钟的时间排干水分。架子必须可以悬挂物品，如同晾晒衣服的衣架，这样有利于衣物排水。有无法关闭的排水孔的口袋应当是空的，但是可以盛水的口袋或物品应装满水。

H2 若称重记录超过允许的数值，选手可以重新在架子上摆放物品，然后负责的技术委员会成员应再次将其浸湿并称重。如果重量依然超过允许的数值，那么可以再重复一次该过程。

H3 身着干式保温服的选手可以选择下列方法称重物品。

（a）干式保温服和穿在其外面的服装以及装备物品均应按上述规定称重。

（b）穿在干式保温服里面的衣服应像在竞赛时的穿着一样，在不需经过控干的情况下称重。

（c）这两项重量应当相加。

# APPENDIX J NOTICE OF RACE AND SAILING INSTRUCTIONS

*See rules 89.2 and 90.2. In this appendix, the term 'race' includes a regatta or other series of races.*

*Care should be taken to ensure that there is no conflict between a rule in the notice of race and a rule in the sailing instructions.*

**J1 NOTICE OF RACE CONTENTS**

**J1.1** The notice of race shall include the following information:

(1) the title, place and dates of the race and name of the organizing authority;

(2) that the race will be governed by the *rules* as defined in *The Racing Rules of Sailing*;

(3) a list of any other documents that will govern the event (for example, *The Equipment Rules of Sailing*, to the extent that they apply), stating where or how each document or a copy of it may be seen;

(4) the classes to race, any handicap or rating system that will be used and the classes to which it will apply, conditions of entry and any restrictions on entries;

(5) the times of registration and warning signals for the practice race, if one is scheduled, and the first race, and succeeding races if known.

**J1.2** The notice of race shall include any of the following that will apply and that would help competitors decide whether to attend the event or that conveys other information they will need before the sailing instructions become available:

(1) changes to the racing rules permitted by rule 86, referring specifically to each rule and stating the change (also, if rule 86.2 applies, include the statement from World Sailing authorizing the change);

(2) that boats will be required to display advertising chosen and supplied by the organizing authority (see rule 80 and World

# 附录J 竞赛通知和航行细则

*参见规则89.2和90.2。本附录中，术语“竞赛”包括一场赛事或其他的系列赛。*

*应仔细确保竞赛通知和航行细则中的规则没有冲突。*

## J1 竞赛通知的内容

**J1.1 竞赛通知应包括以下信息：**

（1）比赛的名称、地点和时间，以及组织机构的名称；

（2）比赛应执行《*帆船竞赛规则*》所定义的*规则*；

（3）该赛事中执行的其他文件的清单（比如《*帆船器材规则*》，它们所适用的范围），指明哪里可以得到或怎样可以看到每个文件或复印件；

（4）比赛的级别、使用的让分系数或分级方法及其所适用的级别，以及报名条件和报名的限制；

（5）报到注册时间、练习赛（如果已安排）和第一轮比赛以及随后比赛的预告信号时间（如果已知）。

J1.2 竞赛通知应包括适用的和可以帮助选手决定是否参赛或在拿到航行细则前选手所需要的其他信息，包括：

（1）规则86允许更改的竞赛规则，具体是哪一条规则和注明更改的内容（并且，当规则86.2适用时，包括世界帆联授权此更改的声明）；

（2）组织机构要求参赛船展示其挑选和提供的广告（参见规则80以及世界帆联规章20，即广告守则）和与规章20相关的其他信息；

Sailing Regulation 20, Advertising Code) and other information related to Regulation 20;

(3) any classification requirements that some or all competitors must satisfy (see rule 79 and World Sailing Regulation 22, Sailor Classification Code);

(4) for an event where entries from other countries are expected, any national prescriptions that may require advance preparation (see rule 88);

(5) the procedures for registration or entry, including fees and any closing dates;

(6) an entry form, to be signed by the boat's owner or owner's representative, containing words such as 'I agree to be bound by *The Racing Rules of Sailing* and by all other *rules* that govern this event.';

(7) times or procedures for equipment inspection or event measurement, or requirements for measurement or rating certificates;

(8) the time and place at which the sailing instructions will be available;

(9) changes to class rules, as permitted under rule 87, referring specifically to each rule and stating the change;

(10) the courses to be sailed;

(11) the time after which no warning signal will be made on the last scheduled day of racing;

(12) the penalty for breaking a rule of Part 2, other than the Two-Turns Penalty;

(13) denial of the right of appeal, subject to rule 70.5;

(14) the scoring system, if different from the Low Point System in Appendix A, included by reference to class rules or other *rules* governing the event. State the number of races scheduled and the minimum number that must be completed to constitute a series;

(15) for chartered or loaned boats, whether rule G3 applies;

(16) prizes.

**J2 SAILING INSTRUCTION CONTENTS**

**J2.1** The sailing instructions shall include the following information:

(1) that the race will be governed by the *rules* as defined in *The Racing Rules of Sailing*;

（3）部分或全体选手必须满足的分级要求（参见规则79和世界帆联规章22，即选手分级法规）；

（4）对于一个有其他国家报名的赛事，应提前准备所有的国家机构的规定（参见规则88）；

（5）报到或报名的程序，包括费用以及截止日期；

（6）由船东或船东代表签字的报名表，包括类似“我同意遵守*《帆船竞赛规则》*和其他所有该赛事执行的*规则*”这样的词句；

（7）器材检查或赛事丈量的时间或程序，或者对丈量证书或分级证书的要求；

（8）可以获取航行细则的时间和地点；

（9）按规则87的要求对级别规则做出的更改，应具体到每一条规则并注明更改部分；

（10）比赛的航线；

（11）在最后一个计划比赛日不再发出预告信号的时间；

（12）当不采用两圈解脱时，违反规则第二章的惩罚办法；

（13）依据规则70.5对上诉权的否决；

（14）如不同于附录A的低分记分法，说明记分方法，包括参考级别规则或其他在该赛事中执行的*规则*。说明计划安排的轮数以及构成系列赛所需完成的最少轮数；

（15）是否可以租船或者借船，规则G3是否适用；

（16）奖励。

## J2　航行细则的内容

J2.1　航行细则应包括以下内容：

（1）比赛应执行*《帆船竞赛规则》*所定义的*规则*；

(2) a list of any other documents that will govern the event (for example, *The Equipment Rules of Sailing*, to the extent that they apply);

(3) the schedule of races, the classes to race and times of warning signals for each class;

(4) the course(s) to be sailed, or a list of *marks* from which the course will be selected and, if relevant, how courses will be signalled;

(5) descriptions of *marks*, including starting and finishing *marks*, stating the order in which *marks* are to be passed and the side on which each is to be left and identifying all rounding *marks* (see rule 28.2);

(6) descriptions of the starting and finishing lines, class flags and any special signals to be used;

(7) the time limit, if any, for *finishing*;

(8) the handicap or rating system to be used, if any, and the classes to which it will apply;

(9) unless stated in the notice of race, the scoring system, if different from the Low Point System in Appendix A, included by reference to class rules or other *rules* governing the event, or stated in full. State the number of races scheduled and the minimum number that must be completed to constitute a series;

(10) unless stated in the notice of race, location(s) of official notice board(s) or address of online notice board.

**J2.2** The sailing instructions shall include those of the following that will apply:

(1) that boats will be required to display advertising chosen and supplied by the organizing authority (see rule 80 and World Sailing Regulation 20, Advertising Code) and other information related to Regulation 20;

(2) replacement of the rules of Part 2 with the right-of-way rules of the *International Regulations for Preventing Collisions at Sea* or other government right-of-way rules, the time(s) or place(s) they will apply, and any night signals to be used by the race committee;

（2）该赛事中执行的其他文件的清单（比如《*帆船器材规则*》，它们所适用的范围）；

（3）比赛日程、比赛级别和每个级别预告信号发出的时间；

（4）比赛的航线或所选航线的*标志*详单，以及相应的航线是如何用信号通知的；

（5）*标志*的描述，包括起航和终点*标志*，说明绕行*标志*的顺序和离开每个*标志*的一侧以及注明所有要绕行的*标志*（参见规则28.2）；

（6）起航线和终点线、级别旗以及任何将会使用的特殊信号的描述；

（7）如果有，*到达终点*的时限；

（8）如果有，将会使用的让分系数或分级方法及其所适用的级别；

（9）除非竞赛通知另有规定不同于附录A的低分记分法的记分方法，包括参照级别规则或赛事执行的其他*规则*，或全文的说明。说明计划安排的轮数以及构成系列赛所需完成的最少轮数；

（10）除非竞赛通知已有陈述，否则要有官方公告栏的地点或者在线公告栏的地址。

J2.2 航行细则应包括下列适用的内容：

（1）组织机构要求参赛船展示其挑选和提供的广告（参见规则80以及世界帆联规章20，即广告守则）和与规章20相关的其他信息；

（2）以《*国际海上避碰规则*》的航行权规则或其他政府航行权规则来替换第二章的规则，它们适用的时间或地点以及竞赛委员会使用的所有夜间信号；

(3) changes to the racing rules permitted by rule 86, referring specifically to each rule and stating the change (also, if rule 86.2 applies, include the statement from World Sailing authorizing the change);

(4) changes to the national prescriptions (see rule 88.2);

(5) prescriptions that will apply if boats will pass through the waters of more than one national authority while *racing*, and when they will apply (see rule 88.1);

(6) when appropriate, at an event where entries from other countries are expected, a copy in English of the national prescriptions that will apply;

(7) changes to class rules, as permitted under rule 87, referring specifically to each rule and stating the change;

(8) restrictions controlling changes to boats when supplied by the organizing authority;

(9) unless included in the notice of race, times or procedures for equipment inspection or event measurement;

(10) procedure for changing the sailing instructions;

(11) procedure for giving oral changes to the sailing instructions on the water (see rule 90.2(c));

(12) safety requirements, such as requirements and signals for personal flotation devices, check-in at the starting area, and check-out and check-in ashore;

(13) declaration requirements;

(14) signals to be made ashore and location of signal station(s);

(15) the racing area (a chart is recommended);

(16) approximate course length and approximate length of windward legs;

(17) description of any area designated by the race committee to be an *obstruction* (see the definition *Obstruction*);

(18) the time after which no warning signal will be made on the last scheduled day of racing;

(19) the time limit, if any, for the first boat to *finish* and the time limit, if any, for boats other than the first boat to *finish*;

（3）规则86允许的对竞赛规则的更改，特别指明更改了哪条规则及更改内容（并且，当规则86.2适用时，包括世界帆联授权此更改的声明）；

（4）对国家管理机构规定的更改（参见规则88.2）；

（5）竞赛中，如果船行驶过的水域不止由一个国家管理机构管辖，相应适用的国家规定以及适用的时间（参见规则88.1）；

（6）若适当，在一个其他国家可以报名的赛事中，所适用的国家规定的英文版的复印件；

（7）按规则87的要求对级别规则的更改，具体到每一条规则并注明更改部分；

（8）当由组织机构提供船时，限制对船只改动的条款；

（9）除非包含在竞赛通知内，否则要有器材检查或赛事丈量的时间和程序；

（10）航行细则更改的程序；

（11）水上给予航行细则口头更改的程序［参见规则90.2(c)］；

（12）安全要求，比如对个人漂浮设备的要求和信号，起航区的检录及岸上的上下水签到；

（13）声明要求；

（14）岸上信号和信号台的位置；

（15）竞赛区域（建议用海图形式呈现）；

（16）航线大致长度和迎风航段的大致长度；

（17）描述竞赛委员会指明的所有*障碍物*的区域（参见*障碍物*定义）；

（18）在最后一个计划比赛日不再发出预告信号的时间；

（19）如果有，第一条船*到达终点*的时限和除了第一条船之外其他船*到达终点*的时限；

(20) time allowances;

(21) location of the starting area and any restrictions on entering it;

(22) any special procedures or signals for individual or general recall;

(23) boats identifying *mark* locations;

(24) any special procedures or signals for changing a leg of the course (see rule 33);

(25) any special procedures for shortening the course or for *finishing* a shortened course;

(26) restrictions on use of support boats, plastic pools, radios, etc.; on trash disposal; on hauling out; and on outside assistance provided to a boat that is not *racing*;

(27) the penalty for breaking a rule of Part 2, other than the Two-Turns Penalty;

(28) whether Appendix P will apply;

(29) when and under what circumstances propulsion is permitted under rule 42.3(i);

(30) time limits, place of hearings, and special procedures for *protests*, requests for redress or requests for reopening;

(31) if rule N1.4(b) will apply, the time limit for requesting a hearing under that rule;

(32) denial of the right of appeal, subject to rule 70.5;

(33) when required by rule 70.3, the national authority to which appeals and requests may be sent;

(34) the national authority's approval of the appointment of an international jury, when required under rule 91(b);

(35) substitution of competitors;

(36) the minimum number of boats appearing in the starting area required for a race to be started;

(37) when and where races *postponed* or *abandoned* for the day will be sailed;

(38) tides and currents;

(39) prizes;

(40) other commitments of the race committee and obligations of boats.

（20）时间宽限；

（21）起航区的位置和进入其中的限制；

（22）任何单召或全召的特殊程序或信号；

（23）展示*标志*位置的船只；

（24）改变航线中某一航段的任何特殊程序或信号（参见规则33）；

（25）任何缩短航线或在缩短航线时*到达终点*的特殊程序；

（26）使用辅助船、塑料池、无线电等的限制；垃圾处理的限制；拖船上岸的限制；对不在*竞赛*中的船提供外部援助的限制；

（27）当不采用两圈解脱时，违反规则第二章的惩罚办法；

（28）附录P是否适用；

（29）何时以及在何种条件下可以根据规则42.3(i)做推进动作；

（30）抗议时限、审理地点以及*抗议*、要求补偿或要求重审的特殊程序；

（31）如果规则N1.4(b)适用，在此规则下要求审理的时限；

（32）受规则70.5 制约的对于上诉权的否决；

（33）根据规则70.3的要求，上诉和请求应递交到国家管理机构；

（34）根据规则91(b)，需要国家管理机构对国际仲裁的任命的批准；

（35）选手的替换；

（36）竞赛起航所需的在起航区出现的最少船数；

（37）当天*推迟*或*放弃*的比赛何时何地再次起航；

（38）潮汐和水流；

（39）奖励；

（40）竞赛委员会的其他义务和船的责任。

# **APPENDIX K** NOTICE OF RACE GUIDE

*This guide provides a notice of race designed primarily for major championship regattas for one or more classes. It therefore will be particularly useful for world, continental and national championships and other events of similar importance. It can be downloaded from the World Sailing website as a basic text for producing a notice of race for any particular event.*

*The guide can also be useful for other events. However, for such events some of the paragraphs will be unnecessary or undesirable. Organizing authorities should therefore be careful in making their choices.*

*This guide relates closely to Appendix L, Sailing Instructions Guide, and its expanded version Appendix LE on the World Sailing website, the introduction to which contains principles that also apply to a notice of race.*

*Rule references within the notice of race use RRS, NoR and SI to denote the source of the rule. 'RRS x' is a rule in* The Racing Rules of Sailing. *'NoR x' is a rule in the notice of race, and 'SI x' is a rule in the sailing instructions.*

*To use this guide, first review rule J1 and decide which paragraphs will be needed. Paragraphs that are required by rule J1.1 are marked with an asterisk (*). Delete all inapplicable or unnecessary paragraphs. Select the version preferred where there is a choice. Follow the directions in the left margin to fill in the spaces where a solid line (____ ) appears and select the preferred wording if a choice or option is shown in brackets* ([ . . . ]).

*After deleting unused paragraphs, renumber all paragraphs in sequential order. Be sure that paragraph numbers are correct where one paragraph refers to another.*

*Care should be taken to ensure that there is no conflict between a rule in the notice of race and a rule in the sailing instructions.*

*If the notice of race is made available electronically, printed copies should be provided on request.*

# 附录K　竞赛通知指南

*本指南提供了特别为单个或多个级别参赛的大多数锦标赛设计的竞赛通知。因此，它特别适合用于世界的、洲际的和国家的锦标赛以及其他同等重要的赛事。本指南可从世界帆联网站下载，可以作为任何赛事竞赛通知的模版。*

*本指南对其他赛事也适用。但是，对于这些赛事，有些段落可能是不必要或不需要的。因此，组委会在选择时应仔细考虑。*

*本指南与附录L、航行细则指南及其扩展版附录LE（见世界帆联网站）的关系紧密，对它的介绍也包括同样适用于竞赛通知的准则。*

*竞赛通知内的规则参考是通过RRS、NoR和SI来显示规则的出处。“RRSx”是帆船竞赛规则中的规则。“NoRx”是竞赛通知中的规则，“SIx”是航行细则中的规则。*

*使用本指南，首先回顾规则J1，决定需要哪些段落。规则J1.1要求的段落用星号（*）标出。删除所有不适用或不需要的段落。在有可选项的地方选择最合适的版本。按照左边的指示在有实线（______）的地方填入内容，在有大括号（[ ... ]）出现的地方选择更合适的词。*

*删掉不用的段落后，重新按顺序编码段落。当在一个段落中说明参照另一段落时，确保段落号码正确。*

*确保竞赛通知和航行细则中的规则没有冲突。*

*如果有电子版的竞赛通知，在有要求的情况下可提供纸质版。*

*The items listed below, when applicable, should be distributed with the notice of race, but should not be included as numbered paragraphs in the notice.*

1 *An entry form, to be signed by the boat's owner or owner's representative, containing words such as 'I agree to be bound by* The Racing Rules of Sailing *and by all other rules that govern this event.'*

2 *For an event where entries from other countries are expected, the applicable national prescriptions in English.*

3 *List of sponsors, if appropriate.*

4 *Lodging and camping information.*

5 *Description of meal facilities.*

6 *Race committee and protest committee members.*

7 *Special mooring or storage requirements.*

8 *Sail and boat repair facilities and ship's chandlers.*

9 *Availability of chartered or loaned boats and whether rule G3 will apply.*

*On separate lines, insert the full name of the regatta, the inclusive dates from equipment inspection, event measurement or the practice race until the final race or closing ceremony, the name of the organizing authority, and the city and country.*

______________________________

______________________________

______________________________

______________________________

## NOTICE OF RACE

*The notation '[DP]' in a rule in the NoR means that the penalty for a breach of that rule may, at the discretion of the protest committee, be less than disqualification.*

**1 RULES**

**1.1 *** The regatta will be governed by the rules as defined in *The Racing Rules of Sailing*.

*以下各项，如果适用，应当同竞赛通知一起公告，但是不得包括在竞赛通知的编号条款中。*

*1. 船东或船东代表签字的报名表，包括类似"我同意遵守《帆船竞赛规则》和其他所有该赛事执行的规则"这样的词句。*

*2. 在一个接受其他国家报名的赛事中，适用的国家规定的英文版。*

*3. 如果合适，列出赞助商的名单。*

*4. 住宿信息。*

*5. 餐饮设施说明。*

*6. 竞赛委员会和抗议委员会成员。*

*7. 特殊停泊或储藏要求。*

*8. 帆和船的维修设施和帆船配件零售商。*

*9. 是否可以租船或者借船，规则G3是否生效。*

*分行填入赛事全称，从器材检查、赛事丈量或练习赛到最后一轮竞赛或闭幕式的日期，组织机构的名称，城市和国家。*

______________________________

______________________________

______________________________

______________________________

______________________________

______________________________

**竞赛通知**

*竞赛通知规则中的标记［DP］意为在经过抗议委员会慎重考虑后，违反某条规则的惩罚可以是轻于取消资格。*

**1　规则**

1.1*　赛事将执行《帆船竞赛规则》所定义的规则。

| | | |
|---|---|---|
| *Use the first sentence if appropriate. Insert the name. List by number and title the prescriptions that will not apply (see RRS 88). Use the second sentence if it applies and if entries from other countries are expected, and state the relevant prescriptions in full.* | **1.2** | [The following prescriptions of the national authority will not apply:___ .] [The prescriptions that may require advance preparation are stated in full below.] |
| | **(OR)** | |
| *Use if appropriate, but only if the national authority for the venue of the event has not adopted a prescription to RRS 88.* | **1.2** | No national prescriptions will apply. |
| *List by name any other documents that govern the event; for example,* The Equipment Rules of Sailing, *to the extent that they apply.* | **1.3*** | ______will apply. |
| *See RRS 86. Insert the rule number(s) and summarize the changes.* | **1.4** | Racing rule(s) will be changed as follows: ____ . The changes will appear in full in the sailing instructions. The sailing instructions may also change other racing rules. |
| | **(OR)** | |
| *See RRS 86. Either insert here the rule number(s) and state the changes, or, if not using this NoR, do the same in each NoR that* | **1.4** | Racing rule(s)______will be changed as follows:______. |

| | |
|---|---|
| *如果合适可以使用第一句话。填入名称。根据号码和名称列出不适用的规定（参见规则88）。如果适用可以使用第二句话，且若接受其他国家报名，则列出相关规定的全文。* | 1.2 ［___国家管理机构的下列规定_____不适用。］［可能要求提前准备的规定全文如下。］ |
| | **（或者）** |
| *只有比赛举办场馆所在地的国家管理机构没有采用规则 88的规定时才可以适当使用。* | 1.2 国家管理机构的规定不适用。 |
| *列出该赛事执行的其他文件名称，例如：《帆船器材规则》及其适用范围。* | 1.3*________适用。 |
| *参见规则86。填入更改的规则编号并概述。* | 1.4 规则______更改如下：_______。更改的全文将体现在航行细则中，航行细则也可能更改其他竞赛规则。 |
| | **（或者）** |
| *参见规则86。在这里填入规则编号并说明更改，或者，若不使用本竞赛通知时，要在每一个竞赛通知中做同样的更改竞赛规则的说明。* | 1.4 规则_______更改如下：_____。 |

*changes a racing rule.*

*Insert the rule number(s) and class name. Make a separate statement for the*

**1.5** Under RRS 87, rule(s) _______ of the class rules [will not apply] [is (are) changed as follows: ].

**1.6** If there is a conflict between languages the English text will take precedence.

*Use only if RRS Appendix S, Standard Sailing Instructions, will be used.*

*Insert the location.*

**1.7** The sailing instructions will consist of the instructions in RRS Appendix S, Standard Sailing Instructions, and supplementary sailing instructions that will be on the official notice board located at .

**2 ADVERTISING**

*See World Sailing Regulation 20, Advertising Code. Include other applicable information related to Regulation 20.*

**2.1** Competitor advertising will be restricted as follows:_______.

*See World Sailing Regulation 20.4.*

**2.2** Boats [shall] [may be required to] display advertising chosen and supplied by the organizing authority. If this rule is broken, World Sailing Regulation 20.9.2 applies. [DP]

**3* ELIGIBILITY AND ENTRY**

*Insert the class(es).*

**3.1** The regatta is open to all boats of the ______class(es).

**(OR)**

*Insert the class(es) and eligibility requirements.*

**3.1** The regatta is open to boats of the ______ class(es) that _____.

*Insert the postal, fax and email addresses and entry closing date.*

**3.2** Eligible boats may enter by completing the attached form and sending it, together with the required fee, to _____ by______.

*填入规则号码和级别名称。分别说明每个级别的规则。*

1.5 根据规则87，________级别规则的规则____________［不适用］［更改如下：______］。

1.6 若有因规则语言版本引起的争议，以英文版内容为准。

*仅在使用RRS附录S，即标准航行细则时使用此条。*
*填入地址。*

1.7 航行细则包括RRS中附录S，标准航行细则中的细则，航行细则的补充将张贴在位于____的官方公告栏上。

## 2 广告

*参见世界帆联规章20，即广告守则。包括其他与规章20相关的适用信息。*

2.1 选手的广告将受到如下限制_______。

*参见世界帆联规章20.4。*

2.2 参赛船［将会］［可能会］被要求展示由组织机构选择并提供的广告。若违反本规则，世界帆联规章20.9.2适用。［DP］

## 3* 参赛资格与报名

*填入级别名称。*

3.1 ______级别的船可报名参加本赛事。

（或者）

*填入级别名称和资格要求。*

3.1 符合____要求的____级别的船可报名参加本赛事。

*填入邮寄地址、传真或电邮地址及报名截止日期。*

3.2 符合报名资格的船可填写附件报名表，并与要求的费用一起于_____前寄达______。

*Insert any conditions.*

**3.3** Late entries will be accepted under the following conditions:______.

*Insert any restrictions.*

**3.4** The following restrictions on the number of boats apply:______.

**4 CLASSIFICATION**

*Insert any requirements.*

The following classification requirements will apply (see RRS 79):______.

**5 FEES**

*Insert all required fees for racing.*

**5.1** Required fees are as follows:

| *Class* | *Fee* |
|---|---|
| ______ | ______ |
| ______ | ______ |
| ______ | ______ |

*Insert optional fees (for example, for social events).*

**5.2** Other fees:

______

______

**6 QUALIFYING SERIES AND FINAL SERIES**

*Use only when a class is divided into fleets racing a qualifying series and a final series.*

The regatta will consist of a qualifying series and a final series.

7 **SCHEDULE**

**7.1*** Registration:

*Insert the day, date and times.*

Day and date ______

From ______ To ______

**7.2** Equipment inspection and event measurement:

*Insert the day, date and times.*

Day and date ______

From______ To ______

| | |
|---|---|
| *填入条件。* | 3.3 符合下列条件的情况，可接受逾期报名。 |
| *填入条件。* | 3.4 适用以下参赛船数的限制：________。 |
| | **4 分级** |
| *填入要求。* | 适用下列分级要求（参见规则79）：________。 |
| | **5 费用** |
| *填入参赛所需的所有费用。* | 5.1 所需费用如下：<br>级别 费用<br>____ ____<br>____ ____<br>____ ____ |
| *填入可选费用（如社交活动费用）* | 5.2 其他费用<br>____________<br>____________ |
| | **6 资格系列赛和决赛** |
| *只有某一级别分组进行资格系列赛和决赛时，才使用本条规则。* | 本赛事包括资格系列赛和决赛。 |
| | **7 日程安排** |
| | 7.1* 报到 |
| *填入星期几、日期和时间。* | 日期：______（星期___）<br>时间：______到______ |
| | 7.2 器材检查和赛事丈量 |
| *填入星期几、日期和时间。* | 日期：______（星期___）<br>时间：______到______ |

*Revise as desired and insert the dates and classes. Include a practice race if any. When the series consists of qualifying races and final races, specify them. The schedule can also be given in an attachment.*

**7.3*** Dates of racing:

| *Date* | *Class* _____ | *Class* _____ |
|---|---|---|
| _____ | racing | racing |
| _____ | racing | reserve day |
| _____ | reserve day | racing |
| _____ | racing | racing |
| _____ | racing | racing |

*Insert the classes and numbers.*

**7.4** Number of races:

| *Class* | *Number* | *Races per day* |
|---|---|---|
| _____ | _____ | _____ |
| _____ | _____ | _____ |

*Insert the time.*

**7.5*** The scheduled time of the warning signal for the [practice race] [first race] [each day] is_____.

*Use when it would be helpful to competitors to know this time before the event. Insert the time.*

**7.6** On the last scheduled day of racing no warning signal will be made after_____.

**8 MEASUREMENT**

**8.1** Each boat shall produce a valid [measurement] [rating] certificate.

**(OR)**

*List the equipment with appropriate references to the class rules.*

**8.1** Each boat shall produce a valid [measurement] [rating] certificate. In addition the following equipment [may] [will] be inspected or measured: .

*Insert the time(s).*

**8.2** A boat shall comply with RRS 78.1 at ____.

*Insert the time, date and location.*

**9 SAILING INSTRUCTIONS**

The sailing instructions will be available after _____on______at_____.

*可按需求更改，填入日期和级别。包括练习赛（如果有）。当系列赛包含资格赛和决赛时，要具体说明。竞赛日程也可作为附件给出。*

7.3*竞赛日程

| *时间* | *级别____* | *级别____* |
| --- | --- | --- |
| ____ | 竞赛日 | 竞赛日 |
| ____ | 竞赛日 | 机动日 |
| ____ | 机动日 | 竞赛日 |
| ____ | 竞赛日 | 竞赛日 |
| ____ | 竞赛日 | 竞赛日 |

*填入级别和数字。*

7.4 竞赛轮次

| *级别* | *轮次* | *每日轮次* |
| --- | --- | --- |
| ____ | ____ | ________ |
| ____ | ____ | ________ |

*填入时间。*

7.5*［练习赛］［第一轮竞赛］［每个竞赛日］的预告信号的计划时间为____。

*使用此条有助于选手在赛前了解该时间。填入时间。*

7.6 最后一个竞赛日_____后不再发出预告信号。

## 8 丈量

8.1 每条船应出具有效的［丈量］［分级］证书。

**（或者）**

*适当参考级别规则列出器材。*

8.1 每条船应出具有效的［丈量］［分级］证书。此外，［可能］［将会］检查或丈量以下器材：_____。

*填入时间。*

8.2 船在_____期间应遵守规则78.1。

## 9 航行细则

*填入日期、时间和地点。*

航行细则将于_____（日期）_____（时间）后在_____（地点）公布。

## 10 VENUE

*Insert a number or letter. Provide a marked map with driving instructions.*

**10.1** Attachment______shows the location of the regatta harbour.

*Insert a number or letter. Provide a marked map or chart.*

**10.2** Attachment______shows the location of the racing areas.

## 11 THE COURSES

*Include the description.*

The courses to be sailed will be as follows: _____.

**(OR)**

*Insert a number or letter. A method of illustrating various courses is shown in Addendum A of Appendix L or LE. Insert the course length if applicable.*

The diagrams in Attachment ____ show the courses, including the approximate angles between legs, the order in which marks are to be passed, and the side on which each mark is to be left. [The approximate course length will be_.]

## 12 PENALTY SYSTEM

*Include paragraph 12.1 only when the Two-Turns Penalty will not be used. Insert the number of places or describe the penalties.*

**12.1** The Scoring Penalty, RRS 44.3, will apply. The penalty will be______places.

**(OR)**

**12.1** The penalties are as follows:______.

*Insert the class(es).*

**12.2** For the _____class(es) RRS 44.1 is changed so that the Two-Turns Penalty is replaced by the One-Turn Penalty.

*Include only if the protest committee is an international jury or another provision of RRS 70.5 applies.*

**12.3** Decisions of the [protest committee] [international jury] will be final as provided in RRS 70.5.

## 10 场地

*填入数字或字母。提供带标注的地图并写明行车路线。*

10.1 附件____为赛事港口位置示意图。

*填入数字或字母。提供带标注的地图或海图。*

10.2 附件____为竞赛区域示意图。

## 11 航线

*填入描述。*

竞赛的航线如下：_________。

**（或者）**

*填入数字或字母。附录L或LE的附件A中有说明不同航线的方法。如果适用，填入航线长度。*

附件_____为航线示意图，包括航段间的大致角度、绕标的顺序以及要求离开标志的一侧。［航线大致长度为________。］

## 12 惩罚方法

*只有不使用两圈解脱时，才使用12.1这一段落。填入名次相应数字或描述惩罚内容。*

12.1 适用规则44.3，分数惩罚。惩罚为___名次。

（或者）

12.1 惩罚如下：_______。

*填入级别名称。*

12.2 对于___级别，规则44.1两圈解脱更改为一圈解脱。

*只有当抗议委员会是国际仲裁委员会或规则70.5的另一条款适用时才使用此条规则。*

12.3 根据规则70.5，［抗议委员会］［国际仲裁委员会］的裁决为最终裁决。

## 13 SCORING

*Include only if the Low Point System of Appendix A will not be used. Describe the system.*

**13.1** The scoring system is as follows:______.

*Insert the number.*

**13.2** ______races are required to be completed to constitute a series.

*Insert the numbers throughout.*

**13.3** (a) When fewer than____ races have been completed, a boat's series score will be the total of her race scores.

(b) When from ______ to ______ races have been completed, a boat's series score will be the total of her race scores excluding her worst score.

(c) When or more races have been completed, a boat's series score will be the total of her race scores excluding her two worst scores.

## 14 SUPPORT BOATS

*Insert the identification markings. National letters are suggested for international events.*

Support boats shall be marked with__. [DP]

## 15 BERTHING

Boats shall be kept in their assigned places while they are in the [boat park] [harbour]. [DP]

## 16 HAUL-OUT RESTRICTIONS

Keelboats shall not be hauled out during the regatta except with and according to the terms of prior written permission of the race committee. [DP]

## 13 记分

*只有不使用附录A的低分计分法时才使用此条规则。描述记分方法。*

13.1记分方法如下：__________。

*填入数字。*

13.2完成___轮竞赛后方能构成系列赛。

*依次填入数字。*

13.3（a）当完成竞赛的轮数少于___时，一条船的系列赛得分为所有轮次得分的总和。

（b）当完成__轮到__轮竞赛时，一条船的系列赛得分为去掉最差一轮成绩的其他所有轮次得分的总和。

（c）当完成__轮或更多轮次竞赛时，一条船的系列赛得分为去掉最差两轮成绩的其他所有轮次得分的总和。

## 14 辅助船

*填入识别标记。在国际赛事中建议使用国家字母代码。*

辅助船应带有_____标志。［DP］

## 15 泊船

船应停放在［陆域停船区］［港池］的指定区域。［DP］

## 16 拖船上岸的限制

除非有竞赛委员会的事先书面许可，否则龙骨船不得在赛事过程中拖到岸上。［DP］

## 17 DIVING EQUIPMENT AND PLASTIC POOLS

Underwater breathing apparatus and plastic pools or their equivalent shall not be used around keelboats between the preparatory signal of the first race and the end of the regatta. [DP]

## 18 RADIO COMMUNICATION

*Insert any alternative text that applies. Describe any radio communication bands or frequencies that will be used or allowed.*

Except in an emergency, a boat that is racing shall not make voice or data transmissions and shall not receive voice or data communication that is not available to all boats. [DP]

## 19 PRIZES

*If perpetual trophies will be awarded state their complete names.*

Prizes will be given as follows:______.

## 20 DISCLAIMER OF LIABILITY

*The laws applicable to the venue in which the event is held may limit disclaimers. Any disclaimer should be drafted to comply with those laws.*

Competitors participate in the regatta entirely at their own risk. See RRS 4, Decision to Race. The organizing authority will not accept any liability for material damage or personal injury or death sustained in conjunction with or prior to, during, or after the regatta.

## 21 INSURANCE

*Insert the currency and amount.*

Each participating boat shall be insured with valid third-party liability insurance with a minimum cover of _____ per incident or the equivalent.

## 22 FURTHER INFORMATION

*Insert necessary contact information.*

For further information please contact _____.

## 17 潜水装备和塑料池

在第一轮准备信号和全部竞赛结束之间，不得在龙骨船周围使用水下呼吸设备、塑料池或类似装置。［DP］

## 18 无线电通讯

*填入任何适用的替代文本。对适用或允许无线电通讯波段或频率做出描述。*

除紧急情况外，参赛船在竞赛时不得发出语音或传输数据，不能接收不针对所有船的语音或数据传输。［DP］

## 19 奖励

*若将颁发永久性奖杯，注明其全称。*

奖励如下：______。

## 20 免责声明

*适用于举行该赛事的场馆所在地的法律可能会限制声明。所有声明应依据这些法律起草。*

参加本赛事的选手完全自担风险。参见规则4，参赛决定。组织机构对赛前、赛中和赛后发生的或与之相关的所有物质损失、人员伤亡不承担任何责任。

## 21 保险

*填入货币种类和数目。*

每条参赛船必须具备有效的第三方责任险，每场赛事的最低保额为____或等价金额。

## 22 更多信息

*填入必要的联系信息。*

若需要更多信息，请联系______。

# APPENDIX L SAILING INSTRUCTIONS GUIDE

*This guide provides a set of tested sailing instructions designed primarily for major championship regattas for one or more classes. It therefore will be particularly useful for world, continental and national championships and other events of similar importance. The guide can also be useful for other events; however, for such events some of these instructions will be unnecessary or undesirable. Race officers should therefore be careful in making their choices.*

*An expanded version of the guide, Appendix LE, is available on the World Sailing website. It contains provisions applicable to the largest and most complicated multi-class events, as well as variations on several of the sailing instructions recommended in this appendix. It will be revised from time to time, to reflect advances in race management techniques as they develop, and can be downloaded as a basic text for producing the sailing instructions for any particular event. Appendix L can also be downloaded from the World Sailing website.*

*The principles on which all sailing instructions should be based are as follows:*

1 *They should include only two types of statement: the intentions of the race committee and protest committee and the obligations of competitors.*

2 *They should be concerned only with racing. Information about social events, assignment of moorings, etc., should be provided separately.*

3 *They should not change the racing rules except when clearly desirable. (When they do so, they must follow rule 86 by referring specifically to the rule being changed and stating the change.)*

4 *They should not repeat or restate any of the racing rules.*

5 *They should not repeat themselves.*

6 *They should be in chronological order; that is, the order in which the competitor will use them.*

7 *They should, when possible, use words or phrases from the racing rules.*

# 附录L　航行细则指南

*本指南提供了特别为单个或多个级别参赛的大多数锦标赛设计的一整套经过测试的航行细则。因此，它特别适合用于世界的、洲际的和国家的锦标赛以及其他同等重要的赛事。该指南对其他赛事也适用。但是，对于这些赛事，有些细则可能是不必要或不需要的。因此，竞赛官在选择时应仔细考虑。*

*本指南的扩展版本，附录LE可以在世界帆联网站上查阅。它包括了适用于最大型、最复杂的多级别赛事的细则，以及本附录建议使用的一些细则的变体。该版本将实时修订，以反映竞赛管理技术在发展中的进步，可以将其从网站上下载下来作为制定某一具体赛事航行细则的基础文本。附录L也可以从世界帆联网站上下载。*

*所有航行细则应遵循的原则如下：*

1. *应只包括两类表述：竞赛委员会和抗议委员会的意图以及选手的义务。*
2. *应只涉及竞赛。有关社会活动、停泊安排等的信息应另行提供。*
3. *除非有明确需求，否则不应更改竞赛规则。（当确实需要更改时，必须根据规则86，指明需更改的规则并说明做出的具体更改。）*
4. *不应重复或赘述任何竞赛规则。*
5. *不应重复本身已有的内容。*
6. *应按时间顺序排列，即选手使用细则的顺序。*
7. *如果可行，应使用竞赛规则中的措辞。*

*Rule references within the sailing instructions use RRS, SI and NoR to denote the source of the rule. 'RRS x' is a rule in* The Racing Rules of Sailing. *'SI x' is a rule in the sailing instructions, and 'NoR x' is a rule in the notice of race.*

*To use this guide, first review rule J2 and decide which instructions will be needed. Instructions that are required by rule J2.1 are marked with an asterisk (*). Delete all inapplicable or unnecessary instructions. Select the version preferred where there is a choice. Follow the directions in the left margin to fill in the spaces where a solid line (____ ) appears and select the preferred wording if a choice or option is shown in brackets* ([ . . . ]).

*After deleting unused instructions, renumber all instructions in sequential order. Be sure that instruction numbers are correct where one instruction refers to another.*

*Care should be taken to ensure that there is no conflict between a rule in the notice of race and a rule in the sailing instructions.*

*If the sailing instructions are made available electronically, printed copies should be provided on request.*

*On separate lines, insert the full name of the regatta, the inclusive dates from equipment inspection, event measurement or the practice race until the final race or closing ceremony, the name of the organizing authority, and the city and country.*

______________________________

______________________________

______________________________

______________________________

## SAILING INSTRUCTIONS

*The notation '[DP]' in a rule in the SI means that the penalty for a breach of that rule may, at the discretion of the protest committee, be less than disqualification.*

**1 RULES**

**1.1*** The regatta will be governed by the rules as defined in *The Racing Rules of Sailing*.

*航行细则内的规则参考是通过RRS、NoR和SI来显示规则的出处。"RRSx"是《帆船竞赛规则》中的规则。"SIx"是航行细则中的规则，"NoRx"是竞赛通知中的规则。*

*使用本指南，首先回顾规则J2，决定需要哪些细则。规则J2.1要求的细则用星号（*）标出。删除所有不适用或不需要的细则。在有可选项的地方选择最合适的版本。按照左边的指示在有实线（___）的地方填入内容，在有大括号（[ ... ]）出现的地方选择更合适的词。*

*删掉不用的细则后，重新按顺序编码所有细则。当在一个细则中说明参照另一细则时，确保细则号码正确。*

*确保竞赛通知和航行细则中的规则没有冲突。*

*如果有电子版的竞赛通知，在有要求的情况下可提供纸质版。*

*分行填入赛事全称，从器材检查、赛事丈量或练习赛到最后一轮竞赛或闭幕式的日期，组织机构的名称，城市和国家。*

______________________________

______________________________

______________________________

______________________________

______________________________

**航行细则**

*竞赛通知规则中的标记［DP］意为在经过抗议委员会慎重考虑后，违反某条规则的惩罚可以是轻于取消资格。*

**1 规则**

1.1*赛事将执行《帆船竞赛规则》所定义的规则。

| | | |
|---|---|---|
| *Use the first sentence if appropriate. Insert the name. List by number and title the prescriptions that will not apply (see RRS 88.2). Use the second sentence if it applies and if entries from other national authorities are expected, and state the prescriptions in full. Include the prescriptions in English when appropriate (see RRS 90.2(b)).* | **1.2** | [The following prescriptions of the national authority will not apply:___ .] [The prescriptions that will apply are stated in full below.] |
| | **(OR)** | |
| *Use if appropriate, but only if the national authority for the venue of the event has not adopted a prescription to RRS 88.* | **1.2** | No national prescriptions will apply. |
| *List by name any other documents that govern the event; for example,* The Equipment Rules of Sailing, *to the extent that they apply.* | **1.3*** | ______will apply. |
| *See RRS 86. Either insert here the rule number(s) and state the changes, or, if not using this instruction, do the same in each instruction that changes a racing rule.* | **1.4** | Racing rule(s)______will be changed as follows:______. |

*如果合适的话，使用第一句话。填入名称。根据号码和名称列出不适用的规定（参见规则88.2）。如果适用使用第二句话，且若接受其他国家报名，则列出相关规定的全文。适当情况下，还应有相关规定的英草药文版［参见规则90.2(b)］。*

1.2 ［____国家管理机构的下列规定________不适用。］［适用的规定全文如下。］

**（或者）**

*只有比赛举办场馆所在地的国家管理机构没有采用规则88的规定时才可以适当使用。*

1.2 国家管理机构的规定不适用。

*列出该赛事执行的其他文件名称，例如：帆《帆船竞赛规则》及其适用范围。*

1.3* ________适用。

*参见规则86。在这里填入规则编号并说明更改，或者，若不使用本细则时，要在每一个细则中做同样的更改竞赛规则的说明。*

1.4 规则_____更改如下：_____。

*Insert the rule number(s) and class name. Make a separate statement for the rules of each class.*

**1.5** Under RRS 87, rule(s)______of the _____ class rules [will not apply] [is (are) changed as follows:_____].

**1.6** If there is a conflict between languages the English text will take precedence.

## 2* NOTICES TO COMPETITORS

*Insert the location(s). If notices are online, state how and where they may be found.*

Notices to competitors will be posted on the official notice board(s) located at ____.

## 3 CHANGES TO SAILING INSTRUCTIONS

*Change the times if different.*

Any change to the sailing instructions will be posted before 0900 on the day it will take effect, except that any change to the schedule of races will be posted by 2000 on the day before it will take effect.

## 4 SIGNALS MADE ASHORE

*Insert the location.*

**4.1** Signals made ashore will be displayed at _____.

*Insert the number of minutes.*

**4.2** When flag AP is displayed ashore, '1 minute' is replaced with 'not less than ——minutes' in the race signal AP.

**(OR)**

*Insert the number of minutes.*

**4.2** Flag D with one sound means 'The warning signal will be made not less than _____minutes after flag D is displayed. [Boats are requested not to leave the harbour until this signal is made.] [Boats shall not leave the harbour until this signal is made. [DP]]'

*填入规则号码和级别名称。分别说明每个级别的规则。*

1.5 根据规则87，___级别规则的规则___［不适用］［更改如下：_____］。

1.6 若有因规则语言版本引起的争议，以英文版内容为准。

**2* 选手通知**

*填入地点。如果是在线通知，说明如何及在哪里可以查询。*

选手通知将张贴在位于___的官方公告栏上。

**3 航行细则更改**

*如果时间不同，更换掉。*

航行细则的任何更改将在生效当天的0900之前公布，此外，对竞赛日程的更改将在其生效的前一天2000之前公布。

**4 岸上信号**

*填入地点。*

4.1 岸上信号将在____展示。

*填入分钟数。*

4.2 当岸上展示AP旗时，有关信号旗AP规则中的“1分钟”替换为“不少于____分钟”。

**（或者）**

*填入分钟数。*

4.2 信号旗D伴随一声音响意为“预告信号将在D旗展示后不少于___分钟发出。［在该信号发出前，参赛船不得离开港池。］［该信号发出前，参赛船不得离开港池。［DP］］”

## 5 SCHEDULE OF RACES

*Revise as desired and insert the dates and classes. Include a practice race if any. When the series consists of qualifying races and final races, specify them. The schedule can also be given in an attachment.*

**5.1 *** Dates of racing:

| *Date* | *Class* ____ | *Class* ____ |
|---|---|---|
| _____ | racing | racing |
| _____ | racing | reserve day |
| _____ | reserve day | racing |
| _____ | racing | racing |
| _____ | racing | racing |

**5.2 *** Number of races:

*Insert the classes and numbers.*

| *Class* | *Number* | *Races per day* |
|---|---|---|
| _____ | _____ | _____ |
| _____ | _____ | _____ |

One extra race per day may be sailed, provided that no class becomes more than one race ahead of schedule and the change is made according to SI 3.

*Insert the time.*

**5.3*** The scheduled time of the warning signal for the first race each day is_____.

**5.4** To alert boats that a race or sequence of races will begin soon, the orange starting line flag will be displayed with one sound at least five minutes before a warning signal is made.

*Insert the time.*

**5.5** On the last scheduled day of racing no warning signal will be made after_____.

## 6* CLASS FLAGS

Class flags will be:

*Insert the classes and names or descriptions of the flags.*

| *Class* | *Flag* |
|---|---|
| _____ | _____ |
| _____ | _____ |
| _____ | _____ |

## 5　竞赛日程安排

| | |
|---|---|
| *可按需求更改，填入日期和级别。包括练习赛（如果有）。当系列赛包含资格赛和决赛时，要具体说明。竞赛日程也可作为附件给出。* | 5.1*竞赛日程 |

| *时间* | *级别____* | *级别____* |
|---|---|---|
| ____ | 竞赛日 | 竞赛日 |
| ____ | 竞赛日 | 机动日 |
| ____ | 机动日 | 竞赛日 |
| ____ | 竞赛日 | 竞赛日 |
| ____ | 竞赛日 | 竞赛日 |

5.2* 竞赛轮次

*填入级别和数字。*

| *级别* | *轮次* | *每日轮次* |
|---|---|---|
| ____ | ____ | ________ |
| ____ | ____ | ________ |

每天可增加一轮竞赛，前提是不会导致任何级别比日程安排提前1轮，且此更改应根据SI3做出。

*填入时间。*

5.3* 每个竞赛日第一轮竞赛的预告信号的计划时间为______。

5.4 为了提醒参赛船1轮竞赛或后续轮次竞赛即将开始，在预告信号发出前至少5分钟时展示橙色旗并伴随一声音响。

*填入时间。*

5.5 最后一个竞赛日____后不再发出预告信号。

## 6*　级别旗

*填入级别和级别旗名称或对其进行描述。*

级别旗为：

| 级别 | 旗帜 |
|---|---|
| ____ | ______ |
| ____ | ______ |
| ____ | ______ |

## 7 RACING AREAS

*Insert a number or letter.*

Attachment______shows the location of racing areas.

## 8 THE COURSES

*Insert a number or letter. A method of illustrating various courses is shown in Addendum A. Insert the course length if applicable.*

**8.1 *** The diagrams in Attachment ____ show the courses, including the approximate angles between legs, the order in which marks are to be passed, and the side on which each mark is to be left. [The approximate course length will be .]

**8.2** No later than the warning signal, the race committee signal vessel will display the approximate compass bearing of the first leg.

**8.3** Courses will not be shortened. This changes RRS 32.

*Include only when changing positions of marks is impracticable.*

**8.4** Legs of the course will not be changed after the preparatory signal. This changes RRS 33.

## 9 MARKS

*Change the mark numbers as needed and insert the descriptions of the marks. Use the second alternative when Marks 4S and 4P form a gate, with Mark 4S to be left to starboard and Mark 4P to port.*

**9.1 *** Marks 1, 2, 3 and 4 will be______.

**(OR)**

**9.1*** Marks 1, 2, 3, 4S and 4P will be______.

**(OR)**

*Insert the number or letter used in SI 8.1.*

**9.1 *** Marks are described in Attachment______.

*Unless it is clear from the course diagrams, list the marks that are rounding marks.*

**9.2** The following marks are rounding marks: ______.

*Insert the descriptions of the marks.*

**9.3** New marks, as provided in SI 12.1, will be ______.

## 7 竞赛区域

*填入数字或字母。*

附件____为竞赛区域示意图。

## 8 航线

*填入数字或字母。附件A中有说明不同航线的方法。如果适用，填入航线长度。*

8.1 附件____为航线示意图，包括航段间的大致角度、绕标的顺序以及要求离开标志的一侧。［航线大致长度为_____。］

8.2 竞赛委员会信号船将不晚于预告信号发出时展示第一航段的大致罗经方位。

8.3 不得缩短航线。此条更改规则32。

*只有在无法改变标志位置时才使用本条细则。*

8.4 准备信号发出后不得更改航段。此条更改了规则33。

## 9 标志

*按需求更改标志号码，填入对标志的表述。当4S和4P标构成门标时，使用第二种选择，以右舷离开4S标，左舷离开4P标。*

9.1* 1、2、3、4标为________。

（或者）

9.1* 1、2、3、4S、4P标为________。

（或者）

*填入SI8.1中使用的数字或字母。*

9.1* 有关标志的描述见附件________。

*列出需绕行的标志，除非在航线图中有明确标示。*

9.2 以下标志为需绕行的标志：______。

*填入标志的描述。*

9.3 SI12.1所述的新的标志为______。

*Describe the starting and finishing marks: for example, the race committee signal vessel at the starboard end and a buoy at the port end. SI 11.2 will describe the starting line and SI 13 the finishing line.*

**9.4 *** The starting and finishing marks will be ______.

*Include if SI 12.2 is included.*

**9.5** A race committee vessel signalling a change of a leg of the course is a mark as provided in SI 12.2.

*Describe each area by its location and any easily recognized details of appearance.*

10 **AREAS THAT ARE OBSTRUCTIONS**
The following areas are designated as obstructions: .

**11 THE START**

*Include only if the asterisked option in RRS 26 will be used. Insert the number of minutes.*

**11.1** Races will be started by using RRS 26 with the warning signal made minutes before the starting signal.

**(OR)**

*Describe any starting system other than that stated in RRS 26.*

**11.1** Races will be started as follows:___ . This changes RRS 26.

**11.2 *** The starting line will be between staffs displaying orange flags on the starting marks.

**(OR)**

**11.2 *** The starting line will be between a staff displaying an orange flag on the starting mark at the starboard end and the course side of the port-end starting mark.

**(OR)**

*Insert the description.*

**11.2*** The starting line will be______.

*描述起点和终点标志：例如，竞赛委员会信号船为右端，浮标为左端。SI11.2描述了起航线，SI13描述了终点线。*

9.4* 起点和终点标志为______。

*采用SI12.2时使用此条。*

9.5 发出航线某一航段更改信号的竞赛委员会船是SI12.2中所述的标志。

## 10 障碍物区域

*描述每个区域的位置及任何易识别的外观细节。*

下列区域为障碍物：________。

## 11 起航

*只有使用规则26的星号选项时才采用此条。填入分钟数。*

11.1 竞赛按规则26起航，在起航信号_____分钟前发出预告信号。

**（或者）**

*对任何不同于规则26所述的起航程序做出描述。*

11.1 竞赛将按下列程序起航_________。此条更改规则26。

11.2* 起航线为起航标志上展示橙色旗的旗杆之间的连线。

**（或者）**

11.2* 起航线为右侧起航标志上展示橙色旗的旗杆和左侧起航标志之间的连线。

**（或者）**

*填入描述。*

11.2* 起航线为_____。

*Insert the number of minutes.*

*Insert the channel number.*

*When SI 12.2 is included, SI 9.5 must also be included. Reverse 'port' and 'starboard' when the mark is to be left to starboard.*

**11.3** Boats whose warning signal has not been made shall avoid the starting area during the starting sequence for other races. [DP]

**11.4** A boat that does not start within minutes after her starting signal will be scored Did Not Start without a hearing. This changes RRS A4 and A5.

**11.5** If any part of a boat's hull, crew or equipment is on the course side of the starting line during the two minutes before her starting signal and she is identified, the race committee will attempt to broadcast her sail number on VHF channel_ . Failure to make a broadcast or to time it accurately will not be grounds for a request for redress. This changes RRS 62.1(a).

## 12 CHANGE OF THE NEXT LEG OF THE COURSE

**12.1** To change the next leg of the course, the race committee will move the original mark (or the finishing line) to a new position.

**(OR)**

**12.1** To change the next leg of the course, the race committee will lay a new mark (or move the finishing line) and remove the original mark as soon as practicable. When in a subsequent change a new mark is replaced, it will be replaced by an original mark.

**12.2** Except at a gate, boats shall pass between the race committee vessel signalling the change of the next leg and the nearby mark, leaving the mark to port and the race committee vessel to starboard. This changes RRS 28.

11.3 未发出预告信号组别的船应避让其他正在进入起航程序的组别的起航区域。[DP]

*填入分钟数。*

11.4 晚于起航信号发出后___分钟起航的船将记为DNS（未起航），无需审理。此条更改规则A4和A5。

*填入频道号码。*

11.5 如果在起航信号发出前2分钟内，一条船的船体、船员或装备的任何部分位于起航线的航线一侧并被识别，竞赛委员会将在VHF___频道广播其帆号。没有广播或没有准确计时不能作为要求补偿的理由。此条更改规则62.1(a)。

## 12 航线下一航段的改变

12.1 如果改变航线的下一航段，竞赛委员会将移动原来的标志（或终点线）到新的位置。

**（或者）**

12.1 如果改变航线的下一航段，竞赛委员会将布设新的标志（或移动终点线）并尽可能地移走原标志。在连续的改变中要替换新标志时，将由原标志替代。

*当采用SI12.2时，必须采用SI9.5。当要以右舷离开标志时，颠倒“左舷”和“右舷”。*

12.2 除在门标处外，参赛船应在发出改变下一航段信号的竞赛委员会船和附近的标志之间通过，以左舷一侧离开标志，右舷一侧离开竞赛委员会船。此条更改规则28。

## 13 THE FINISH

**13.1** * The finishing line will be between staffs displaying orange flags on the finishing marks.

**(OR)**

**13.1** * The finishing line will be between a staff displaying an orange flag on the finishing mark at the starboard end and the course side of the port-end finishing mark.

**(OR)**

*Insert the description.*

**13.1*** The finishing line will be_____.

**13.2** If the race committee is absent when a boat finishes, she should report her finishing time, and her position in relation to nearby boats, to the race committee at the first reasonable opportunity.

## 14 PENALTY SYSTEM

*Include SI 14.1 only when the Two-Turns Penalty will not be used. Insert the number of places or describe the penalties.*

**14.1** The Scoring Penalty, RRS 44.3, will apply. The penalty will be______places.

**(OR)**

**14.1** The penalties are as follows:______.

*Insert the class(es).*

**14.2** For the _____class(es) RRS 44.1 is changed so that the Two-Turns Penalty is replaced by the One-Turn Penalty.

*Unless all of Appendix P applies, state any restrictions.*

**14.3** Appendix P will apply [as changed by SI(s) [14.2] [and] [14.4]].

*Recommended only for junior events.*

**14.4** RRS P2.3 will not apply and RRS P2.2 is changed so that it will apply to any penalty after the first one.

## 13　终点

13.1* 终点线为终点标志上展示橙色旗的旗杆间的连线。

**（或者）**

13.1* 终点线为右侧终点标志上展示橙色旗的旗杆和左侧终点标志航线一侧之间的连线。*填入描述*。

**（或者）**

13.1* 终点线为________。

13.2 如果一条船到达终点时，竞赛委员会不在场，她应将其到达终点的时间、排名位置以及和她临近的船的关系在最初出现的合理时机报告给竞赛委员会。

## 14　惩罚方法

*只有不适用两圈解脱时才采用此条规则。*

14.1 规则44.3的分数惩罚将适用。惩罚为___名次。

*填入排名数字或对惩罚进行描述。*

**（或者）**

14.1 惩罚方法如下：______。

*填入级别名称。*

14.2 对于___级别，规则44.1的两圈解脱更改为一圈解脱。

*除非附录P全文适用，否则说明其适用限制。*

14.3 附录P［按照本细则14.2］［和］［14.4］［更改后］适用。

*仅推荐青少年赛事使用。*

14.4 规则P2.3不适用，更改规则P2.2，使其适用于第一个解脱后的所有惩罚。

## 15 TIME LIMITS AND TARGET TIMES

*Insert the classes and times. Omit the Mark 1 time limit and target time if inapplicable.*

**15.1 *** Time limits and target times are as follows:

| *Class* | *Time limit* | *Mark 1 time limit* | *Target time* |
|---|---|---|---|
| ______ | ______ | ______ | ______ |
| ______ | ______ | ______ | ______ |
| ______ | ______ | ______ | ______ |

If no boat has passed Mark 1 within the Mark 1 time limit the race will be abandoned. Failure to meet the target time will not be grounds for redress. This changes RRS 62.1(a).

*Insert the time (or different times for different classes).*

**15.2** Boats failing to finish within ____ after the first boat sails the course and finishes will be scored Did Not Finish without a hearing. This changes RRS 35, A4 and A5.

## 16 PROTESTS AND REQUESTS FOR REDRESS

*State the location if necessary.*

**16.1** Protest forms are available at the race office[, located at _]. Protests and requests for redress or reopening shall be delivered there within the appropriate time limit.

*Change the time if different.*

**16.2** For each class, the protest time limit is 90 minutes after the last boat has finished the last race of the day or the race committee signals no more racing today, whichever is later.

*Change the posting time if different. Insert the protest room location and, if applicable, the time for the first hearing.*

**16.3** Notices will be posted no later than 30 minutes after the protest time limit to inform competitors of hearings in which they are parties or named as witnesses. Hearings will be held in the protest room,

## 15 时间限制和目标时间

*填入级别名称和时间。如果不适用，省略1标时限和目标时间。*

15.1* 时间限制和目标时间如下：

| 级别 | 时间限制 | 1标时限 | 目标时间 |
| --- | --- | --- | --- |
| ____ | ________ | _______ | ________ |
| ____ | ________ | _______ | ________ |
| ____ | ________ | _______ | ________ |

若在1标时限内没有船通过1标，则该轮竞赛将被放弃。未能达成目标时间不能作为要求补偿的依据。此条更改规则62.1(a)。

*填入时间（或不同级别的不同时间）*

15.2 在第一条船行驶航线并到达终点后____分钟内仍未到达终点的船，将被记为DNF而无需审理。此条更改规则35、A4和A5。

## 16 抗议和补偿要求

*若需要，注明地点。*

16.1 抗议表在竞赛办公室［，位于____］领取。抗议表和要求补偿表或重新审理表应在规定时限内递交。

*如有不同，更改时间。*

16.2 抗议时限为各级别最后一条船完成当天最后一轮竞赛或竞赛委员会发出今天再没有竞赛的信号后90分钟内，以较晚的为准。

*如有不同，更改张贴时间。填入抗议审理室的地点，如果适用，填入第一个审理的时间。*

16.3 将于抗议时限结束后30分钟内张贴抗议通知以告知审理各方或被点名的证人选手。审理将于［张贴的时间］［____］在位于_____的抗议审理室进行。

located at______, beginning at [the time posted] [_____].

**16.4** Notices of protests by the race committee, technical committee or protest committee will be posted to inform boats under RRS 61.1(b).

**16.5** A list of boats that, under SI 14.3, have been penalized for breaking RRS 42 will be posted.

**16.6** Breaches of SIs 11.3, 18, 21, 23, 25, 26 and 27 will not be grounds for a protest by a boat. This changes RRS 60.1(a).

**16.7** On the last scheduled day of racing a request for redress based on a protest committee decision shall be delivered no later than 30 minutes after the decision was posted. This changes RRS 62.2.

*Include only if RRS 70.5 applies.*

**16.8** Decisions of the [protest committee] [international jury] will be final as provided in RRS 70.5.

**17 SCORING**

*Include only if the Low Point System of Appendix A will not be used. Describe the system.*

**17.1** The scoring system is as follows:______.

*Insert the number.*

**17.2** ______races are required to be completed to constitute a series.

*Insert the numbers throughout.*

**17.3** (a) When fewer than____ races have been completed, a boat's series score will be the total of her race scores.

(b) When from _______ to _______ races have been completed, a boat's series score will be the total of her race scores excluding her worst score.

16.4 按照规则61.1(b)的竞赛委员会、技术委员会或抗议委员会的抗议通知将被张贴以通知相关各船。

16.5 根据本细则14.3，将张贴违反规则42的参赛船名单。

16.6 违反本细则11.3、18、21、23、25、26和27不能作为一条船抗议的依据。此条更改规则60.1(a)。

16.7 在最后一个竞赛日，以仲裁委员会的裁决为依据的补偿申请应在该裁决张贴后的30分钟内提出。此条更改规则62.2。

*仅在规则70.5适用时采用此条。*

16.8 根据规则70.5，［抗议委员会］［国际仲裁委员会］的裁决为最终裁决。

## 17 记分

*只有不使用附录A低分记分法时才采用此条。描述记分方法。*

17.1 记分方法如下：______。

*填入数字。*

17.2 完成 轮竞赛后方能构成系列赛。

*依次填入数字。*

17.3 （a）当完成竞赛的轮数少于___时，一条船的系列赛得分为所有轮次得分的总和。

（b）当完成___轮到___轮竞赛时，一条船的系列赛得分为去掉最差一轮成绩的其他所有轮次得分的总和。

(c) When or more races have been completed, a boat's series score will be the total of her race scores excluding her two worst scores.

**18 SAFETY REGULATIONS**

*Insert the procedure for check-out and check-in.*

**18.1** Check-Out and Check-In:______. [DP]

**18.2** A boat that retires from a race shall notify the race committee as soon as possible. [DP]

**19 REPLACEMENT OF CREW OR EQUIPMENT**

**19.1** Substitution of competitors will not be allowed without prior written approval of the [race committee] [protest committee]. [DP]

**19.2** Substitution of damaged or lost equipment will not be allowed unless authorized by the [race committee] [protest committee]. Requests for substitution shall be made to the committee at the first reasonable opportunity. [DP]

**20 EQUIPMENT AND MEASUREMENT CHECKS**

On the water, a boat can be instructed by a member of the race committee or the technical committee to proceed immediately to a designated area for inspection. Ashore, equipment may be inspected or measured at times specified in the class rules, the notice of race, and at the following time(s) __.

*Insert the time(s).*

（c）当完成___轮或更多轮次竞赛时，一条船的系列赛得分为去掉最差两轮成绩的其他所有轮次得分的总和。

## 18 安全规定

*填入上下水签到程序。*

18.1 上下水签到：_____。［DP］

18.2 退出竞赛的船应尽快通知竞赛委员会。［DP］

## 19 船员或器材的替换

19.1 若没有事先得到［竞赛委员会］［抗议委员会］的书面许可，不得更换选手。［DP］

19.2 除非得到［竞赛委员会］［抗议委员会］的授权，否则不得替换损坏或丢失的器材。替换的请求应在最先出现的合理时机向委员会提出。

## 20 器材和丈量检查

在水上，一条船可以被竞赛委员会或技术委员会的一员带到指定区域进行器材检查。在岸上，器材可能被按照级别规则、竞赛通知的规定，在如下时间_______接受检查或丈量。

*填入时间。*

**21 EVENT ADVERTISING**

*See World Sailing Regulation 20.4. Insert necessary information on the display of event advertising material.*

Boats shall display event advertising supplied by the organizing authority as follows:___. If this rule is broken, World Sailing Regulation 20.9.2 applies. [DP]

**22 OFFICIAL BOATS**

*Insert the descriptions. If appropriate, use different identification markings for boats performing different duties.*

Official boats will be marked as follows: _____.

**23 SUPPORT BOATS**

**23.1** Team leaders, coaches and other support persons shall stay outside areas where boats are racing from the time of the preparatory signal for the first class to start until all boats have finished or retired or the race committee signals a postponement, general recall or abandonment. [DP]

*Insert the identification markings. National letters are suggested for international events.*

**23.2** Support boats shall be marked with______. [DP]

**24 TRASH DISPOSAL**

Trash may be placed aboard support or official boats.

**25 HAUL-OUT RESTRICTIONS**

Keelboats shall not be hauled out during the regatta except with and according to the terms of prior written permission of the race committee. [DP]

## 21 赛事广告

*参见世界帆联规章20.4。填入赛事广告材料的必要信息。*

参赛船应展示组织机构提供的如下赛事广告：______。若违反此规则，世界帆联规章20.9.2适用。［DP］

## 22 官方船只

*填入描述。若可行，为不同职责的船配以不同的识别标志。*

官方船只的标志如下：_____。

## 23 辅助船

23.1 从第一个级别的准备信号开始到所有船到达终点或退出比赛，或竞赛委员会发出推迟、全召或放弃信号为止，领队、教练和其他辅助人员不得进入竞赛区域。

*填入识别标志。在国际赛事中建议使用国家字母代码。*

23.2 辅助船应带有______标志。［DP］

## 24 垃圾处理

垃圾可以放置到辅助船或竞赛委员会船上。

## 25 拖船上岸的限制

除非有竞赛委员会的事先书面许可，否则龙骨船不得在赛事过程中拖到岸上。［DP］

## 26 DIVING EQUIPMENT AND PLASTIC POOLS

Underwater breathing apparatus and plastic pools or their equivalent shall not be used around keelboats between the preparatory signal of the first race and the end of the regatta. [DP]

## 27 RADIO COMMUNICATION

*Insert any alternative text that applies. Describe any radio communication bands or frequencies that will be used or allowed.*

Except in an emergency, a boat that is racing shall not make voice or data transmissions and shall not receive voice or data communication that is not available to all boats. [DP]

## 28 PRIZES

*If perpetual trophies will be awarded state their complete names.*

Prizes will be given as follows:_.

## 29 DISCLAIMER OF LIABILITY

*The laws applicable to the venue in which the event is held may limit disclaimers. Any disclaimer should be drafted to comply with those laws.*

Competitors participate in the regatta entirely at their own risk. See RRS 4, Decision to Race. The organizing authority will not accept any liability for material damage or personal injury or death sustained in conjunction with or prior to, during, or after the regatta.

## 30 INSURANCE

*Insert the currency and amount.*

Each participating boat shall be insured with valid third-party liability insurance with a minimum cover of ________per incident or the equivalent.

## 26 潜水装备和塑料池

在第一轮准备信号和全部竞赛结束之间，不得在龙骨船周围使用水下呼吸设备、塑料池或类似装置。[DP]

## 27 无线电通讯

*填入任何适用的替代文本。对适用或允许无线电通讯波段或频率做出描述。*

除紧急情况外，参赛船在竞赛时不得发出语音或传输数据，不能接收不针对所有船的语音或数据传输。[DP]

## 28 奖励

*若将颁发永久性奖杯，注明其全称。*

奖励如下：__________。

## 29 免责声明

*适用于举行该赛事的场馆所在地的法律可能会限制声明。所有声明应依据这些法律起草。*

参加本赛事的选手完全自担风险。参见规则4，参赛决定。组织机构对赛前、赛中和赛后发生的或与之相关的所有物质损失、人员伤亡不承担任何责任。

## 30 保险

*填入货币种类和数目。*

每条参赛船必须具备有效的第三方责任险，每场赛事的最低保额为____或等价金额。

## ADDENDUM A ILLUSTRATING THE COURSE

*Shown here are diagrams of course shapes. The boat's track is represented by a discontinuous line so that each diagram can describe courses with different numbers of laps. If more than one course may be used for a class, state how each particular course will be signalled.*

### A Windward-Leeward Course

**Start – 1 – 2 – 1 – 2 – Finish**

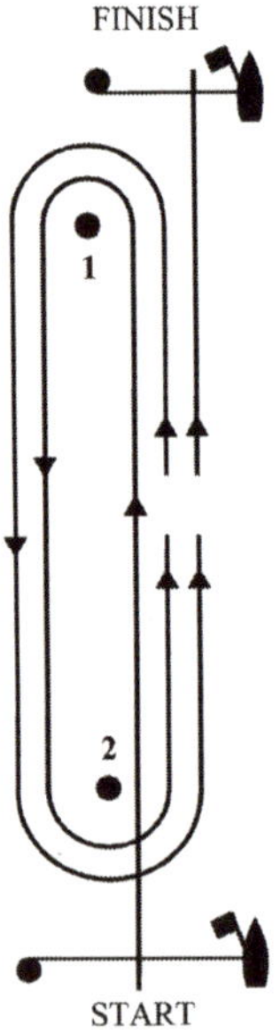


*Options for this course include*

*(1)* *increasing or decreasing the number of laps,*

*(2)* *deleting the last windward leg,*

*(3)* *using a gate instead of a leeward mark,*

*(4)* *using an offset mark at the windward mark, and*

*(5)* *using the leeward and windward marks as starting and finishing marks.*

## 附件A　航线描述

*以下为航线形状示意图。船的航行轨迹由一条不连续的线表示，这样每一个示意图可以描述不同绕行圈数的航线。如果一个级别可能使用1个以上的航线，要说明每一个特定航线的信号。*

**迎尾风航线**

Start - 1 - 2 - 1 - 2 - Finish

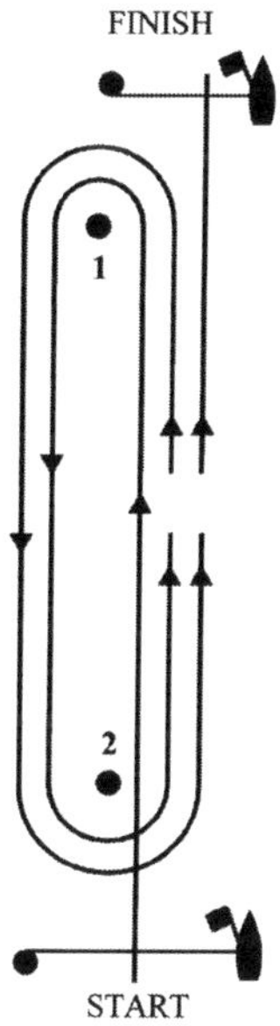


*此航线的可选项包括：*

*（1）增加或减少绕行的圈数，*

*（2）去掉最后一个迎风航段，*

*（3）使用门标代替下风标，*

*（4）在上风标处使用外设标，*

*（5）使用下风标和上风标作为起航标起和终点标志。*

## A Triangle-Windward-Leeward Course

**Start – 1 – 2 – 3 – 1 – 3 – Finish**

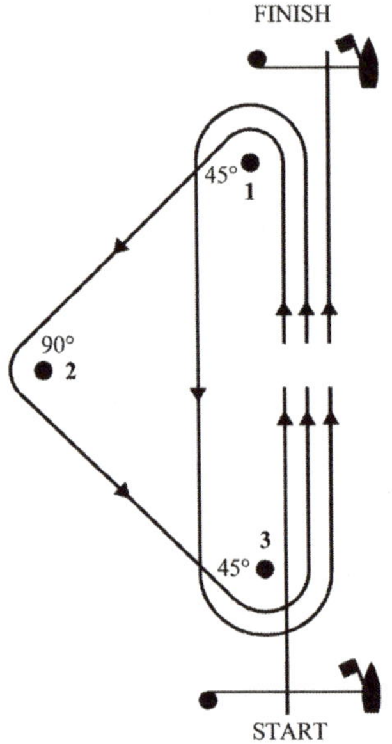


*Options for this course include*

*(1)* *increasing or decreasing the number of laps,*

*(2)* *deleting the last windward leg,*

*(3)* *varying the interior angles of the triangle (45°–90°–45° and 60°–60°–60° are common),*

*(4)* *using a gate instead of a leeward mark for downwind legs,*

*(5)* *using an offset mark at the beginning of downwind legs, and*

*(6)* *using the leeward and windward marks as starting and finishing marks.*

*Be sure to specify the interior angle at each mark.*

**三角形迎尾风航线**

Start – 1 – 2 – 3 – 1 – 3 – Finish

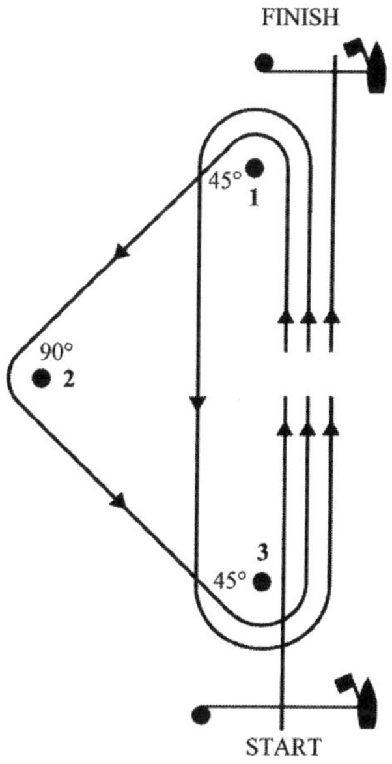


*此航线的可选项包括：*

*（1）增加或减少绕行圈数，*

*（2）去掉最后一个迎风航段，*

*（3）变化三角形的内角（通常为45°–90°–45°和60°–60°–60°），*

*（4）在顺风航段上使用门标代替下风标。*

*（5）在顺风航段的起点使用外设标，以及*

*（6）使用下风标和上风标作为起点和终点标志。*

*确保注明每个标志的内角度数。*

## Trapezoid Courses

**Start – 1 – 2 – 3 – 2 – 3 – Finish**

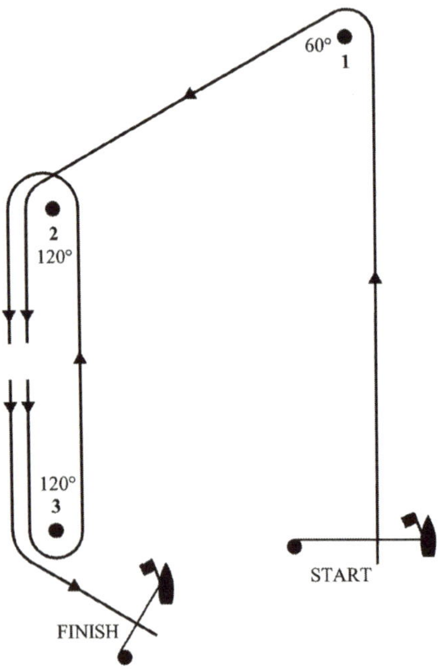


**Start – 1 – 4 – 1 – 2 – 3 – Finish**

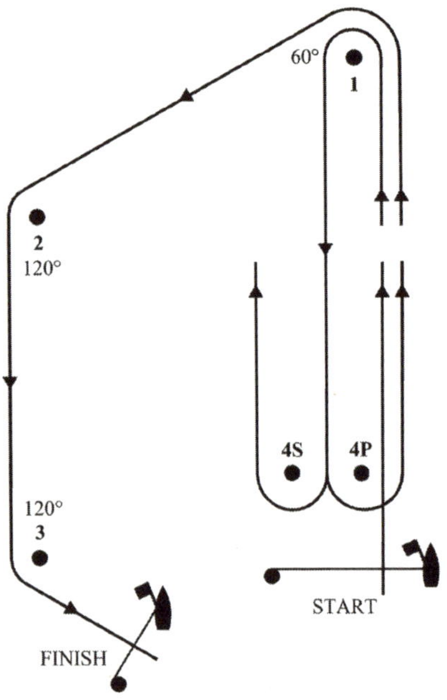


*Options for these courses include*

*(1) adding additional legs,*

*(2) replacing the gate shown by a single mark, or using a gate also in the outer loop,*

*(3) varying the interior angles of the reaching legs,*

*(4) using an offset mark at the beginning of downwind legs, and*

*(5) finishing boats upwind rather than on a reach.*

*Be sure to specify the interior angle of each reaching leg.*

**梯形航线**

Start - 1–2–3–2–3 - Finish

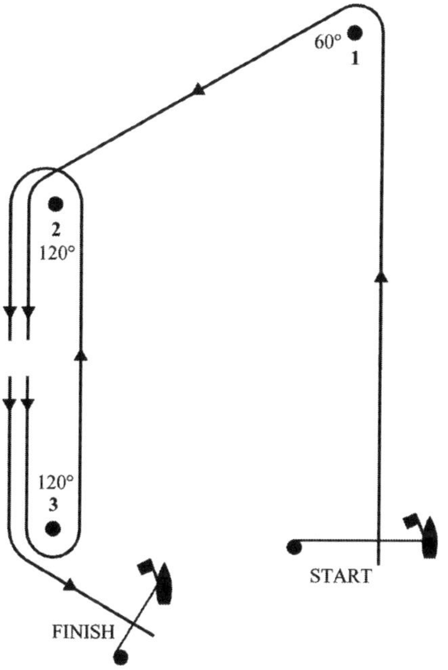


Start - 1 - 4 - 1 - 2 - 3 - Finish

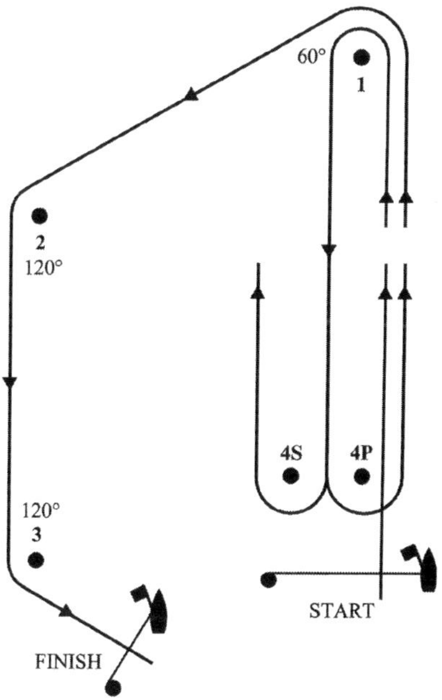


*此航线的可选项包括：*

*（1）增加额外的航段，*

*（2）用单一标志替代所示门标，或者在外绕航线也使用门标，*

*（3）变化横风航段的内角角度，*

*（4）下顺风航段的起点使用外设标，以及*

*（5）迎风到达终点而不是横风到达终点。*

*确保注明每个横风航段的内角度数。*

## **ADDENDUM B** BOATS PROVIDED BY THE ORGANIZING AUTHORITY

*The following sailing instruction is recommended when all boats will be provided by the organizing authority. It can be changed to suit the circumstances. When used, it should be inserted after SI 3.*

**4 BOATS**

**4.1** Boats will be provided for all competitors, who shall not modify them or cause them to be modified in any way except that

(a) a compass may be tied or taped to the hull or spars;

(b) wind indicators, including yarn or thread, may be tied or taped anywhere on the boat;

(c) hulls, centreboards and rudders may be cleaned, but only with water;

(d) adhesive tape may be used anywhere above the water line; and

(e) all fittings or equipment designed to be adjusted may be adjusted, provided that the class rules are complied with.

**4.2** All equipment provided with the boat for sailing purposes shall be in the boat while afloat.

**4.3** The penalty for not complying with one of the above instructions will be disqualification from all races sailed in which the instruction was broken.

**4.4** Competitors shall report any damage or loss of equipment, however slight, to the organizing authority's representative immediately after securing the boat ashore. The penalty for breaking this instruction, unless the protest committee is satisfied that the competitor made a determined effort to comply, will be disqualification from the race most recently sailed.

**4.5** Class rules requiring competitors to be members of the class association will not apply.

## 附件B　组织机构提供的参赛船

*当组织机构提供所有参赛船时，建议使用以下细则。可根据情况做出更改。使用时，应插入到SI3之后。*

**4　参赛船**

4.1　将为所有选手提供参赛船，选手不得以任何方式对其改造或致使其被改造，除了

（a）罗经可以系于或用带子固定在船体或杆具上；

（b）风向标，包括细绳或线，可以系于或用带子固定在船的任何地方；

（c）船体、稳向板和舵可以被清洗，但只能用水；

（d）可以在水线以上的任何地方使用胶带；以及

（e）在遵守级别规则的前提下，所有设计初衷为可调节的配件或装备均可进行调节。

4.2　在水上时，随参赛船提供的所有用于航行的装备均应置于船上。

4.3　违反上述任一细则，将取消该船违反细则所航行的所有轮次的资格。

4.4　选手在岸上系牢参赛船后，应立即向组织机构的代表报告器材的所有损坏和遗失，不论情况有多轻微。除非抗议委员会认为选手已尽力遵守了细则，否则违反此细则的惩罚将是取消最近一轮竞赛的资格。

4.5　要求选手是该级别协会会员的级别规则不适用。

# APPENDIX M RECOMMENDATIONS FOR PROTEST COMMITTEES

*This appendix is advisory only; in some circumstances changing these procedures may be advisable. It is addressed primarily to protest committee chairmen but may also help judges, protest committee secretaries, race committees and others connected with protest and redress hearings.*

In a protest or redress hearing, the protest committee should weigh all testimony with equal care; should recognize that honest testimony can vary, and even be in conflict, as a result of different observations and recollections; should resolve such differences as best it can; should recognize that no boat or competitor is guilty until a breach of a *rule* has been established to the satisfaction of the protest committee; and should keep an open mind until all the evidence has been heard as to whether a boat or competitor has broken a *rule*.

## M1 PRELIMINARIES (may be performed by race office staff)

- Receive the *protest* or request for redress.
- Note on the form the time the *protest* or request is delivered and the protest time limit.
- Inform each *party*, and the race committee when necessary, when and where the hearing will be held.

## M2 BEFORE THE HEARING

**M2.1** Make sure that

- each *party* has a copy of or the opportunity to read the *protest* or request for redress and has had reasonable time to prepare for the hearing.
- only one person from each boat (or *party*) is present unless an interpreter is needed.
- all boats and people involved are represented. If they are not, however, the committee may proceed under rule 63.3(b).

# 附录M　对抗议委员会的建议

*本附录只作建议性使用；在一些情况下，更改这些步骤或许是明智的。本附录主要针对抗议委员会主席，但也能帮助到裁判、抗议委员会秘书、竞赛委员会和其他与抗议和补偿审理相关的部分。*

在抗议或补偿审理中，抗议委员会应以相同标准对待所有证词；应意识到，由于不同的观察角度和回忆，即便是诚实的证词也可能存在差异和矛盾之处；应尽可能地解决好这些差异；应认可在抗议委员会认定某船或选手确实违反了某一*规则*前，其应是无辜的；应在没有审完某船或选手是否违反了*规则*的全部证据前不抱成见。

## M1　初期工作（可由竞赛办公室工作人员办理）

- 接收*抗议*或补偿请求。
- 在表上注明*抗议*或请求递交的时间以及抗议时限。
- 将审理于何时何地举行通知到每一方，必要时还有竞赛委员会。

## M2　审理前

M2.1 确保

- 每一方都有一份*抗议*或补偿申请的复印件，或有机会能够看到，并有合理的时间为审理做准备。
- 每条船（或一方）只能有1人出席，除非需要翻译。
- 涉及审理的所有船和人派代表出席。但是，如果做不到，委员会可按照规则63.3(b)继续进行。

- boats' representatives were on board when required (rule 63.3(a)). When the *parties* were in different races, both organizing authorities must accept the composition of the protest committee (rule 63.8). In a *protest* concerning class rules, obtain the current class rules and identify the authority responsible for interpreting them (rule 64.3(b)).

**M2.2** Determine if any members of the protest committee saw the incident. If so, require each of them to state that fact in the presence of the *parties* (rule 63.6).

**M2.3** Assess *conflicts of interest.*

- Ensure that all protest committee members declare any possible *conflicts of interest.* At major events this will often be a formal written declaration made before the event starts that will be kept with the protest committee records.
- At the start of any hearing, ensure that the *parties* are aware of any *conflicts of interest* of protest committee members. Ask the *parties* if they consent to the members. If a *party* does not object as soon as possible after a *conflict of interest* has been declared, the protest committee may take this as consent to proceed and should record it.
- If a *party* objects to a member, the remainder of the protest committee members need to assess whether the *conflict of interest* is significant. The assessment will consider the level of the event, the level of the conflict and the perception of fairness. It may be acceptable to balance conflicts between protest committee members. Guidance may be found on the World Sailing website. Record the decision and the grounds for that decision.
- In cases of doubt it may be preferable to proceed with a smaller protest committee. Except for hearings under rule 69, there is no minimum number of protest committee members required.
- When a request for redress is made under rule 62.1(a) and is based on an improper action or omission of a body other than the protest committee, a member of that body should not be a member of the protest committee.

- 有要求时，代表需要是船上的人［规则63.3(a)］。当*各方*是来自不同的赛事时，双方的组织机构必须接受抗议委员会的构成（规则63.8）。在涉及级别规则的*抗议*中，要掌握先行的级别规则并确定负责解释规则的机构［规则64.3(b)］。

M2.2 确定是否有抗议委员会的成员看到了事件的发生。如果有人看到，每个人都要在*各方*面前陈述事件发生的事实。

M2.3 评估*利益*冲突。

- 确保所有抗议委员会的成员都声明了任何有可能的*利益冲*突。在多数赛事中，开赛前会有一份正式的书面声明并保存在抗议委员会的记录里。
- 在任何审理开始时，确保*各方*都了解抗议委员会成员的*利益冲*突。询问*各方*是否同意委员会成员的构成。如果一方在声明*利益冲*突后没有马上反对，委员会将视为同意并记录在案。
- 如果一方反对委员会的一个成员，委员会的其他成员需要评估这个*利益冲*突是否显著。评估将会考虑赛事的等级、冲突的程度和对公平的认知。平衡抗议委员会成员之间的冲突是可以接受的。关于这方面的指导可以参见世界帆联的官网。记录该决定及其依据。
- 如果有疑虑，最好是以更少成员的抗议委员会继续推进工作。除了根据规则69召开的审理，对抗议委员会成员的最低人数没有要求。
- 根据规则62.1(a)做出补偿要求时，如果补偿是由于除抗议委员会之外的别的主体的不恰当行为或疏忽而造成，该主体的成员不能作为抗议委员会的成员。

## M3 THE HEARING

**M3.1** Check the validity of the *protest* or request for redress.

- Are the contents adequate (rule 61.2 or 62)?
- Was it delivered in time? If not, is there good reason to extend the time limit (rule 61.3 or 62.2)?
- When required, was the protestor involved in or a witness to the incident (rule 60.1(a))?
- When necessary, was 'Protest' hailed and, if required, a red flag displayed correctly (rule 61.1(a))?
- When the flag or hail was not necessary, was the protestee informed?
- Decide whether the *protest* or request for redress is valid (rule 63.5).
- Once the validity of the *protest* or request has been determined, do not let the subject be introduced again unless truly new evidence is available.

**M3.2** Take the evidence (rule 63.6).

- Ask the protestor and then the protestee to tell their stories. Then allow them to question one another. In a redress matter, ask the *party* to state the request.
- Invite questions from protest committee members.
- Make sure you know what facts each *party* is alleging before calling any witnesses. Their stories may be different.
- Allow anyone, including a boat's crew, to give evidence. It is the *party* who normally decides which witnesses to call, although the protest committee may also call witnesses (rule 63.6). The question asked by a *party* 'Would you like to hear N?' is best answered by 'It is your choice.'
- Call each *party's* witnesses (and the protest committee's if any) one by one. Limit *parties* to questioning the witness(es) (they may wander into general statements).
- Invite the protestee to question the protestor's witness first (and vice versa). This prevents the protestor from leading his witness from the beginning.

## M3　审理

M3.1 检查*抗议*或补偿请求的有效性。

- 内容是否充实（规则61.2或62.1）？
- 是否按时递交？若没有，是否有延长时限的充分理由（规则61.3或62.2）？
- 若有要求，抗议者是事件的当事人还是目击者［规则60.1(a)］？
- 必要时，是呼喊“Protest（抗议）”还是有要求正确地展示红旗［规则61.1(a)］？
- 当无需红旗和呼喊时，是否通知了被抗议人？
- 决定*抗议*或补偿请求是否有效（规则63.5）。
- 一旦确定了*抗议*或请求的有效性，除非有真正的新证据，否则不要再次探讨该问题。

M3.2 取证（规则63.6）。

- 请抗议人和被抗议人先后陈述经历。然后允许他们相互提问。在补偿事件中，请一方陈述请求。
- 请抗议委员会成员提问。
- 在传召证人前，确定你已知晓每一方所宣称的事实。他们的陈述会有所不同。
- 允许包括船员在内的任何人提供证据。虽然抗议委员会也可以传召证人，但通常是由一方决定证人人选（规则63.6）。一方提出的问题“你是否想听N的证词？”的最好答案是“这是你的选择”。
- 逐一传召每一方的证人（以及抗议委员会的证人，如果有的话）。限制各方对证人的提问（他们可能在一般陈述时偏题）。
- 先请被抗议人提问抗议人的证人（然后反过来）。这样可以防止抗议人从一开始就引导证人。

- Allow members of the protest committee who saw the incident to give evidence (rule 63.6), but only while the *parties* are present. Members who give evidence may be questioned, should take care to relate all they know about the incident that could affect the decision, and may remain on the protest committee (rule 63.3(a)).
- Try to prevent leading questions or hearsay evidence, but if that is impossible discount the evidence so obtained.
- Accept written evidence from a witness who is not available to be questioned only if all *parties* agree. In doing so they forego their rights to question that witness (rule 63.6).
- Ask one member of the committee to note down evidence, particularly times, distances, speeds, etc.
- Invite first the protestor and then the protestee to make a final statement of her case, particularly on any application or interpretation of the *rules*.

**M3.3** Find the facts (rule 63.6).

- Write down the facts; resolve doubts one way or the other.
- Call back *parties* for more questions if necessary.
- When appropriate, draw a diagram of the incident using the facts you have found.

**M3.4** Decide the *protest* or request for redress (rule 64).

- Base the decision on the facts found (if you cannot, find some more facts).
- In redress cases, make sure that no further evidence is needed from boats that will be affected by the decision.

**M3.5** Inform the *parties* (rule 65).

- Recall the *parties* and read them the facts found, conclusions and *rules* that apply, and the decision. When time presses it is permissible to read the decision and give the details later.
- Give any *party* a copy of the decision on request. File the *protest* or request for redress with the committee records.

- 允许目睹了该事件的抗议委员会成员作证（规则63.6），但是只能在各方都在场的情况下。作证的成员可能会被提问，应小心陈述他们知晓的可能会影响到裁决的全部事件事实，并且可以留在抗议委员会［规则63.3(a)］。
- 尽力防止引导性问题或传闻证据，但若无法避免，所获证据的可靠性需打折扣。
- 只有在各方都同意的前提下，才可以接受不能到场被提问的证人的书面证词。这样做说明他们放弃了提问证人的权利（规则63.6）。
- 请委员会的一人记录证词，特别是时间、距离、速度等。
- 先请抗议人再请被抗议人对自身情况做最后陈述，特别是对*规则*的任何适用和解释。

M3.3 认定事实（规则63.6）。

- 写下事实；用同一种方式或其他方式解决疑问。
- 若必要，召回各方进行更多提问。
- 若可行，根据认定的事实画出事件示意图。

M3.4 裁决*抗议*或补偿请求（规则64）。

- 基于认定的事实（如果不行，寻求更多事实）。
- 在补偿事件中，确保无需从会受到裁决影响的船那里寻求更多证据。

M3.5 通知每一方（规则65）。

- 重新召回各方，宣读认定的事实、结论、适用的*规则*和裁决。时间紧张时，允许先宣布裁决，稍后再给出细节。
- 任何一方有要求时可提供裁决的复印件。将*抗议*或补偿请求连同委员会记录一同归档。

## M4 REOPENING A HEARING (rule 66)

**M4.1** When a *party*, within the time limit, has asked for a hearing to be reopened, hear the *party* making the request, look at any video, etc., and decide whether there is any significant new evidence that might lead you to change your decision. Decide whether your interpretation of the *rules* may have been wrong; be open-minded as to whether you have made a mistake. If none of these applies refuse to reopen; otherwise schedule a hearing.

**M4.2** Evidence is 'new'

- if it was not reasonably possible for the *party* asking for the reopening to have discovered the evidence before the original hearing,
- if the protest committee is satisfied that before the original hearing the evidence was diligently but unsuccessfully sought by the *party* asking for the reopening, or
- if the protest committee learns from any source that the evidence was not available to the *parties* at the time of the original hearing.

## M5 MISCONDUCT (rule 69)

**M5.1** An action under this rule is not a *protest,* but the protest committee gives its allegations in writing to the competitor before the hearing. The hearing is conducted under rules similar to those governing a protest hearing but the protest committee must have at least three members (rule 69.2(a)). Use the greatest care to protect the competitor's rights.

**M5.2** A competitor or a boat cannot protest under rule 69, but the protest form of a competitor who tries to do so may be accepted as a report to the protest committee, which can then decide whether or not to call a hearing.

**M5.3** Unless World Sailing has appointed a person for the role, the protest committee may appoint a person to present the allegation. This person might be a race official, the person making the allegation or other appropriate person. When no reasonable alternative person is available, a person who was appointed as a member of the protest committee may present the allegation.

## M4 重新审理（规则66）

M4.1 如果一方在时限内提出进行重新审理，听取提出要求的一方的陈述及查看录像等，然后决定是否找到能导致你改变裁决的任何实质性的新证据。确定对于*规则*的解释是否出现错误；要正确对待自己是否犯了错误。如果均不符合上述情况，则拒绝重审，否则应安排审理时间。

M4.2 证据是“新的”

- 如果是要求重新审理的一方在最初审理前无法发现的证据，
- 如果抗议委员会认定要求重新审理的一方在最初审理前虽无果但已努力寻找过证据，或者
- 如果抗议委员会从任何渠道得到的证据在最初审理时对各方不可用。

## M5 品行不端（规则69）

M5.1 依照此规则采取的措施不是*抗议*，但是抗议委员会应在审理前将书面形式的意见交给选手。违反此规则的审理将和审理其他*抗议*的程序类似，但是抗议委员会至少需有3名成员［规则69.2(a)］。应尽力保护选手的权益。

M5.2 选手或船不能根据规则69提出抗议，但是力图这样做的选手的抗议表可以作为给抗议委员会的报告被接收，之后抗议委员会可以决定是否召集审理。

M5.3 抗议委员会可以指定一人提出指控，除非世界帆联已经委派他人。这个人可以是竞赛官、提出指控的人或其他合适人选。在没有合适备用人选的情况下，被任命为竞赛委员会成员的一个人可以提出指控。

**M5.4** When it is desirable to call a hearing under rule 69 as a result of a Part 2 incident, it is important to hear any boat-vs.-boat *protest* in the normal way, deciding which boat, if any, broke which *rule*, before proceeding against the competitor under rule 69.

**M5.5** Although action under rule 69 is taken against a competitor, boat owner or *support person*, and not a boat, a boat may also be penalized (rules 69.2(h)(2) and 64.4).

**M5.6** When a protest committee upholds a rule 69 allegation it will need to consider if it is appropriate to report to either a national authority or World Sailing. Guidance on when to report may be found in the World Sailing Case Book. When the protest committee does make a report it may recommend whether or not further action should be taken.

**M5.7** Unless the right of appeal is denied in accordance with rule 70.5, a *party* to a rule 69 hearing may appeal the decision of the protest committee.

**M5.8** Further guidance for protest committees about misconduct may be found on the World Sailing website.

## M6 APPEALS (rule 70 and Appendix R)

When decisions can be appealed,

- retain the papers relevant to the hearing so that the information can easily be used for an appeal. Is there a diagram endorsed or prepared by the protest committee? Are the facts found sufficient? (Example: Was there an *overlap*? Yes or No. 'Perhaps' is not a fact found.) Are the names of the protest committee members and other important information on the form?
- comments by the protest committee on any appeal should enable the appeals committee to picture the whole incident clearly; the appeals committee knows nothing about the situation.

## M7 PHOTOGRAPHIC EVIDENCE

Photographs and videos can sometimes provide useful evidence but protest committees should recognize their limitations and note the following points:

M5.4 当由于规则第二章的时间需要根据规则69召集审理时，在指控选手违反规则69前以常态听取任何船对船的*抗议*是非常重要的，如果有船违反*规则*，要裁决出是哪条船违反了哪条*规则*。

M5.5 虽然根据规则69采取的措施是针对选手、船东或*后援人员*的，而不是某条船，但是该船可能也会被惩罚［规则69.2(h)(2)和 64.4］。

M5.6 当抗议委员会支持规则69的指控时，需要考虑其是否适合报告给国家管理机构或世界帆联。世界帆联案例书里有关于何时报告的指导。当抗议委员会做出报告时，会给出是否应采取进一步措施的建议。

M5.7 除非根据规则70.5否决了上诉权，否则规则69审理的一方可以对抗议委员会的裁决提出上诉。

M5.8 关于抗议委员会处理品行不端的进一步指导可参见世界帆联网站。

## M6 上诉（规则70和附录R）

对裁决提出上诉时，

- 保留有关审理的纸质文件，这样方便于在上诉中使用这些信息。是否有抗议委员会批注或准备的示意图？认定的事实是否充分？（如：是否有*相联*？ 是或否。“可能”不能作为认定的事实。）抗议委员会成员的姓名和其他重要信息是否都在表上？
- 抗议委员会对任何上诉的评论应该能使上诉委员会清楚地勾画出整个事件；上诉委员会对当前情况一无所知。

## M7 图像证据

照片和录像带有时可以提供有用的证据，但抗议委员会应认识到其局限性并注意以下几点：

- The *party* producing the photographic evidence is responsible for arranging the viewing.
- View the video several times to extract all the information from it.
- The depth perception of any single-lens camera is very poor; with a telephoto lens it is non-existent. When the camera views two *overlapped* boats at right angles to their course, it is impossible to assess the distance between them. When the camera views them head on, it is impossible to see whether an *overlap* exists unless it is substantial.
- Ask the following questions:
  - Where was the camera in relation to the boats?
  - Was the camera's platform moving? If so in what direction and how fast?
  - Is the angle changing as the boats approach the critical point? Fast panning causes radical change.
  - Did the camera have an unrestricted view throughout?

- 提供图像证据的一方有责任安排观看。
- 多看几遍录像带以从中提取所有信息。
- 任何单镜头相机的深度感都很差；使用长焦镜头时则不存在深度感。当相机的取景点与两条*相联*的船的航线成直角时，是无法估算她们之间的距离的。当相机的取景点与她们正面相对时，除非是重叠的情况，否则是无法看到*相联*是否存在的。
- 询问以下问题：
  - 相机与船的相对位置？
  - 相机的底座是否移动？如果移动，移动的方向和速度如何？
  - 当船接近关键点时角度是否发生变化？快速平移会导致彻底改变。
  - 相机镜头是否全程不受镜像限制？

# APPENDIX N
# INTERNATIONAL JURIES

*See rules 70.5 and 91(b). This appendix shall not be changed by the notice of race, sailing instructions or national prescriptions.*

## N1 COMPOSITION, APPOINTMENT AND ORGANIZATION

**N1.1** An international jury shall be composed of experienced sailors with excellent knowledge of the racing rules and extensive protest committee experience. It shall be independent of and have no members from the race committee, and be appointed by the organizing authority, subject to approval by the national authority if required (see rule 91(b)), or by World Sailing under rule 89.2(c).

**N1.2** The jury shall consist of a chairman, a vice chairman if desired, and other members for a total of at least five. A majority shall be International Judges.

**N1.3** No more than two members (three, in Groups M, N and Q) shall be from the same national authority.

**N1.4** (a) The chairman of a jury may appoint one or more panels composed in compliance with rules N1.1, N1.2 and N1.3. This can be done even if the full jury is not composed in compliance with these rules.

(b) The chairman of a jury may appoint panels of at least three members each, of which the majority shall be International Judges. Members of each panel shall be from at least three different national authorities except in Groups M, N and Q, where they shall be from at least two different national authorities. If dissatisfied with a panel's decision, a *party* is entitled to a hearing by a panel composed in compliance with rules N1.1, N1.2 and N1.3, except concerning the facts found, if requested within the time limit specified in the sailing instructions.

# 附录N　国际仲裁委员会

*参见规则 70.5 和 91(b)。竞赛通知、航行细则或国家规定不能更改本附录。*

**N1　构成、任命和组织**

N1.1 国际仲裁委员会成员应为具有丰富竞赛规则知识和资深抗议委员会经验的帆船水手。国际仲裁委员会应独立于竞赛委员会且没有来自竞赛委员会的成员，是由组织机构任命的，如有要求应得到国家管理机构许可［参见规则91(b)］，或根据规则89.2(c)由世界帆联任命。

N1.2 仲裁委员会应包括一名主席，如需要可以包括一名副主席，以及其他成员，总人数最少5名。其中大多数应为国际裁判。

N1.3 来自同一国家管理机构的成员不得超过2名（在 M、N 和 Q 组为3名）。

N1.4 （a）仲裁委员会主席可以根据规则 N1.1、N1.2 和 N1.3 任命一个或多个小组。即使整个仲裁委员会没有按照这些规则完整建制也可以执行这一点。

（b）仲裁委员会的主席可以任命每组至少3人的小组，其大多数成员应当是国际裁判。每组成员应当至少来自3个不同的国家管理机构；除非是在M、N 和 Q 组里，成员可以至少来自于2个不同的国家管理机构。如果对小组的裁决不满，除了考虑到认定的事实外，如果是在航行细则规定的时限内提出，审理的一方有权要求一个按照规则 N1.1、N1.2和N1.3 组成的仲裁小组进行审理。

**N1.5** When a full jury, or a panel, has fewer than five members, because of illness or emergency, and no qualified replacements are available, it remains properly constituted if it consists of at least three members and if at least two of them are International Judges. When there are three or four members they shall be from at least three different national authorities except in Groups M, N and Q, where they shall be from at least two different national authorities.

**N1.6** When it is considered desirable that some members not participate in discussing and deciding a *protest* or request for redress, and no qualified replacements are available, the jury or panel remains properly constituted if at least three members remain and at least two of them are International Judges.

**N1.7** In exception to rules N1.1 and N1.2, World Sailing may in limited circumstances (see World Sailing Regulation 25.8.13) authorize an international jury consisting of a total of only three members. All members shall be International Judges. The members shall be from three different national authorities (two, in Groups M, N and Q). The authorization shall be stated in a letter of approval to the organizing authority and in the notice of race and sailing instructions, and the letter shall be posted on the event's official notice board.

**N1.8** When the national authority's approval is required for the appointment of an international jury (see rule 91(b)), notice of its approval shall be included in the sailing instructions or be posted on the official notice board.

**N1.9** If the jury or a panel acts while not properly constituted, its decisions may be appealed.

## N2 RESPONSIBILITIES

**N2.1** An international jury is responsible for hearing and deciding all *protests*, requests for redress and other matters arising under the rules of Part 5. When asked by the organizing authority or the race committee, it shall advise and assist them on any matter directly affecting the fairness of the competition.

N1.5 当整个仲裁委员会或小组因病或紧急事件导致不足5人且没有具备资质的替补人员时，只要还有至少3名成员并且其中至少有2名是国际裁判时，那么其仍是正常建制。当有3或4名成员时，他们应至少来自3个不同的国家管理机构，除非是在M、N和Q组里，成员可以至少来自于2个不同的国家管理机构。

N1.6 当考虑到一些成员不适合参加某一抗议或补偿要求的讨论和决策，且没有具备资质的替补人员在场时，若仲裁委员会或小组有至少3名成员且其中至少2名为国际裁判，那么其仍为正常建制。

N1.7 除了规则N1.1和N1.2，世界帆联在有限的范围内可以授权总共由3人构成的国际仲裁委员会（参见世界帆联规章25.8.13）。所有的成员必须是国际裁判。成员必须来自于3个（在 M、N和Q组里可以是2个）不同的国家管理机构。授权应该以授权函件的形式发送给国家管理机构，且体现在竞赛通知和航行细则中，并张贴在赛事官方公告栏上。

N1.8 当对国际仲裁委员会的任命需要得到国家管理机构的许可时［参见规则91(b)］，该许可的通知应包括在航行细则里或张贴于官方公告栏。

N1.9 如果仲裁委员会或一个小组在没有正常建制的情况下行事，可以对其裁决提出上诉。

## N2 责任

N2.1 国际仲裁委员会对审理和裁决所有*抗议*、补偿请求和其他根据第五章规则所产生的事件负责。当组织机构或竞赛委员会要求时，国际仲裁委员会应当在任何直接影响到比赛公正性的事件中给予建议和帮助。

**N2.2** Unless the organizing authority directs otherwise, the jury shall decide

(a) questions of eligibility, measurement or rating certificates; and

(b) whether to authorize the substitution of competitors, boats or equipment when a *rule* requires such a decision.

**N2.3** The jury shall also decide matters referred to it by the organizing authority or the race committee.

## N3 PROCEDURES

**N3.1** Decisions of the jury, or of a panel, shall be made by a simple majority vote of all members. When there is an equal division of votes cast, the chairman of the meeting may cast an additional vote.

**N3.2** Members shall not be regarded as having a significant *conflict of interest* (see rule 63.4) by reason of their nationality, club membership or similar. When otherwise considering a significant *conflict of interest* as required by rule 63.4, considerable weight must be given to the fact that decisions of an international jury cannot be appealed and this may affect the perception of fairness and lower the level of conflict that is significant. In case of doubt, the hearing should proceed as permitted by rule N1.6.

**N3.3** If a panel fails to agree on a decision it may adjourn, in which case the chairman shall refer the matter to a properly constituted panel with as many members as possible, which may be the full jury.

## N4 MISCONDUCT (Rule 69)

**N4.1** World Sailing Regulation 35, Disciplinary Code, contains procedures that apply to specific international events with regard to the appointment of a person to conduct any investigation. These procedures override any conflicting provision of this appendix.

**N4.2** A person shall be responsible for presenting to the hearing panel any allegations of misconduct under rule 69. This person shall not be a member of the hearing panel but may be a member of the jury. Such a person shall be required to make full disclosure of all material that may come into his possession in the course of his investigation to the person subject to allegations of a breach of rule 69.

N2.2 除非组织机构另有指示，否则仲裁委员会必须裁决：

（a）资格、丈量或分级证书的问题；和

（b）当*规则*要求做出裁决时，是否批准选手、船或器材的替换。

N2.3 仲裁委员会还应对组织机构或竞赛委员会向其提出的事件做出裁决。

**N3 程序**

N3.1 仲裁委员会或小组的裁决应以全体投票的形式通过（多数即为通过）。当出现票数相等的情况时，仲裁委员会主席可以多投一票。

N3.2 成员不应该因为国籍、俱乐部会员或者相似的因素被认为有显著*利益冲突*（参见规则 63.4）。否则当根据规则63.4考虑显著*利益冲突*时，必须慎重考虑不能对国际仲裁的裁决进行上诉这一事实，因为这可能会影响对公平的认知和降低明显*利益冲突*的等级。如有异议，应根据规则N1.6 召集审理。

N3.3 如果一个小组没有对裁决达成一致，它可以休会；在这种情况下，仲裁委员会主席可以将此事件转交给一个正常建制的小组，其成员越多越好，甚至可以是全体仲裁委员会成员。

**N4 品行不端（规则69）**

N4.1 世界帆联规章35，即处罚条例里面有适用于特定国际比赛中任命某人执行调查的程序，这些程序可推翻该附录中任何冲突的条款。

N4.2 根据规则 69，应有一人承担向审理小组陈述任何品行不端指控的责任。这个人不应该是审理小组的成员，但可以是仲裁委员会的成员。这个人被要求向违反规则69的被指控人充分披露调查的过程中自己获得的所有材料。

**N4.3** Prior to a hearing, the hearing panel, to the extent practically possible, shall not act as an investigator of any allegations made under rule 69. However, during the hearing the panel shall be entitled to ask any investigative questions it may see fit.

**N4.4** If the panel decides to call a hearing, all material disclosed to the panel in order for them to make that decision must be disclosed to the person subject to the allegations before the hearing begins.

N4.3 在任何根据规则69的审理中，在审理前，审理小组在可能的范围内不应该充当调查者的角色。但是，在审理过程中，审理小组有权询问任何其认为适宜的调查性问题。

N4.4 如果小组决定召开审理，所有为了帮助小组做决策而披露给小组的材料必须在审理前同样披露给受指控的当事人。

# APPENDIX P SPECIAL PROCEDURES FOR RULE42

*All or part of this appendix applies only if the notice of race or sailing instructions so state.*

## P1 OBSERVERS AND PROCEDURE

**P1.1** The protest committee may appoint observers, including protest committee members, to act in accordance with rule P1.2. A person with a significant *conflict of interest* shall not be appointed as an observer.

**P1.2** An observer appointed under rule P1.1 who sees a boat breaking rule 42 may penalize her by, as soon as reasonably possible, making a sound signal, pointing a yellow flag at her and hailing her sail number, even if she is no longer *racing*. A boat so penalized shall not be penalized a second time under rule 42 for the same incident.

## P2 PENALTIES

### P2.1 First Penalty

When a boat is first penalized under rule P1.2 her penalty shall be a Two-Turns Penalty under rule 44.2. If she fails to take it she shall be disqualified without a hearing.

### P2.2 Second Penalty

When a boat is penalized a second time during the regatta, she shall promptly retire. If she fails to do so she shall be disqualified without a hearing and her score shall not be excluded.

### P2.3 Third and Subsequent Penalties

When a boat is penalized a third or subsequent time during the regatta, she shall promptly retire. If she does so her penalty shall be disqualification without a hearing and her score shall not be excluded. If she fails to do so her penalty shall be disqualification without a hearing from all races in the regatta, with no score excluded, and the protest committee shall consider calling a hearing under rule 69.2.

# 附录P　规则42的特殊程序

*只有竞赛通知或航行细则中注明时，本附录的全部或部分才适用。*

## P1　观察员和程序

P1.1　抗议委员会可以指定包括抗议委员会成员在内的人担任观察员，来执行规则P1.2的规定。有明显*利益冲突*的人不能被指定为观察员。

P1.2　根据规则P1.1指定的观察员看到有船违反规则42时，可以尽快发出音响信号，用黄色旗指向该船并呼喊其帆号来判罚她，即使她已经不在*竞赛*中。在同一事件中，已经被判罚的船不应再次被判罚。

## P2　判罚

### P2.1　第一次判罚

根据规则 P1.2，当一条船第一次被判罚时，根据规则 44.2 对其惩罚是做一个两圈解脱。如果她没有做解脱，将无须审理，取消她的资格。

### P2.2　第二次判罚

当一条船在一场赛事中第二次被判罚，她应该尽快退出当轮比赛。如果她没有这样做，将无须审理，取消其资格而且该分数不能被去掉。

### P2.3　第三次及其后的判罚

当一条船在一场赛事中第三次或更多次被判罚，她应当尽快退出。如果她这样做了，将无须审理，取消其资格而且该分

### P2.4 Penalties Near the Finishing Line

If a boat is penalized under rule P2.2 or P2.3 and it was not reasonably possible for her to retire before *finishing*, she shall be scored as if she had retired promptly.

## P3 POSTPONEMENT, GENERAL RECALL OR ABANDONMENT

If a boat has been penalized under rule P1.2 and the race committee signals a *postponement*, general recall or *abandonment*, the penalty is cancelled, but it is still counted to determine the number of times she has been penalized during the regatta.

## P4 REDRESS LIMITATION

A boat shall not be given redress for an action by a member of the protest committee or its designated observer under rule P1.2 unless the action was improper due to a failure to take into account a race committee signal or a class rule.

## P5 FLAGS O AND R

### P5.1 When Rule P5 Applies

Rule P5 applies if the class rules permit pumping, rocking and ooching when the wind speed exceeds a specified limit.

### P5.2 Before the Starting Signal

(a) The race committee may signal that pumping, rocking and ooching are permitted, as specified in the class rules, by displaying flag O before or with the warning signal.

(b) If the wind speed becomes less than the specified limit after flag O has been displayed, the race committee may *postpone* the race. Then, before or with a new warning signal, the committee shall display either flag R, to signal that rule 42 as changed by the class rules applies, or flag O, as provided in rule P5.2(a).

数不能被减去。如果她没有这样做，对她的惩罚是无须审理而取消其在该赛事中所有轮次的资格，分数带入总分不得去掉，而且抗议委员会将根据规则69.2考虑召集审理。

**P2.4 靠近终点线处的判罚**

根据规则 P2.2 或者 P2.3 ，如果一条船被判罚，同时在其*到达终点*之前没有合理的可能来退出比赛，该船应当被记为已经即刻退出了比赛。

## P3 推迟、全召或放弃

根据规则P1.2，如果一条船被判罚，之后竞赛委员会发出*推迟*、全召或*放弃*信号，那么对她的判罚将被取消，但是她在此赛事中被判罚的次数将被累计。

## P4 补偿的限制

只有当抗议委员会成员或者其指定的观察员因为没有考虑到竞赛委员会信号或级别规则时，根据规则P1.2做出的错误行动才可以被给予补偿。

## P5 O旗和R旗

**P5.1 当规则P5适用时**

如果级别规则允许当风速超过某一限定值可以摇帆、滚动和前冲，那么规则P5适用。

**P5.2 在起航信号发出前**

（a）竞赛委员会可按级别规则的规定，通过在预告信号之前或与预告信号一起展示O旗来发出信号，表明允许摇帆、滚动和前冲动作。

（b）如果风速在展示O旗后变得比规定的风速限制小，竞委会可能*推迟*竞赛。接下来，在新的预告信号发出前，竞赛委员会应该会展示 R 旗表示被级别规则更改的规

(c) If flag O or flag R is displayed before or with the warning signal, it shall be displayed until the starting signal.

**P5.3 After the Starting Signal**

After the starting signal,

(a) if the wind speed exceeds the specified limit, the race committee may display flag O with repetitive sounds at a *mark* to signal that pumping, rocking and ooching are permitted, as specified in the class rules, after passing the *mark*;

(b) if flag O has been displayed and the wind speed becomes less than the specified limit, the race committee may display flag R with repetitive sounds at a *mark* to signal that rule 42, as changed by the class rules, applies after passing the *mark*.

则42已适用，或者根据规则 P5.2(a)展示 O 旗。

（c）如果 O 旗或 R 旗在预告信号之前或与预告信号一起展示，该旗应当一直展示至起航信号发出。

**P5.3 在起航信号发出后**

在起航信号发出后，

（a）如果风速超过了规定的限制，竞委会应根据级别规则在标志旁展示O旗同时伴随重复音响，船通过该标志后可以进行摇帆、滚动和前冲；

（b）当O旗已经被展示，但是风力变得小于规定的限制，竞委会应根据级别规则在标志旁展示R旗同时伴随重复音响，船通过该标志后规则42适用。

# **APPENDIX R** PROCEDURES FOR APPEALS AND REQUESTS

*See rule 70. A national authority may change this appendix by prescription but it shall not be changed by sailing instructions.*

**R1 APPEALS AND REQUESTS**

Appeals, requests by protest committees for confirmation or correction of their decisions, and requests for interpretations of the *rules* shall be made in compliance with this appendix.

**R2 SUBMISSION OF DOCUMENTS**

**R2.1** To make an appeal,

(a) no later than 15 days after receiving the protest committee's written decision or its decision not to reopen a hearing, the appellant shall send an appeal and a copy of the protest committee's decision to the national authority. The appeal shall state why the appellant believes the protest committee's decision or its procedures were incorrect;

(b) when the hearing required by rule 63.1 has not been held within 30 days after a *protest* or request for redress was delivered, the appellant shall, within a further 15 days, send an appeal with a copy of the *protest* or request and any relevant correspondence. The national authority shall extend the time if there is good reason to do so;

(c) when the protest committee fails to comply with rule 65, the appellant shall, within a reasonable time after the hearing, send an appeal with a copy of the *protest* or request and any relevant correspondence.

If a copy of the *protest* or request is not available, the appellant shall instead send a statement of its substance.

# 附录R 上诉和申请程序

*参见规则70。国家管理机构可以通过其特别规定来更改本附录，但是不得通过航行细则进行更改。*

## R1 上诉和申请

上诉，抗议委员会就其裁决提出的要确认或更正的申请，以及要求对某些*规则*进行解释的申请应按本附录执行。

## R2 文件的递交

R2.1 提请一个上诉：

（a）在收到抗议委员会书面裁决或其不重新审理的决定之后的15天内，申诉人应向国家管理机构递交一份上诉申请和抗议委员会的裁决复印件。该上诉应写明申诉人认为抗议委员会的裁决或其程序不正确的原因；

（b）如果按照规则63.1要求的审理没有在抗议或者要求补偿的申请递交后的 30 日内召开的话，申诉人应当在此后的15日内，连同抗议书或者补偿申请书以及与此有任何关联的信件的复印件，递交一份上诉申请。如果有合理的原因，国家管理机构应当延长这个时限；

（c）当抗议委员会没有能遵守规则65，申诉人应当在审理后适当的时间内，连同抗议书或补偿申请书以及与此有任何关联的信件的复印件，递交一份上诉申请。

如果无法获得抗议书或者补偿申请书的复印件，申诉人应当递交一份相关事实陈述作为替代。

**R2.2** The appellant shall also send, with the appeal or as soon as possible thereafter, all of the following documents that are available to her:

(a) the written *protest*(*s*) or request(s) for redress;

(b) a diagram, prepared or endorsed by the protest committee, showing the positions and tracks of all boats involved, the course to the next *mark* and the required side, the force and direction of the wind, and, if relevant, the depth of water and direction and speed of any current;

(c) the notice of race, the sailing instructions, any other conditions governing the event, and any changes to them;

(d) any additional relevant documents; and

(e) the names, postal and email addresses, and telephone numbers of all *parties* to the hearing and the protest committee chairman.

**R2.3** A request from a protest committee for confirmation or correction of its decision shall be sent no later than 15 days after the decision and shall include the decision and the documents listed in rule R2.2. A request for an interpretation of the *rules* shall include assumed facts.

## R3 RESPONSIBILITIES OF NATIONAL AUTHORITY AND PROTEST COMMITTEE

Upon receipt of an appeal or a request for confirmation or correction, the national authority shall send to the *parties* and protest committee copies of the appeal or request and the protest committee's decision. It shall ask the protest committee for any relevant documents listed in rule R2.2 not sent by the appellant or the protest committee, and the protest committee shall promptly send them to the national authority. When the national authority has received them it shall send copies to the *parties*.

## R4 COMMENTS AND CLARIFICATIONS

**R4.1** The *parties* and protest committee may make comments on the appeal or request or on any of the documents listed in rule R2.2 by sending them in writing to the national authority.

**R4.2** The national authority may seek clarifications of *rules* governing the event from organizations that are not *parties* to the hearing.

R2.2 申诉人还应在上诉时或上诉后尽早递交下列其所拥有的材料：

（a）书面*抗议*或补偿申请；

（b）由抗议委员会准备或认可的示意图，其中展示了所有涉及该事件船只的位置和轨迹、到下一标志的航线和规定的一侧、风力和风向，如果相关的话，还应注明水深及水流的方向与速度；

（c）竞赛通知、航行细则、赛事执行的其他条件及对它们的更改；

（d）任何其他相关的文件；以及

（e）审理各方和抗议委员会主席的姓名、邮政编码、电子邮箱地址和电话号码。

R2.3 来自抗议委员会的对其裁决的确认和更正的请求应在做出裁决后的15天内提请，且须包括裁决内容和规则R2.2列出的文件。对规则解释的请求应当包括假定的事实。

## R3 国家管理机构和抗议委员会的责任

当收到上诉或者要求确认或更正的请求时，国家管理机构应向审理*各方*和抗议委员会发出该上诉或请求以及抗议委员会裁决的复印件。国家管理机构可以要求抗议委员会提交规则R2.2列出的申诉人和抗议委员会没有递交的任何相关材料，抗议委员会应立即向国家管理机构递交这些材料。国家管理机构收到这些材料后应将其复印件发送给审理*各方*。

## R4 意见与说明

R4.1 审理*各方*和抗议委员会可以通过向国家管理机构递交书面报告的形式，对上诉或请求，或规则R2.2中列出的任何文件提出意见。

R4.2 国家管理机构可以向不作为审理*各方*的组织机构寻求对管理赛事的*规则*进行说明。

**R4.3** The national authority shall send copies of comments and clarifications received to the *parties* and protest committee as appropriate.

**R4.4** Comments on any document shall be made no later than 15 days after receiving it from the national authority.

**R5 INADEQUATE FACTS; REOPENING**

The national authority shall accept the protest committee's finding of facts except when it decides they are inadequate. In that case it shall require the committee to provide additional facts or other information, or to reopen the hearing and report any new finding of facts, and the committee shall promptly do so.

**R6 WITHDRAWING AN APPEAL**

An appellant may withdraw an appeal before it is decided by accepting the protest committee's decision.

R4.3 国家管理机构应根据情况向审理各方和抗议委员会发送其收到的意见和说明材料的复印件。

R4.4 对任何文件的意见应在不晚于收到国家管理机构发出的文件后15天内提出。

## R5 事实不足；重新审理

国家管理机构应接受抗议委员会认定的事实，除非它认为这些事实不充分。在这种情况下，国家管理机构可以要求抗议委员会提交事实补充材料或其他信息，或要求其重新审理，并报告任何新认定的事实，抗议委员会应立即按此执行。

## R6 撤销上诉

申诉人可以接受抗议委员会的裁决，在上诉被裁决前将其撤销。

# APPENDIX S STANDARD SAILING INSTRUCTIONS

*This appendix applies only if the notice of race so states.*

*These Standard Sailing Instructions may be used at an event in place of printed sailing instructions made available to each boat. To use them, state in the notice of race that 'The sailing instructions will consist of the instructions in RRS Appendix S, Standard Sailing Instructions, and supplementary sailing instructions that will be on the official notice board located at_.'*

*The supplementary sailing instructions will include:*

1. *A table showing the schedule of races, including the day and date of each scheduled day of racing, the number of races scheduled each day, the scheduled time of the first warning signal each day, and the latest time for a warning signal on the last scheduled day of racing (see SI 5 below).*
2. *The location of the race office and of the flag pole on which signals made ashore will be displayed (SI 4.1).*
3. *A list of the marks that will be used and a description of each one (SI 8). How new marks will differ from original marks (SI 10).*
4. *The time limits, if any, that are listed in SI 12.*
5. *Any changes or additions to the instructions in this appendix.*

*A copy of the supplementary sailing instructions will be available to competitors on request.*

# 附录S　标准航行细则

*本附录只有在竞赛通知中有这样的陈述时才适用。*

*这些标准航行细则在一场赛事中可以替代纸质版航行细则提供给各参赛船。使用时，应在竞赛通知中写明“航行细则包括《帆船竞赛规则》附录S中的细则、标准航行细则，补充的航行细则将张贴在位于____的官方公告栏上。”*

*补充的航行细则将包括：*

1. *竞赛日程安排的表格，包括竞赛日安排的天数和时间、每个竞赛日计划竞赛的轮数、每个竞赛日第一次预告信号的计划时间，以及最后一个竞赛日发出预告信号的最晚时间（参见以下SI5）。*
2. *竞赛办公室和展示岸上信号的旗杆的位置（SI 4.1）。*
3. *所使用标志的清单以及每个标志的描述（SI 8）。新标志与原标志如何区分（SI 10）。*
4. *若有时间限制，在SI 12中列明。*
5. *对本附录中细则的所有更改和添加。*

*选手索要时向其提供补充航行细则的复印件。*

# SAILING INSTRUCTIONS

## 1 RULES

1.1 The regatta will be governed by the rules as defined in *The Racing Rules of Sailing*.

## 2 NOTICES TO COMPETITORS

2.1 Notices to competitors will be posted on the official notice board.

2.2 Supplementary sailing instructions (called 'the supplement' below) will be posted on the official notice board.

## 3 CHANGES TO SAILING INSTRUCTIONS

3.1 Any change to the sailing instructions will be posted before 0800 on the day it will take effect, except that any change to the schedule of races will be posted by 2000 on the day before it will take effect.

## 4 SIGNALS MADE ASHORE

4.1 Signals made ashore will be displayed from the flag pole. The supplement will state its location.

4.2 When flag AP is displayed ashore, '1 minute' is replaced with 'not less than 60 minutes' in the race signal AP.

## 5 SCHEDULE OF RACES

5.1 The supplement will include a table showing the days, dates, number of races scheduled, the scheduled times of the first warning signal each day, and the latest time for a warning signal on the last scheduled day of racing.

# 航行细则

## 1　规则

1.1　赛事将执行《帆船竞赛规则》所定义的规则。

## 2　选手通知

2.1　选手通知将张贴于官方公告栏上。

2.2　补充的航行细则（以下简称“补充”）将张贴于官方公告栏上。

## 3　航行细则更改

3.1　航行细则的任何更改将在生效当天的0800之前公布，此外，对竞赛日程的更改将在其生效的前一天2000之前公布。

## 4　岸上信号

4.1　岸上信号将在旗杆上展示。补充将注明其位置。

4.2　当岸上展示AP旗时，有关信号旗AP规则中的“1分钟”替换为“不少于60分钟”。

## 5　竞赛日程

5.1　补充中将包括一个表格，写明日期、时间、计划竞赛轮数、每个竞赛日第一次预告信号的计划时间，以及最后一个竞赛日预告信号发出的最晚时间。

6 **CLASS FLAGS**

6.1 Each class flag will be the class insignia on a white background or as stated in the supplement.

7 **THE COURSES**

7.1 No later than the warning signal, the race committee will designate the course by displaying one or two letters followed by a number, and it may also display the approximate compass bearing of the first leg.

7.2 The course diagrams are on the pages following SI 13. They show the courses, the order in which marks are to be passed, and the side on which each mark is to be left. The supplement may include additional courses.

8 **MARKS**

8.1 A list of the marks that will be used, including a description of each one, will be included in the supplement.

9 **THE START**

9.1 Races will be started by using RRS 26.

9.2 The starting line will be between a staff displaying an orange flag on the race committee vessel and the course side of the starting mark.

10 **CHANGE OF THE NEXT LEG OF THE COURSE**

10.1 To change the next leg of the course, the race committee will lay a new mark (or move the finishing line) and remove the original mark as soon as practicable. When in a subsequent change a new mark is replaced, it will be replaced by an original mark.

11 **THE FINISH**

11.1 The finishing line will be between a staff displaying an orange flag on the race committee vessel and the course side of the finishing mark.

12 **TIME LIMITS**

12.1 The supplement will state which of the following time limits, if any,

## 6 级别旗

6.1 每面级别旗为白底上印有级别标志或如补充中所述。

## 7 航线

7.1 竞赛委员会将不晚于预告信号通过1个或2个字母并伴随1个数字来展示所要行驶的航线，并且可能还会展示第一行段的大致罗经方位。

7.2 航线示意图在后续SI 13那一页。它们展示了航线、绕标顺序以及离开每个标志的一侧。补充可能包括其他航线。

## 8 标志

8.1 补充中将包括要使用的标志列表，包括每个标志的描述。

## 9 起航

9.1 竞赛按规则26起航。

9.2 起航线为竞赛委员会船上展示橙色旗的旗杆与起航标志航线一侧之间的连线。

## 10 航线下一航段的改变

10.1 如果改变航线的下一行段，竞赛委员会将布设新的标志（或移动终点线）并尽快地移走原标志。在连续的改变中要替换新标志时，将由原标志替代。

## 11 终点

11.1 终点线为竞赛委员会船上展示橙色旗的旗杆与终点标志航线一侧之间的连线。

## 12 时间限制

12.1 补充将说明以下时间限制哪个适用，如果适用，列出每个时

will apply and, for each, the time limit.

| | |
|---|---|
| • Mark 1 Time Limit | Time limit for the first boat to pass Mark 1. |
| • Race Time Limit | Time limit for the first boat to sail the course and finish. |
| • Finishing Window | Time limit for boats to finish after the first boat sails the course and finishes. |

12.2 If no boat has passed Mark 1 within the Mark 1 Time Limit, the race shall be abandoned.

12.3 Boats failing to finish within the Finishing Window shall be scored Did Not Finish without a hearing. This changes RRS 35, A4 and A5.

## 13 PROTESTS AND REQUESTS FOR REDRESS

13.1 Protest forms are available at the race office. Protests and requests for redress or reopening shall be delivered there within the appropriate time limit.

13.2 For each class, the protest time limit is 60 minutes after the last boat has finished the last race of the day or the race committee signals no more racing today, which ever is later.

13.3 Notices will be posted no later than 30 minutes after the protest time limit to inform competitors of hearings in which they are parties or named as witnesses and where the hearings will be held.

13.4 Notices of protests by the race committee, technical committee or protest committee will be posted to inform boats under RRS 61.1(b).

13.5 On the last scheduled day of racing a request for redress based on a protest committee decision shall be delivered no later than 30 minutes after the decision was posted. This changes RRS 62.2.

间限制。

- 1标时限　　第一条船通过1标的时间限制。
- 竞赛时限　　第一条船行驶航线并到达终点的时间限制。
- 终点封闭时间　第一条船行驶航线并到达终点后其他船的时间限制。

12.2 若在1标时限内没有船通过1标，则该轮竞赛将被放弃。

12.3 没有在封闭时间内到达终点的船将被记为DNF而无需审理。此条更改规则35、A4和A5。

## 13 抗议和补偿要求

13.1 抗议表在竞赛办公室领取。抗议表、要求补偿表或重新审理表应在规定时限内递交至竞赛办公室。

13.2 抗议时限为各级别最后一条船完成当天最后一轮竞赛后或竞赛委员会发出今天再没有竞赛的信号后60分钟内，以较晚的时间为准。

13.3 将于抗议时限结束后不晚于30分钟张贴抗议通知以告知审理各方或被点名的证人以及审理的地点。

13.4 按照规则61.1(b)的竞赛委员会、技术委员会或抗议委员会的抗议通知将被张贴以通知相关各船。

13.5 在最后一个竞赛日，以仲裁委员会的裁决为依据的补偿申请应在该裁决张贴后的30分钟内提出。此条更改规则62.2。

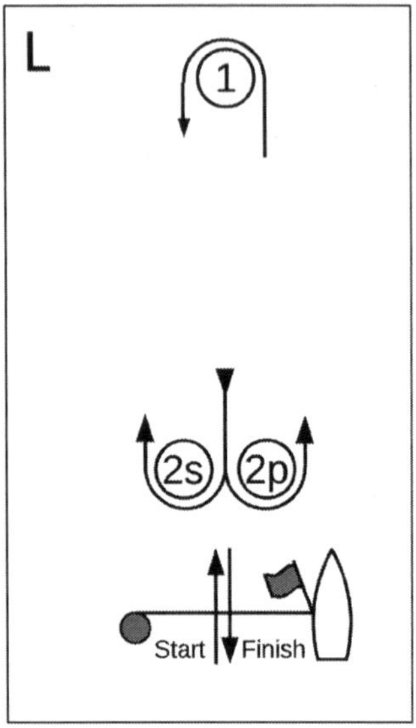


| Course L – Windward/Leeward, Leeward Finish | |
|---|---|
| *Signal* | *Mark Rounding Order* |
| L2 | Start – 1 – 2s/2p – 1 – Finish |
| L3 | Start – 1 – 2s/2p – 1 – 2s/2p – 1 – Finish |
| L4 | Start – 1 – 2s/2p – 1 – 2s/2p – 1 – 2s/2p – 1 – Finish |

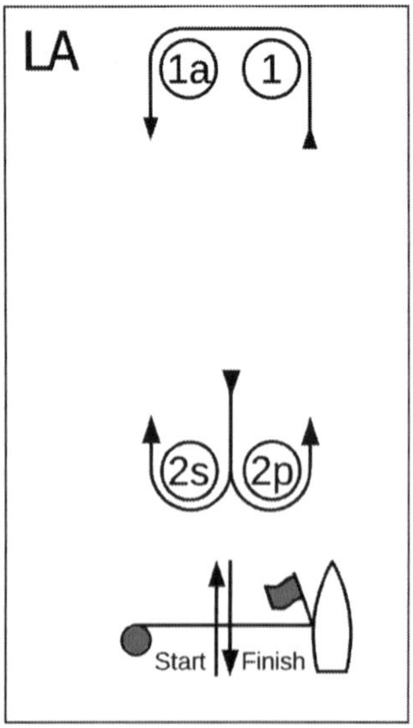


| Course LA – Windward/Leeward with Offset Mark, Leeward Finish | |
|---|---|
| *Signal* | *Mark Rounding Order* |
| LA2 | Start – 1 – 1a – 2s/2p – 1 – 1a – Finish |
| LA3 | Start – 1 – 1a – 2s/2p – 1 – 1a – 2s/2p – 1 – 1a – Finish |
| LA4 | Start – 1 – 1a – 2s/2p – 1 – 1a – 2s/2p – 1 – 1a – 2s/2p – 1 – 1a – Finish |

# 航线示意图

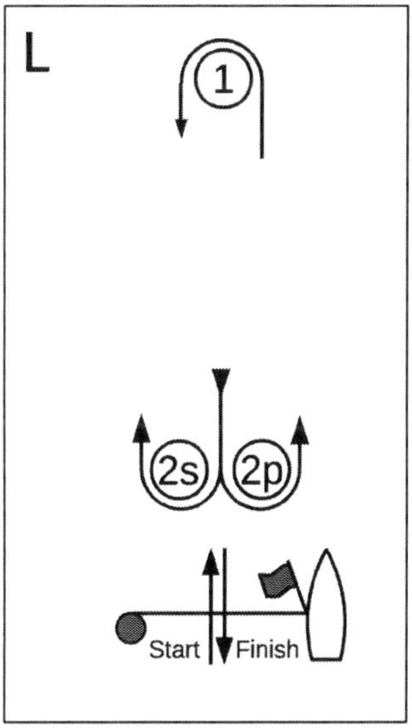


| L航线——迎尾风航线，顺风冲终点 | |
|---|---|
| 信号 | 绕标顺序 |
| L2 | Start - 1 - 2s/2p - 1 - Finish |
| L3 | Start - 1 - 2s/2p - 1 - 2s/2p - 1–Finish |
| L4 | Start - 1 - 2s/2p - 1 - 2s/2p - 1 - 2s/2p - 1 - Finish |

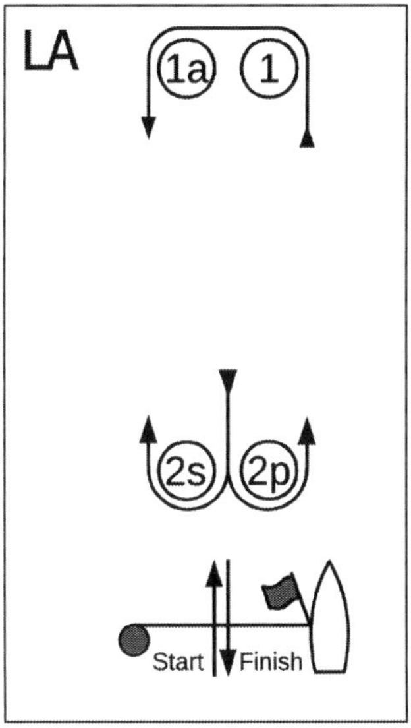


| LA航线——有外设标的迎尾风航线，顺风冲终点 | |
|---|---|
| 信号 | 绕标顺序 |
| LA2 | Start - 1 - 1a - 2s/2p - 1 - 1a - Finish |
| LA3 | Start - 1 - 1a - 2s/2p - 1 - 1a - 2s/2p - 1 - 1a - Finish |
| LA4 | Start - 1 - 1a - 2s/2p - 1 - 1a - 2s/2p - 1 - 1a - 2s/2p - 1 - 1a - Finish |

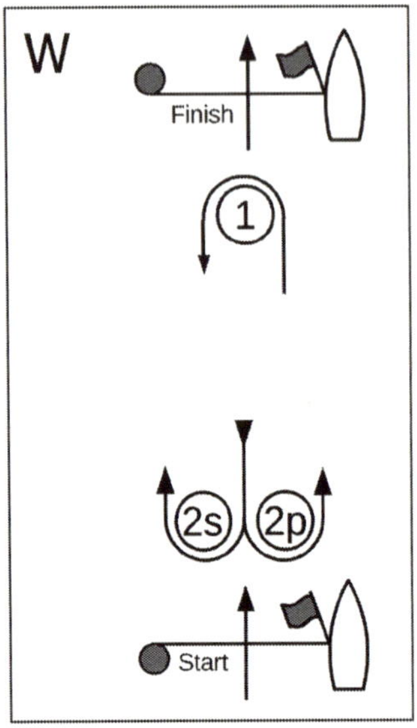


| Course W – Windward/Leeward, Windward Finish | |
|---|---|
| *Signal* | *Mark Rounding Order* |
| W2 | Start – 1 – 2s/2p – Finish |
| W3 | Start – 1 – 2s/2p – 1 – 2s/2p – Finish |
| W4 | Start – 1 – 2s/2p – 1 – 2s/2p – 1 – 2s/2p – Finish |

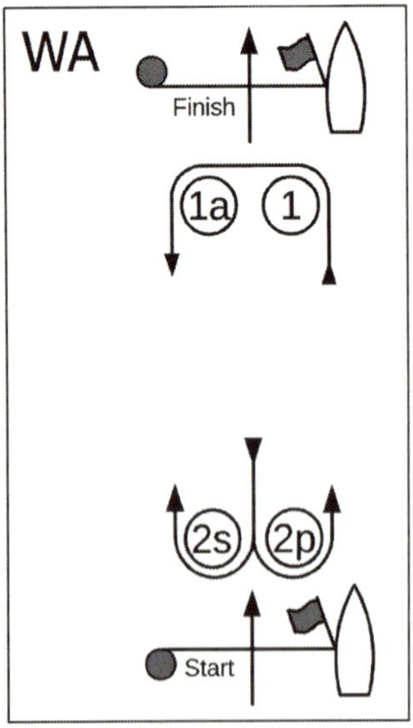


| Course WA – Windward/Leeward with Offset Mark, Windward Finish | |
|---|---|
| *Signal* | *Mark Rounding Order* |
| WA2 | Start – 1 – 1a - 2s/2p – Finish |
| WA3 | Start – 1 – 1a – 2s/2p – 1 – 1a - 2s/2p – Finish |
| WA4 | Start – 1 – 1a – 2s/2p – 1 – 1a – 2s/2p – 1 – 1a – 2s/2p – Finish |

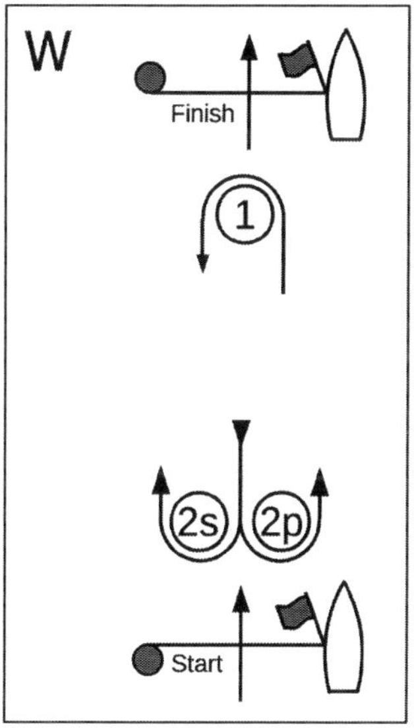


| W航线——迎尾风航线，迎风冲终点 | |
|---|---|
| 信号 | 绕标顺序 |
| W2 | Start – 1 – 2s/2p – Finish |
| W3 | Start – 1 – 2s/2p – 1 – 2s/2p – Finish |
| W4 | Start – 1 – 2s/2p – 1 – 2s/2p – 1 – 2s/2p – Finish |

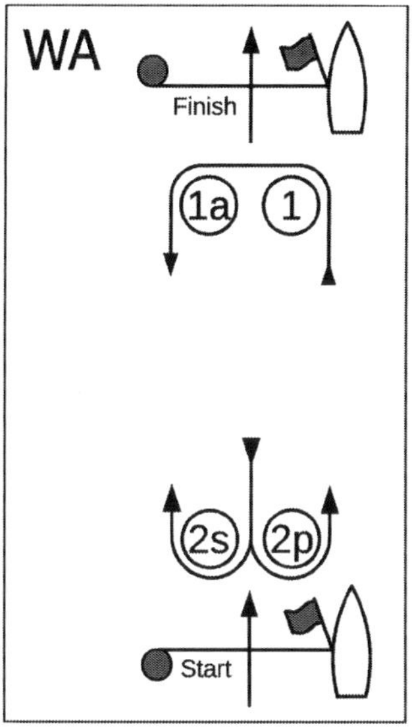


| WA航线——有外设标的迎尾风航线，迎风冲终点 | |
|---|---|
| 信号 | 绕标顺序 |
| WA2 | Start – 1 – 1a–2s/2p – Finish |
| WA3 | Start – 1 – 1a – 2s/2p – 1 – 1a–2s/2p – Finish |
| WA4 | Start – 1 – 1a – 2s/2p – 1 – 1a – 2s/2p – 1 – 1a – 2s/2p – Finish |

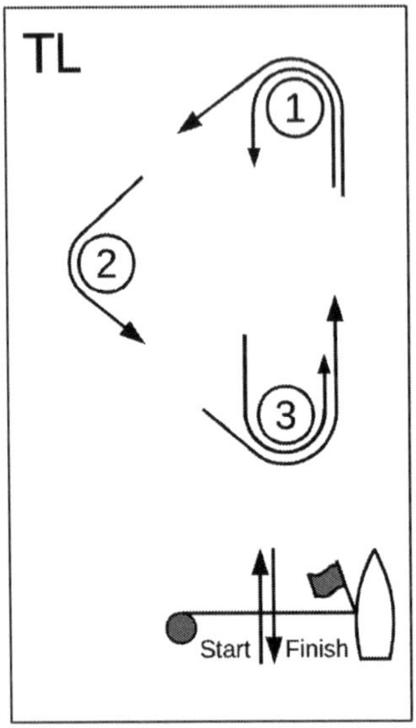


| Course TL – Triangle, Leeward Finish | |
|---|---|
| *Signal* | *Mark Rounding Order* |
| TL2 | Start – 1 – 2 – 3 – 1 – Finish |
| TL3 | Start – 1 – 2 – 3 – 1 – 3 – 1 – Finish |
| TL4 | Start – 1 – 2 – 3 – 1 – 3 – 1 – 3 – 1 – Finish |

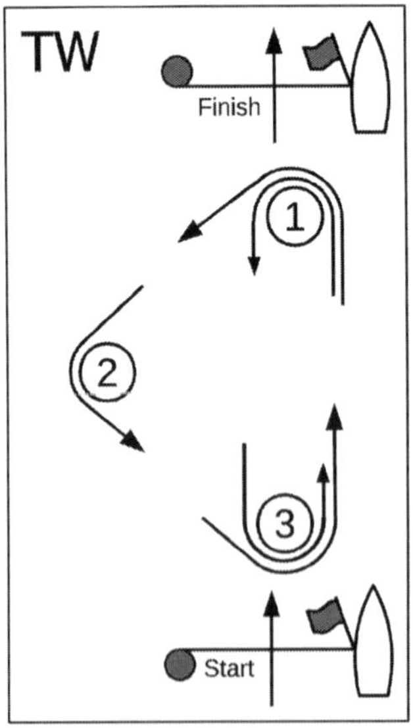


| Course TW – Triangle, Windward Finish | |
|---|---|
| *Signal* | *Mark Rounding Order* |
| TW2 | Start – 1 – 2 – 3 – Finish |
| TW3 | Start – 1 – 2 – 3 – 1 – 3 – Finish |
| TW4 | Start – 1 – 2 – 3 – 1 – 3 – 1 – 3 – Finish |

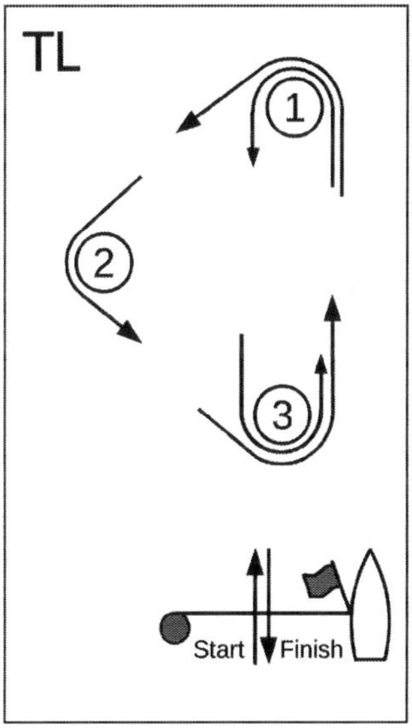


| TL航线——三角形航线，顺风冲终点 | |
|---|---|
| *信号* | *绕标顺序* |
| TL2 | Start - 1 - 2 - 3 - 1 - Finish |
| TL3 | Start - 1 - 2 - 3 - 1 - 3 - 1 - Finish |
| TL4 | Start - 1 - 2 - 3 - 1 - 3 - 1 - 3 - 1 - Finish |

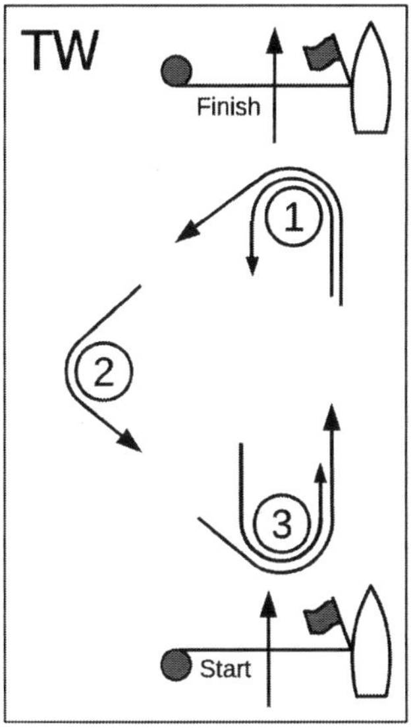


| TW航线——三角形航线，迎风冲终点 | |
|---|---|
| *信号* | *绕标顺序* |
| TW2 | Start - 1 - 2 - 3 - Finish |
| TW3 | Start - 1 - 2 - 3 - 1 - 3 - Finish |
| TW4 | Start - 1 - 2 - 3 - 1 - 3 - 1 - 3 - Finish |

# APPENDIX T ARBITRATION

*This appendix applies only if the notice of race or sailing instructions so state.*

*Arbitration adds an extra step to the protest resolution process but can eliminate the need for some protest hearings, thus speeding up the process for events in which many protests are expected. Arbitration may not be appropriate for all events as it requires an additional knowledgeable person to act as the arbitrator. Further guidance on arbitration can be found in the World Sailing International Judges Manual, which can be downloaded from the World Sailing website.*

## T1 POST-RACE PENALTIES

(a) Provided that rule 44.1(b) does not apply, a boat that may have broken one or more rules of Part 2 or rule 31 in an incident may take a Post-Race Penalty at any time after the race until the beginning of a protest hearing involving the incident.

(b) A Post-Race Penalty is a 30% Scoring Penalty calculated as stated in rule 44.3(c). However, rule 44.1(a) applies.

(c) A boat takes a Post-Race Penalty by delivering to the arbitrator or a member of the protest committee a written statement that she accepts the penalty and that identifies the race number and where and when the incident occurred.

## T2 ARBITRATION MEETING

An arbitration meeting will be held prior to a protest hearing for each incident resulting in a *protest* by a boat involving one or more rules of Part 2 or rule 31, but only if each *party* is represented by a person who was on board at the time of the incident. No witnesses will be permitted. However, if the arbitrator decides that rule 44.1(b) may apply or that arbitration is not appropriate, the meeting will not be held, and if a meeting is in progress, it will be closed.

# 附录T 仲裁调解

*只有在竞赛通知和航行细则中有相关说明时，本附录才适用。*

*仲裁调解给抗议决策过程添加了额外步骤，但是能够减少一些抗议受理的必要，因此加速了预期会有很多抗议的赛事的进程。仲裁可能不适合所有赛事，因为其要求一个额外的具有相关知识的人担任调解仲裁一职。可以从世界帆联网站下载《世界帆联国际裁判手册》来进一步了解。*

## T1 赛后惩罚

（a）如果规则44.1(b)不适用，一条在一次事件中打破一条或多条第二章规则或规则31的船，可能在赛后的任一时间直至涉及该事件的抗议审理开始前受到赛后惩罚。

（b）赛后惩罚是根据规则44.3(c)的规定计算的30%的分数惩罚。但是，规则 44.1(a)适用。

（c）受到赛后惩罚的船需要通过向调解仲裁或一名抗议委员会成员递交一份书面声明来表明她接受了惩罚，并确认轮次和事件发生的时间和地点。

## T2 调解仲裁会议

每一个涉及一条船因违反一条或多条第二章规则或规则31而导致*抗议*的事件，将在*抗议*审理前召开仲裁调解会议，但前提是每一方的代表在事件发生时都在船上。不允许有证人。但是，如果调解仲裁认定规则44.1(b)可能适用或仲裁调

## T3 ARBITRATOR'S OPINION

Based on the evidence given by the representatives, the arbitrator will offer an opinion as to what the protest committee is likely to decide:

(a) the *protest* is invalid,

(b) no boat will be penalized for breaking a rule, or

(c) one or more boats will be penalized for breaking a rule, identifying the boats and the penalties.

## T4 ARBITRATION MEETING OUTCOMES

After the arbitrator offers an opinion,

(a) a boat may take a Post-Race Penalty, and

(b) a boat may ask to withdraw her *protest.* The arbitrator may then act on behalf of the protest committee in accordance with rule 63.1 to allow the withdrawal.

Unless all *protests* involving the incident are withdrawn, a protest hearing will be held.

解不适用，将不会进行会议，如果会议正在进行中，则结束会议。

**T3　调解仲裁的意见**

根据代表们提供的证据，仲裁调解将就抗议委员会可能做出的裁决提出意见：

（a）抗议无效；

（b）没有船因违反规则而被判罚，或

（c）一条或多条船将因违反规则而被判罚，确定船和惩罚。

**T4　调解仲裁会议的结果**

在仲裁出意见后，

（a）一条船可能受到赛后惩罚，以及

（b）一条船可能被要求撤销*抗议*。之后调解仲裁可以根据规则63.1采取措施，允许其撤回。

除非涉及该事件的所有*抗议*都撤销，否则将举行抗议审理。

**Received by race office: Date and time ....................Signature ..................................Number ........**

**Protest Time Limit .................................**

## PROTEST FORM – also for requests for redress and reopening

***Fill in and tick as appropriate***

**1. EVENT** ................................. **Organizing authority** .................. **Date** .................. **Race no.** ...........

**2. TYPE OF HEARING**

| | | | |
|---|---|---|---|
| Protest by boat against boat | ☐ | Request for redress by boat or race committee | ☐ |
| Protest by race committee against boat | ☐ | Consideration of redress by protest committee | ☐ |
| Protest by protest committee against boat | ☐ | Request by boat or race committee to reopen hearing | ☐ |
| | | Consideration of reopening by protest committee | ☐ |

**3. BOAT PROTESTING, OR REQUESTING REDRESS OR REOPENING**

**Class** ................................ **Fleet** .............. **Sail no.** .......................... **Boat's name** ............................

**Represented by** .......................................... **Phone** ................................ **Email** ..................................

**4. BOAT(S) PROTESTED OR BEING CONSIDERED FOR REDRESS**

**Class** ................................ **Fleet** .............. **Sail no.** ......................... **Boat's name** ............................

**5. INCIDENT**

**Where and when the incident occurred** ..........................................................................................

**Rules alleged to have been broken** .............................. **Witnesses** .....................................................

**6. INFORMING PROTESTEE How did you inform the protestee of your intention to protest?**

**By hailing** ☐ **When?** .......................... **Word(s) used** .........................

**By displaying a red flag** ☐ **When?** ..................................................................................

**By informing her in some other way** ☐ **Give details** .....................................................................

**7. DESCRIPTION OF INCIDENT (use another sheet if necessary)**

**Diagram: one square = hull length; show positions of boats, wind and current directions, marks.**

..............................................................................

..............................................................................

..............................................................................

..............................................................................

..............................................................................

..............................................................................

..............................................................................

..............................................................................

..............................................................................

..............................................................................

..............................................................................

..............................................................................

由竞赛办公室接收：日期和时间.............. 签名.................... 编号............
抗议时限........................

**抗议表**——也可作为补偿申请表和重新审理申请表

*在适当的位置填空和勾选*

1. 赛事名称.............. 组织机构.............. 日期.............. 轮次.................
2. 审理类型

   船与船之间的抗议 □　　船或竞赛委员会的补偿申请 □
   竞赛委员会抗议参赛船 □　　抗议委员会对补偿的考虑 □
   抗议委员会抗议参赛船 □　　船或竞赛委员会对重新审理的申请 □
   抗议委员会对重新审理的考虑 □

3. 提出抗议、要求补偿或重新审理的船

   级别...................... 组别..................... 帆号................ 船名..............
   代表................................. 电话........................ 邮箱.............................

4. 被抗议或被考虑给予补偿的船

   级别................ 组别................ 帆号...................... 船名....................

5. 事件

   事件发生的时间和地点..............................................................................
   被控违反的规则.......................................... 证人.......................................

6. 通知被抗议人　　你是如何通知被抗议人你的抗议意图的？

   通过呼喊 □ 时间？.......................... 如何说的....................
   通过展示红旗 □ 时间？..................................................................
   通过其他方式通知 □ 提供细节..................................................................

7. 事件的描述（若需要可加页）

   示意图：1个方格=1倍船长；标示出船的位置、风向和水流方向、标志的位置。

**THIS SIDE FOR PROTEST COMMITTEE USE** Number ........

*Fill in and tick as appropriate* Heard together with numbers ...............

Withdrawal requested ☐ Signature ........................................................ Withdrawal permitted ☐

Class ............................. Fleet ..................... Race ..................

Protest, or request for redress or reopening, received within time limit ☐ Time limit extended ☐

Protestor, or party requesting redress or reopening, represented by ......................................................

Other party, or boat being considered for redress, represented by ..........................................................

Names of witnesses ........................................................................................................................

Interpreters ...............................................................................................

Remarks

Conflict of interest declared ☐ Objections: Yes ☐ No ☐ ..........................................

Written protest or request identifies incident ☐ ..........................................

'Protest' hailed at first reasonable opportunity ☐ ..........................................

No hail needed; protestee informed at first reasonable opportunity ☐ ..........................................

Red flag conspicuously displayed at first reasonable opportunity ☐ ..........................................

Protest or request valid; hearing will continue ☐ Protest or request invalid; hearing is closed ☐

FACTS FOUND .......................................................................................................................

.......................................................................................................................................

.......................................................................................................................................

.......................................................................................................................................

.......................................................................................................................................

.......................................................................................................................................

.......................................................................................................................................

.......................................................................................................................................

Diagram of boat .................. is endorsed by committee ☐ Committee's diagram is attached ☐

CONCLUSIONS AND RULES THAT APPLY ..........................................................................................

.......................................................................................................................................

.......................................................................................................................................

DECISION

Protest: dismissed ☐ Boat(s) ............................................... is (are) disqualified from race(s) ......

penalized as follows ☐ : .......................................................................................

Redress: not given ☐ given as follows ☐ : ..............................................................................

Request to reopen a hearing: denied ☐ granted ☐

Protest committee chairman and other members ..........................................................................

.......................................................................................................................................

Chairman's signature ......................................................... Date and time ...............................

此页供抗议委员会使用

编号....................

合并审理编号....................

*在适当的位置填空和勾选*

要求撤销 □ 签字............................................................ 允许撤销 □

级别.................... 组别.................... 轮次....................

抗议、补偿申请、重新审理申请在时间限制内接收 □ 抗议时限延长 □

抗议人、补偿申请或重新审理一方的代表..............................................................

另一方或被考虑给予补偿的船的代表....................................................................

证人姓名..................................................................................................

翻译.........................................................................................................

备注

利益冲突声明 □ 是否反对：是 □ 否 □ ................................

确定事件的书面抗议或请求 □ ................................

在最先出现的合理时机呼喊“Protest（抗议）” □ ................................

无需呼喊；在最先出现的合理时机通知被抗议人 □ ................................

在最先出现的合理时机清楚地展示红旗 □ ................................

抗议或申请有效；继续审理 □ 抗议或申请无效；停止审理 □

认定事实..................................................................................................

.................................................................................................................

.................................................................................................................

.................................................................................................................

.................................................................................................................

船的示意图..........被委员会认可 □ 委员会的示意图附后 □

结论及适用的规则......................................................................................

.................................................................................................................

.................................................................................................................

裁决

抗议：不予受理 □ 船............................被取消第....................轮的资格。

惩罚如下 □：.......................................................................

补偿：不予批准 □ 给予补偿如下 □：............................................

重新审理的申请：驳回 □ 同意 □

抗议委员会主席及其他成员..........................................................................

.................................................................................................................

主席签名............................ 日期和时间............................

**图书在版编目(CIP)数据**

帆船竞赛规则.2017—2020 / 世界帆船运动联合会编著
.—北京：人民体育出版社，2019（2019.11.重印）
ISBN 978-7-5009-5529-0

Ⅰ.①帆… Ⅱ.①世… Ⅲ.①帆船运动－竞赛规则－世界－2017-2020 Ⅳ.①G861.44

中国版本图书馆 CIP 数据核字（2019）第 034684 号

*

人 民 体 育 出 版 社 出 版 发 行
北京中献拓方科技发展有限公司印刷
新 华 书 店 经 销

*

880×1230 32 开本 11.5 印张 300 千字
2019 年 4 月第 1 版 2019 年 11 月第 2 次印刷
印数：2,001—2,500 册

*

ISBN 978-7-5009-5529-0
定价：58.00 元

社址：北京市东城区体育馆路 8 号（天坛公园东门）
电话：67151482（发行部） 邮编：100061
传真：67151483 邮购：67118491
网址：www.sportspublish.cn
（购买本社图书，如遇有缺损页可与邮购部联系）